THE
CORBETTS
& OTHER SCOTTISH HILLS

Published with support from VisitScotland

VisitScotland

First published in Great Britain by the Scottish Mountaineering Trust in 1990

Reprinted with ammendments 1993
Reprinted with ammendments 1996
Second Edition 2002

ISBN 0 907521 71 1
A catalogue record for this book is available from the British Library

Illustrations
Front Cover: Suilven: Looking east along its spectacular ridge *Hugh Barron*
Previous Page: Streap, centre, and Sgurr an Utha, right, from Glas-charn *Andrew Dempster*
Facing Page: Beinn na Caillich *Jim Teesdale*

Production: Scottish Mountaineering Trust (Publications) Ltd
Design concept: Curious Oranj, Glasgow
Typesetting: Aileen Scott
Maps: Craig Green, David Langworth, Tom Prentice
Colour separations: Digital Imaging, Glasgow
Printing: GNP Booth, Glasgow
Binding: Hunter and Foulis, Edinburgh

Distributed by Cordee, 3a DeMonfort Street, Leicester. LE1 7HD
(t) 0116 254 3579, (f) 0116 247 1176, (e) sales@cordee.co.uk

For details of other SMC guidebooks see back endpaper

THE
CORBETTS
& OTHER SCOTTISH HILLS

SCOTTISH MOUNTAINEERING CLUB

HILLWALKERS' GUIDE

Edited by
Rob Milne and Hamish Brown

Contents

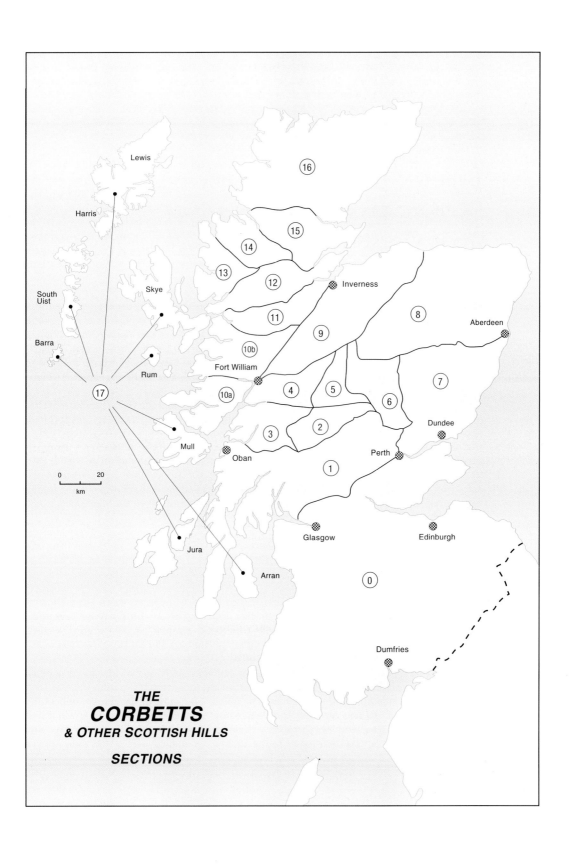

Lewis

Harris

South
Uist

Barra

Skye

Rum

Mull

⑯

⑮

⑭

⑬

⑫

Inverness

⑪

⑩b

Fort William

⑩a

④

⑤

⑨

⑧

Aberdeen

⑦

⑥

Dundee

③

②

Perth

①

Oban

⑰

Jura

Glasgow

Edinburgh

Arran

⓪

Dumfries

0   20
km

THE
CORBETTS
& OTHER SCOTTISH HILLS

SECTIONS

Introduction

John Rooke Corbett was a district valuer based in Bristol and a keen member of the Scottish Mountaineering Club (SMC) in the years between the two World Wars. He was a distinguished student at Cambridge University and an original member of the Rucksack Club. Corbett was a regular attendee at SMC meets, a committee member and joint editor of the second edition of the *Northern Highlands* guidebook. He completed the Munros and Tops in 1930, only the second person to do so and, more remarkably, he climbed all Scotland's 2000ft hills.

Out of this extensive experience and knowledge came Corbett's eponymous tables in which he listed all those hills of height between 2500ft (762m) and 3000ft (914.4m) with a drop of at least 500ft (152.4m) between each listed hill and any adjacent higher one. In this way the separation between the Corbetts is more clearly defined than is the case with the Munros. The fairly large height drop between Corbetts ensures that they are quite distinct hills, unlike the Munros where the criterion for separation does not involve a rigidly fixed drop between adjacent summits. When Corbett died, his list was passed to the SMC by his sister. As has been the case with the Munros, the list of Corbetts has changed over the years as a result of changes in hill and bealach heights measured by the Ordnance Survey (OS). The present list contains 219 Corbetts.

Corbett's list, along with Percy Donald's list of 2000ft hills in Southern Scotland, has been added to Munro's tables to create the book *Munro's Tables* of which the most recent edition came out in 1997. One additional section has been introduced for the Corbetts, namely Section 0 - Galloway and the Borders - which does not feature in the list of the Munros. In addition, a new sub-section has been introduced in this book: Section 10a for Morvern, Sunart, Ardgour and Moidart, an area of the Western Highlands which has no Munros and which, if added to the existing Section 10, would cover a disproportionately large area of the Highlands. The area of Section 10 of the Munros becomes Section 10b in this book.

The geographical division between Sections 5 and 6 goes through the Gaick Pass between the neighbouring hills of An Dun and A' Chaoirnich, which can be climbed most logically together. These two hills are described together in Section 6.

Corbetts's list includes so many fine and favourite hills that any hillwalker with much experience of the Highlands and Islands is certain to have climbed many of them, even if they have not set out systematically to climb all the Corbetts. The Munros may well form the mountain heartland of most of the Highlands, but the Corbetts have their place in the geography of our hills. In some areas, for example the Cairngorms, they are the outliers of the main mountains; in others they fill the gaps between them; thirdly (and most impressively) they are the principal peaks in those parts of the Highlands where there are few if any Munros.

Hillwalkers who concentrate their efforts entirely on the Munros will be in danger of missing many of the best of Scottish mountains. Height alone is no criterion and there are in the ranks of the Corbetts many peaks of great character, interest and beauty that are the equal of all but a few Munros. Dedicated Munroists in their travels will acquire a detailed knowledge of many parts of the Highlands, but not all. There will be gaps in their knowledge which an exploration of the Corbetts will fill, and this provides another very good reason for climbing these hills. Many a remote and unfrequented Corbett commands summit views of great quality. Exploration can and should be extended still further by climbing some other lower hills which are included in this book, hills chosen for inclusion by reason of their character and interest.

It would be wrong to think of the Corbetts as 'lesser' hills, giving shorter and easier expeditions than the Munros. Many of them, particularly those which rise from near sea-level in the Western and Northern Highlands and the islands and some of the remote hills of the Grampians, give climbs that are long and demanding. Baosbheinn, Beinn Dearg Mhor and Foinaven are just three examples of Corbetts whose traverses are major hillwalking days. The separateness of the Corbetts resulting from the 500ft drop criterion means that there are few instances where three or four or more can be combined in long traverses such as are possible with the Munros. There is only one example in this book where a traverse of more than three Corbetts is described.

In no part of the mainland do the Corbetts contribute more to the mountainous character of the land than in the Western and Northern Highlands. In Ardgour and Moidart, for example, where there are no Munros, peaks such as Garbh Bheinn, Sgurr Dhomhnuill, Sgurr Ghiubhsachain and Rois-Bheinn dominate the wild landscape. Just to their north, Streap, Bidean a' Chabhair and Ben Aden yield nothing except a few metres of height to the big peaks of western Lochaber and Knoydart.

Quinag, Spidean Coinich from Sail Gharbh

In Applecross, Coulin and Torridon the Corbetts may be rather overshadowed by the three great mountains - Beinn Alligin, Liathach and Beinn Eighe, but Beinn Bhan, Fuar Tholl, Beinn Dearg and Baosbheinn are splendid peaks which equally exhibit the classic features of Torridonian mountain architecture. Beinn Lair to the north of Loch Maree has on its north face an array of buttresses and gullies almost equal to the two greatest mountain cliffs in Scotland - the north face of Ben Nevis and Sron na Ciche in Skye. In the far north-west the Corbetts are the dominant mountains. Cul Mor, Quinag, Foinaven and Ben Loyal are just a few of the very fine peaks in that area, which also includes some of the best of the `lower hills' - Ben Mor Coigach, Stac Pollaidh and Suilven.

The Corbetts also contribute much to the mountain scenery of the islands. Arran, Jura, Rum and Harris owe their mountainous character to a few Corbetts and many more lower hills of outstanding interest. The ridges of Arran and Rum, although not on the same scale as the Black Cuillin of Skye, have a distinctive quality that fully compensates for their smaller scale. Surprisingly, Skye has only two Corbetts, but some of its lower hills give superb high-level walks. Most of the larger islands of the Outer Hebrides have their hills, some of them of modest height. The quality of an island hill, however, is not judged by height, but rather by its situation bounded by the limitless horizons of the sea.

In the southern part of Scotland the Corbetts are the highest hills in Galloway and the Borders. The Merrick, Corserine, White Coomb and Broad Law may overtop their neighbours, but there are lower hills too, such as Tinto, the Eildon Hills and the Pentlands that inspire great affection among hillwalkers.

In the Southern Highlands there are many fine hills in the list of Corbetts, but none can match The Cobbler. The outline of its three rocky peaks makes it one of the best-known mountains of the Highlands, and is certainly one of the most frequently climbed. The Arrochar Alps have other fine little mountains such as The Brack and Beinn an Lochain (once a Munro). Further east Ben Ledi is one of the most distinctive outposts of the Highlands.

Going further north into the Central Highlands, the Corbetts are a less distinctive part of the landscape. There are some good ones on both sides of Glen Etive and in Appin, but in Lochaber and Badenoch, which may be considered to be the heart of the Highlands, there are no Corbetts of particular interest. To the east, in the Grampians, Ben Vrackie is a well-known and prominent hill. Elsewhere the Corbetts form part of the vast undulating plateau that is characteristic of the country that stretches north-east from Blair Atholl towards Braemar, and in Deeside and around the Cairngorms they form a discontinuous ring of outlying hills among which Morven and Ben Rinnes are especially prominent.

Climbing the Corbetts is becoming increasingly popular. By early 2002, 175 people were known to have completed rounds of Corbetts, ending on around 80 different hills. Five people were known to have been round them all twice.

Notes

The layout of this book will be familiar to those who know *The Munros*. The scope and purpose are the same, namely to provide a concise and practical guide describing natural day expeditions which may be either a single Corbett or the traverse of two or three. Most routes are described as starting and finishing at convenient points on public roads as it is recognised that most hillwalkers use cars to reach their chosen hills. However, this should not be interpreted as a discouragement to multi-day bothy or tent based exploration, which brings far greater rewards. The length and difficulty of each day may vary considerably, and as noted, the Corbetts should not be regarded as `lesser Munros'. Some of the days described in this book are long, but they have been chosen as providing routes which may be the easiest or the natural choice, or following well-defined natural features or paths, or being of particular scenic interest. Many variations and alternatives may exist, but lack of space precludes a complete description of them. The hillwalker is encouraged to explore and have adventures.

The descriptions apply to summer ascents, but most of them can be applied in winter as well, bearing in mind the hazards of snow and ice, the shorter hours of daylight and the need for additional equipment. A good number of the routes described may become quite intimidating and dangerous in winter, and the Torridonian peaks in particular present difficulties which may be beyond the competence of some hillwalkers. To keep within one's capabilities is the basic principle of safe winter hillwalking in Scotland.

The standard heading for each Corbett or lower hill or the practical combination of such gives the following information:

The hill's name (those not Corbetts are marked by an asterisk *); the height (if differing from the OS Landranger a more accurate height has been obtained); the number of the OS Landranger sheet(s); a six figure grid reference for the summit; the meaning of the hill's name if reasonably clear.

In order to distinguish between the Corbetts and the Lower Hills, the latter are denoted by asterisks in any listing, and are also noted separately in the Index.

In the text, to distinguish between heights and distances, the abbreviation 'm' (e.g. 650m) is used to denote a height, and the word 'metre' (e.g. 200 metres) is used to denote a distance. Distances and heights are rounded up to the nearest 0.5km and 10m respectively, and times for ascents are calculated on the basis of 4.5km per hour for distance walked, plus 10m per minute for climbing uphill. Times are rounded up to the nearest 10 minutes, but no allowance is made for stops nor the extra time required by rough or difficult ground. (The above times are a close metric approximation to Naismith's time-honoured formula). Times quoted are for ascents only, so extra must be added for stops and the descent. Where two or more hills are traversed in succession, the times at each summit are cumulative from the day's starting point.

The maps in this book are intended to illustrate the text and serve as aids to route planning. They cannot take the place of a proper map in the field. The recommended maps for hillwalking are Ordnance Survey Landranger 1:50,000 maps. The Ordnance Survey Sheets referred to with each hill description are the 1:50,000 series. Hill heights quoted in this book are generally taken from Ordnance Survey 1:50,000 maps except in a few cases where 1:25,000 maps are used for greater accuracy. Harvey, Main Street, Doune, FK16 6BJ (tel: 0178 841 202) produce maps designed for walkers, many at 1:25,000 and these cover many areas: Pentlands, Arrochar Alps, Trossachs, Lawers, Glen Coe, Ben Nevis, Cairngorms, Lochnager, Kintail, Torridon, Arran and Skye.

The maps in this book use the following symbols to indicate the status of a summit or high point:

▲   Munro   summit heights 3,000ft (914.5m) and higher

△   Munro Top   summit heights 3,000ft (914.5m)and higher with a drop of at least 98.4ft (30m)

●   Corbett   summit heights 2,500ft (762m) and higher, but below 3,000ft (914.4m) with a drop of at least 500ft (152.4m)

○   Corbett Top   summit heights 2,500ft (762m) and higher, but below 3,000ft (914.4m) with a drop of at least 98.4ft (30m) within the above.

◆   Graham   summit heights 2,000ft (606m) and higher, but below 2,500ft (762m)

⊗   other summit

Six figure grid references for key locations are given in the text, for example "leave the track at 983572..." or as "cross the stream at a small bridge (274592) and continue ...".

9

Beinn Bheula from Lochan nan Cnaimh

Throughout the text, 'road' means a tarmac surface (usually public), 'track' any unsurfaced way such as used by forestry or estate vehicles (usually private) and 'path', a clear on the ground pedestrian only route (often a stalkers path). These are clearly differentiated on the maps. A publicly maintained car park is indicated with a P on the maps, while a P indicates that there is adequate off road parking for vehicles. Otherwise parking may not always be easy and convenient and walkers should avoid blocking gates or hindering local needs.

Hills are sometimes given two route descriptions and it is often possible, without stating it every time, that linking these can give a satisfying and often recommended traverse, though some transport arrangements may be needed. Plenty of time should be allowed for longer expeditions and those into remoter areas. The potential hazards of winter conditions, rivers in spate or challenging navigation from changes in weather should not be forgotten. In the interest of topographical accuracy and therefor safety, the most recent map is best used in the field.

For those dependent on public transport in the Highlands such as bus, postbus, train, ferry and air services in the Highlands up to date timetables are available on the World Wide Web. The Scottish Mountaineering Club web site maintains up to date links.

A few points of interest and changes should be noted.

In one case, this books lists two hills as Corbetts, although only one of the two can be a Corbett. Sgurr a' Bhac Chaolais (south Glen Sheil) and Buidhe Bheinn both have summit heights of 885m, but the drop between them is less than the requisite 152.4m to make them separate Corbetts. No one, including the Ordnance Survey, knows which is higher and hence which one of the pair should be considered the Corbett summit. A prudent hill walker should visit both summits. Carn Liath has two tops of the same height (862m), 1km apart. Although clearly only one hill, the prudent walker should visit both high points to be sure of having visited the summit. They are also counted as one Corbett.

The high ridge on the north side of Glen Kinglas in the Arrochar Alps has the name Binnein an Fhidhleir given to its 811m west top, but no name for its 817m highest point 1.5 km to the east. The name Stob Coir Creagach has been used for this point, Coire Creagach being the corrie to its NE overlooking upper Glen Kinglas.

The highest point of the hill on the south side of Loch Voil is un-named, although it has the trig point (771m). From features on the eastern ridge the name Beinn Stacath has been adopted. The northern top overlooking Loch Voil is named Ceann na Baintighearna by the OS.

The flat-topped hill to the east of Loch an Duin at the Gaick Pass has now been given a name by the OS: A' Chaoirnich, so this superceeds Maol Creag an Loch or Craig an Loch.

At the head of the Cona Glen in north Ardgour the name Druim Tarsuinn refers to the ridge extending NW beyond the Bealach an Sgriodain. As no local name has been found, the name Stob a' Bhealach an Sgriodain has been introduced for the Corbett.

The name Beinn Bharain was used rather loosely for the hills on the west of Arran but as the OS shows the highest point as Mullach Buidhe this name is now used.

Names of hills in the Outer Hebrides have now been given Gaelic forms by the OS and these are followed in this guide. The older names, often little different, are also given where possible and are often a guide to pronunciation. Ironically, most of the names are of Norse origin.

Place name meanings are from the most recent research. No meaning indicates it is already in English or simple not known. These lists come from extensive studies by Peter Drummond and are culled from his exhaustive listings.

Those interested in Corbetts and other, lower hills will find the following of interest: Brown, H.: *Hamish's Mountain Walk* & *Climbing the Corbetts* (Bâton Wicks, narrative compendium); Dempster, A.: *The Grahams* (Mainstream, guidebook); Dawson, A. and Hewitt, D.: *Corbett Tops and Corbetteers* (TACit Tables, the minutiae on Corbetts). The Corbett Tops indicated on the maps were compiled by Alan Dawson and full details are in this publication. The periodically updated booklet *Heading for the Scottish Hills* has information on access, contacts, etc. and can be obtained from the Mountaineering Council of Scotland office The Old Granary, West Mill Street, Perth PH1 5QP, telephone 01738 638 227, email: info@mountaineering-scotland.org.uk; web site: **www.mountaineering-scotland.org.uk.**

Available from the SMC is a CD ROM with detailed GPS route information for the primary routes in this book. The GPS routes are in several popular GPS formats. The routes are also given in text format, providing detailed waypoints and grid references for any hillwalker. Details are available from the SMC web site. There is also a CD ROM version of this book available.

There are links on the The Scottish Mountaineering Club web site: **www.smc.org.uk** for any updates or corrections to this book, tourist information centres, train, bus and ferry schedules. Please send any corrections to the SMC via the contact information on the web site.

Lastly, the editors would welcome any updating and correcting for future editions and would like to thank the large number of people including the administrative support of Linsay Turbert and those who have contributed to this popular volume over the years.

The Campsie Fells across Srath Blane

Environment

With ever larger numbers of hill walkers and climbers going to the Scottish hills, countryside and coasts, it is important that all who do so recognise their responsibilities to those who live and work in these environments, to our fellow climbers and to the environment in which we find our pleasure and recreation.

The Scottish Mountaineering Club and Scottish Mountaineering Trust, who jointly produce this and other guidebooks, wish to point out that it is in everybody's interests that good relations are maintained between visitors and landowners. The right of access to and on to a climbing, walking or skiing route in any of these publications is based on the individual abiding by responsible Access Codes.

Access

The stag stalking season is from 1st July to 20th October. Hinds continue to be culled until 15th February. The grouse shooting season is from 12th August until 10th December. These sporting activities can be important to the economy of highland estates and it would be a responsible approach to keep disturbance to a minimum during these seasons by following advice from the MCofS (see below) and any reasonable local advice about alternative routes.

It is also important to avoid disturbance to sheep, particularly during the lambing season between March and May. Dogs should not be taken onto the hills at this time, and at all times should be kept under close control. The MCofS and Scottish Natural Heritage also operate a Hillphones service giving daily recorded information of the location of stalking on some estates in the popular hill walking areas.

Climbers and hill walkers are recommended to consult *Heading For The Scottish Hills*, published by the SMT on behalf of the Mountaineering Council of Scotland and the Scottish Landowners' Federation, which gives the names and addresses of factors and keepers who may be contacted for information regarding access to the hills.

Footpath Erosion

The number of walkers and climbers on the hills is leading to increased, and in some cases, very unsightly footpath erosion. Part of the revenue from the sale of this and other Scottish Mountaineering Club books is granted by the Scottish Mountaineering Trust as financial assistance towards the repair and maintenance of hill paths in Scotland.

However, it is important for all of us to recognise our responsibility to minimise our erosive effect, so that the enjoyment of future hill walkers shall not be spoiled by our damage of the landscape.

As a general rule, if a path exists then try to stay on it. If the path is wet and muddy avoid walking along its edges as this only extends the erosion sideways. Do not take short-cuts at the corners of zig-zag paths. The worst effects of erosion are likely to be caused during or soon after prolonged wet weather when the ground is soft and waterlogged. At such times a route on stony or rocky hillside is likely to cause less erosion than one on bare soil or grass.

Always try to follow a path or track through cultivated land and forests, and avoid causing damage to fences, walls (dykes in Scotland) and gates by climbing over them carelessly.

James Lamb

Beinn Trilleachan and Loch Etive

Bird Life

When on the hills, don't cause direct disturbance to nesting birds (between 1st February and the end of July), particularly the rarer species, which are often found on crags (eg, Golden Eagle, White Tailed (Sea) Eagle, Peregrine Falcon, Razorbill, Guillemot, Puffin, Fulmar, Kittiwake, Cormorant, Shag, Buzzard, Kestrel, Raven).

Intentional disturbance of nesting birds is a criminal offence and if convicted, you face a fine of up to £5000 and confiscation of equipment.

It is the individual's responsibility to find out from the MCofS (see below) about voluntary restrictions at any particular location and to obtain advice as to whether their presence might disturb any nesting birds.

Litter and Pollution

Do not leave litter of any sort anywhere, take it down from the hill or in your rucksack. Do not cause pollution, and bury human waste carefully out of sight far away from any habitation or water supply. Avoid burying rubbish as this may also pollute the environment.

Cycles

Although the use of cycles can often be helpful for reaching remote hills, they can cause severe erosion and damage when used 'off road' on soft footpaths and open hillsides. Cycles should only be used on hard tracks such as vehicular or forest tracks.

Cairns

The proliferation of navigation cairns detracts from the feeling of wildness, and may be confusing rather than helpful as regards route-finding. The indiscriminate building of cairns on the hills is discouraged.

Car Use

Do not drive along private roads without permission, and when parking, avoid blocking access to private roads and land or causing any hazard to other road users.

General Privacy

Respect for personal privacy around people's homes is nothing less than good manners.

Bothies

The Mountain Bothies Association has about 100 buildings on various estates throughout Scotland which it maintains as bothies. The MBA owns none of these buildings, they belong to estates which generously allow their use as open bothies. Bothies are there for use by small groups (less than six) for a few days. If you wish to stay longer permission should be sought from the owners. The increased number of hill users has put a greater strain on the bothies and their surrounding environment. It is therefore more important than ever that the simple voluntary bothy code be adhered to, this and more information can be found on the MBA website: **www.mountainbothies.org.uk**.

If you carry it in, then carry it out and have respect for the bothy, its owners and its users.

Leave the bothy clean and dry, guard against fire and don't cause vandalism or graffiti.

Bury human waste carefully out of sight far away from the bothy and the water supply and avoid burying rubbish.

Mountaineering Council of Scotland

The MCofS is the representative body for climbers and hill walkers. One of its primary concerns is the continued free access to the hills and crags.

Information about bird restrictions, stalking and general access issues can be obtained from the MCofS. Should any climber or hill walker encounter problems regarding access they should contact the MCofS, whose current address is: The Old Granary, West Mill Street, Perth PH1 5QP, tel 01738 638 227, fax 01738 442 095, email: **info@mountaineering-scotland.org.uk**, website: **www.mountaineering-scotland.org.uk**.

SAFETY
Participation

"Climbing and mountaineering are activities with a danger of personal injury or death. Participants in these activities should be aware of and accept these risks and be responsible for their own actions and involvement."

UIAA participation statement.

Liabilities

You are responsible for your own actions and should not hold landowners liable for an accident (even if a 'no win, no fee' solicitor tempts you), even if it happens while climbing over a fence or dyke.

Mountain Rescue

Contact the police, either by phone (999) or in person. Give concise information about the location and injuries of the victim and any assistance available at the accident site. It is often better to stay with the victim, but in a party of two, one may have to leave to summon help. Leave the casualty warm and comfortable in a sheltered, well marked place.

Equipment and Planning

Good navigation skills, equipment, clothing and forward planning can all help reduce the chance of an accident. While mobile phones and GPS can help in communications and locating your position, consider that the former do not work over all of Scotland and both rely on batteries and electronics which can fail or be easily damaged. Consequently, they can never be a substitute for good navigation, first aid or general mountain skills.

Avalanches

Hill walkers venturing onto the hills in winter should be familiar with the principles of snow structure and avalanche prediction. All gullies and most slopes between 22 and 60 degrees should then be suspect. The greater the amount of fresh snow, the higher the risk. Fresh snow can include wind-blown deposits, so that stormy weather can maintain an avalanche risk for prolonged spells. Past and present weather conditions are very important.

Hill walkers preparing for winter journeys should familiarise themselves with basic avalanche theory. In the field, much can be learned by digging a pit and examining the snow profile, looking especially for different layers of snow with different degrees of bonding. Slab avalanches, for example, will be caused when a weakly cohesive layer of snow collapses underfoot. Such a weak layer is usually hidden under a firmer layer, hence its great potential as a killer. The top layer will often break into slabby fragments, the first warning.

If avalanched, try and either jump free, or anchor yourself for as long as possible, depending on circumstances. If swept down protect your access to oxygen by 'swimming' to stay on the surface, by keeping your mouth closed, and by preserving a space in front of your face if buried. Wet snow avalanches harden rapidly on settling, so try and break free if possible at this point. If trapped try to stay calm, which will reduce oxygen demand. If a witness to an avalanche it is vital to start a search immediately, given it is safe to do so. Victims will often be alive at first, but their chances of survival lessen rapidly if buried. Unless severely injured, some 80% may live if found immediately, but only 10% after a three-hour delay.

Mark the burial sight if known, listen for any sound, look for any visual clue, search until help arrives if possible. Again, a working knowledge of first aid may save a life, as many victims may have stopped breathing.

A Chance in a Million? by Bob Barton and Blyth Wright, published by the SMC, is the classic work on Scottish avalanches. While the ability to make your own assessment of risk is vital to anyone venturing into the area, avalanche predictions for the major mountain areas, produced by the Scottish Avalanche Information Service (01463 713191), or website: **www.sais.gov.uk** are readily available during the winter. These can be found at police stations, sports shops, tourist information centres and on display boards in mountain areas.

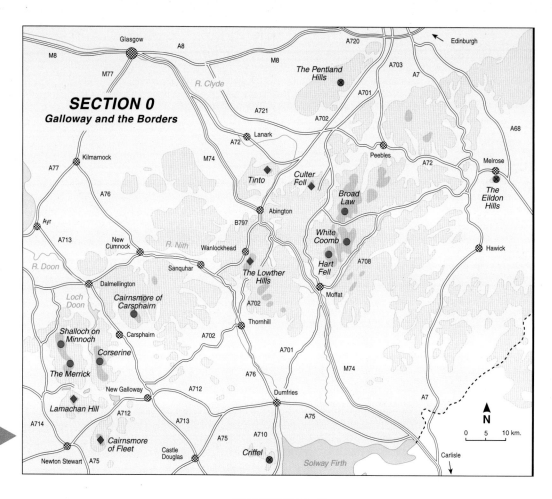

SECTION 0

Galloway and the Borders

Tom Prentice

Shalloch on Minnoch from the flanks of Tarfessock

Shalloch on Minnoch; 775m; (OS Sheet 77; NX405907); *middle heel*

Shalloch on Minnoch is the furthest of the three hills immediately north of The Merrick and east of the hilly minor road between Straiton and Bargrennan in the Galloway Forest Park. The highest and closest to The Merrick is Kirriereoch Hill (786m), formerly a Corbett, while the middle hill is Tarfessock (697m). After the approach through the forest which covers their western slopes, the three hills are easily linked to form a circuit, which can be extended to include The Merrick.

15

The best approach is from the Bell Memorial car park (353907) near Rowantree Toll on the Straiton road. This is just north of the point where the Straiton road meets the minor road from Barr.

SHALLOCH ON
MINNOCH

From the car park walk north up the road to meet a forest track on the right which leads down past Laglanny to Shalloch on Minnoch farm. Go through the farmyard on the left and follow the burn to a sleeper bridge. Cross over and follow the left (S) bank of the Shalloch Burn NE, to where it is joined by the minor Shiel Rig Burn (376900). Follow the burn and firebreak to the grassy west ridge of Shalloch on Minnoch. The true summit lies 300 metres SE of the trig point at 768m. (6km; 537m; 2h 20min).

Leave the summit in a SE direction and descend SSE to the Nick of Carclach and climb to Tarfessock. A long ill-defined ridge continues SSE, pitted with lochans and decorated with dark grey and pinkish outcrops and light grey erratics. After crossing a fence, steep uphill work on grass and scree leads to Kirriereoch Hill. The small summit cairn is 150 metres south of a ruined wall. The summit of The Merrick (843m) lies 2km to the south and can be linked to this route by descending Kirriereoch's SE ridge to the col at 637m.

Retrace the route to Tarfessock and descend its broad west ridge in a NW direction to a fence dividing open hillside from recently felled forest. Follow the fence north to cross the Knochlach Burn (386895), and descend the right (N) bank of the burn, with occasional squeezes between conifers, back to the Shalloch Burn at Shalloch on Minnoch farm. The sleeper bridge is a short distance back upstream.

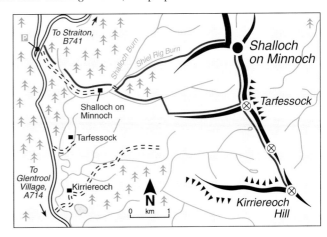

Corserine and Harrow Loch

Corserine; 814m; (OS Sheet 77; NX497870); *cross of the Rhinns*

Corserine is the central and highest point of a long, high, curving ridge which runs from north to south between Loch Doon and Clatteringshaws Loch. The range is called the Rhinns of Kells. The shortest ascent of Corserine is from the east. Follow the single track road which leaves the A713 at Polharrow Bridge and goes to a car park near Forrest Lodge. From the car park go towards Forrest Lodge, turn left before the bridge and follow the road west along the south side of the Polharrow Burn past Fore Bush and into the forest.

Where the road splits near Loch Harrow follow the right branch NW to 525875, where a path leads west across a gully by a bridge. Follow the fire-break NW to 517876 from where open slopes rise to Corserine. (6km; 690m; 2h 30min). The return can be made along the ridge SSE over Millfire and Milldown to Meikle Millyea. From there descend the NE ridge, turning east to reach the lower slopes. Continue east along the edge of the forest to a stile and fire-break leading north for about 300 metres to reach the forest road past Burnhead and back to the Forrest Lodge car park.

Infrequently, at times of high fire danger, hillwalkers are asked to avoid the Polharrow Glen approach. An alternative route which avoids any walking through forest can be accessed from the minor road which leaves the A762 at Glenlee (611803). Follow the road by the Garroch Burn for 6km to a car park at 558826. From there climb west over Rig of Clenrie to Meikle Millyea, and continue NNW for 4.5km along the undulating ridge to Corserine.

The traverse of the whole 13km-long Rhinns of Kells ridge is a fine expedition. However, it ends a long way from the start, so suitable transport arrangements are necessary. Starting from the north, a public road along the west side of Loch Doon leads to the Carrick Forest Drive. Leave this on the left and follow the track across the Carrick Lane and Gala Lane to park at the head of the loch. Follow the forest track round the end of Loch Doon and then north up the east bank.

At its end forest rides cross the Polrobin Burn and give access to slopes below Coran of Portmark. Follow the ridge south over Bow, Meaul and Carlin's Cairn to Corserine, then over Millfire and Milldown to Meikle Millyea, and finally east over Rig of Clenrie to the car park at 558826 near the end of the Garroch Burn road.

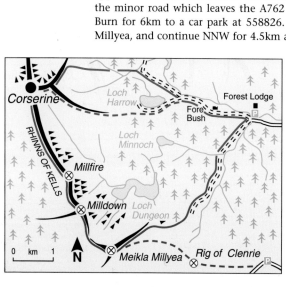

The Merrick above Loch Enoch

The Merrick; 843m; (OS Sheet 77; NX427855); *fingered or branched hill*

The Merrick is the highest point of the range containing Shalloch on Minnoch and Kirriereoch Hill and it is also the highest hill in the Southern Uplands.

The quickest and easiest route to the hill is also one of the finest, and starts from the end of the public road in Glen Trool. From opposite the Bruce's Stone a well-used path signposted to The Merrick goes up the west bank of the Buchan Burn, with grand views of its cataracts and over the oakwoods and conifers fringing Loch Trool to the surrounding hills.

The path starts above the burn, but joins it where it leaves its hanging valley, then swings away higher and enters the forest and emerges at Culsharg bothy (415821). A path leads

NW from there through the forest close to the Whiteland Burn. Cross the burn at the bridge and continue ascending beside the burn to a stile and open hillside. Ascend north to a wall running to the top of Benyellary (719m).

Continue along the wall in a north then NE direction to a col. When the slope broadens out leave the wall and ascend the grassy hillside by the path. The upper slopes leading to the summit of The Merrick are studded with granite boulders left by the ice ages. (6km; 770m; 2h 40min).

To the north. a col separates The Merrick's north ridge, known as the Little Spear, from Kirriereoch Hill and the broad ridge linking it with Tarfessock and Shalloch on Minnoch beyond. The numerous lochs below The Merrick's east and SE faces enliven the scenery and on a clear day it is possible to see the Scottish Highlands, Ireland's Mourne Mountains and England's Lake District.

An interesting return route descends east then SE to pass between Loch Enoch and the Buchan Burn. The rock face known as The Grey Man is nearby at 437846, while an island in Loch Enoch carries its own little loch. The Rig of Loch Enoch gives a good ridge-walk back SSW over Buchan Hill to Glen Trool.

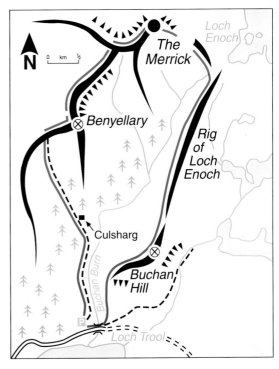

Tom Prentice

Lamachan Hill from Curleywee

Lamachan Hill*; 716m; (OS Sheet 77; NX435769); *hill of the hand*

18

The high ground south of the Loch Trool – Loch Dee gap is dominated by the ridge joining Larg Hill (675m), Lamachan Hill and Curleywee (674m). Curleywee's underlying shale makes it both rocky and distinctive, surrounded as it is by rounded granite summits, and the change in geology between it and Lamachan Hill is very marked.

LAMACHAN HILL*

The best starting point is the Bruce's Stone car park (416804), at the end of Glen Trool. This is also the start of the path for The Merrick. Continue on the road down to Buchan and then SE along the track. Before Glenhead leave the track for a path on the right and cross Glenhead Burn at a wooden bridge, the route of the Southern Upland Way. Continue SE along the south bank of the burn beside the forest, continuing on the path when it turns into the forest

following the Sheil Burn. Turn left onto the forestry track and follow it to about 454785, its high point below White Hill from where there are views of Loch Dee below. Ascend the NW flank of White Hill to gain the broad north ridge and follow it to Curleywee. (2h 30min).

Steep scree covered slopes west of Curleywee lead down to the Nick of Curleywee and then a surprisingly rocky ridge to Bennanbrack. From there turn SW again along grassy slopes to the summit of Lamachan Hill. (8km; 800m; 3h 20min). Larg Hill, which lies about 2km SW, can be included in the traverse, following a ruined fence down to the narrow col and a stone wall from there to the top. (4h from the start). Return across the col and ascend towards Lamachan Hill before contouring north to Cambrick Hill. From there the descent to Glen Trool goes down the east side of the Sheil Burn to the forestry track.

Ronald Turnbull

Cairnsmore of Fleet

Cairnsmore of Fleet*; 711m; (OS Sheet 83; NX501670); *Fleet's big cairn*

This hill forms a long ridge running in a NW to SE direction 9km east of Newton Stewart. The ridge is steep and bouldery on the east, but the most popular route to the summit follows an excellent and easily graded path up the gently sloping, grassy western face, where the granite bedrock is mostly hidden.

To reach this route leave the A75 5km SE of Newton Stewart at the white farmhouse of Muirfad (457628). This is the second turn on the left after leaving Palnure. Follow the road to a three-way junction under the disused sandstone railway viaduct. Turn right, leaving the tarmaced road and follow the track through the centre of the viaduct, past iron gates, and into the Cairnsmore Estate. Continue on this track alongside the Cairnsmore Burn, to skirt the large white estate building on the left. Turn left to a small car park (472641).

Follow the track to its end and cross the field to a gate, hidden by gorse bushes, in the far left-hand corner. Follow a path through woodland, then over a stile into the modern plantation of Bardrochwood Moor. The path is easily followed as it climbs steadily through the trees, over a forestry track and onto the moors north of Crammery Hill. Continues NE up the open slopes to cross a wall and then turns north following cairns along the ridge to the summit cairn and trig point, passing a granite memorial to airmen from Canada, UK, New Zealand, Holland and the USA, killed on this hill in several crashes between 1940 and 1979. Assorted small pieces of wreckage can be found on the summit plateau. (4.75km; 635m; 2h 20min).

The south top (655m) is 2km away, and is easily reached in 30 minutes along the fairly level and generally firm grassy ridge. By retracing your steps for 1km, an easy horizontal traverse leads back NW to the path for the descent.

CAIRNSMORE OF FLEET*

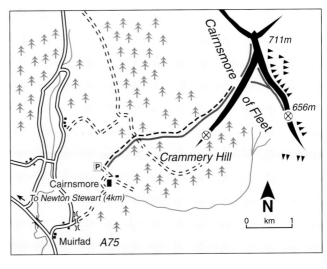

Criffel from the Nith estuary

Criffel*; 569m; (OS Sheet 84; NX957619); *crow or raven hill*

CRIFFEL*

Criffel is an isolated granite hill rising to the north of the Solway Firth on the west side of the estuary of the River Nith 4km south of New Abbey, and is bounded on the east and south by the A710 from Newton Abbey to Sandyhills.

On the west side of Criffel there are a few lesser ridges, but that side of the hill has little attraction for walkers as the approaches are long and tedious through coarse grass, heather and forest. Forestry developments have added to the defences on the north side of Criffel also, so the east side of the hill offers the best approach.

Start at Ardwall 1km west of the A710, where cars can be left just before the farm (971635). Parking is restricted, so please observe the requests to keep farm access clear. The route is signposted through the gate on the left. Follow the track for 100 metres, then turn right and ascend the track passing Ardwell farm to another gate leading into the forest covering the east side of the hill.

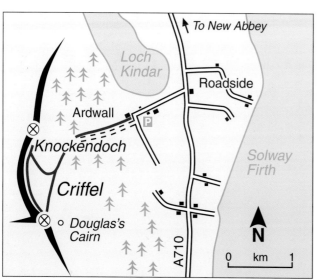

A well-marked path leads directly up a fire-break on the south side of the Craigrockall Burn which flows down to Loch Kindar. This route is taken to a stile above the forest from where the path turns more towards the south and heads straight up to the large summit cairn which is associated with the Earl of Douglas. (3km; 530m; 1h 40min).

Before descending, the north ridge can be followed for 1km to Knockendoch (429m) for a good view of New Abbey to add to the summit views, which on a good day include the Isle of Man and the Lake District fells as well as the expanse of the Solway Firth. At the summit the compass is unreliable so careful navigation is required in cloudy conditions.

Ken Andrew

Cairnsmore of Carsphairn from the Water of Deugh

Cairnsmore of Carsphairn; 797m; (OS Sheet 77; NX594979; *big cairn of the alder glen*

Cairnsmore of Carsphairn lies 6km NE of the village of Carsphairn, which is the mid-point of the A713 road between Ayr and Castle Douglas. The B729 from Carsphairn to Moniaive crosses south of the hill and sends off a minor branch up the Water of Ken.

The approach from Green Well of Scotland is very direct and easy along a rough track starting at Bridgend, just east of the A713 bridge over the Water of Deugh. Walkers are requested to avoid the Green Well approach between April 1 and May 28 due to lambing (see below).

Follow the track through a gate by the nearby bungalow and pass various cattle sheds. The track leads up past sheep pens and a small plantation, to skirt the flanks of Willieanna and Dunool to its end in the broad corrie below Cairnsmore of Carsphairn. Continue alongside the wall, cross the Polsue Burn and follow the wall up the broad SW ridge of Cairnsmore of Carsphairn to the trig point and large summit cairn. (5.5km; 600m; 2h 20min).

An enjoyable circuit can be made by descending the broad south ridge to Black Shoulder (688m) and then the start of another wall. This leads down past a small lochan to the SW and then over Dunool (541m) towards Willieanna. Leave the wall before the summit of Willieanna and descend NW to meet the access track at a gate above the small plantation.

During lambing time the easiest approach is from Craigengillan (637948) beside the Water of Ken. Follow the track past houses, ignoring left-turnings into the forest. When the track finally enters the forest at 633962, cross the bridge over the burn and follow an overgrown track to the new access track to Moorbrock. Continue on the track past Moorbrock, cross the Poltie Burn and follow the track round Green Hill until opposite the craggy east face of Beninner Gairy. Drop down through the first fire-break to the Poldores Burn. Follow the fence where it crosses the burn and skirt Beninner into the boulder strewn corrie. Ascend easily to the col (Nick of the Lochans) and follow Carsphairn's broad SE ridge to the summit. (7km; 500m; 1hr 45min).

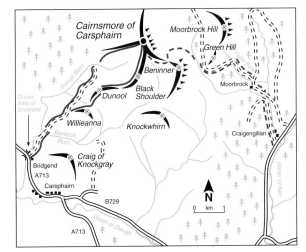

North to Hart Fell from Nether Coomb Craig

Tom Prentice

HART FELL   Hart Fell; 808m; (OS Sheet 78; NT113135)

The hills between Moffat and the Talla Reservoir are mostly steep-sided and rounded on top. The walking is mostly over grass with wet ground in the valleys. This is sheep country, and the fences along the crests of most of the ridges are invaluable aids to navigation in bad weather, especially where changes in direction occur at strategic points.

Although Hart Fell is easily accessed from the west via Hartfell Spa (076104) or the Devil's Beef Tub a much more interesting round can be had from Cappelgill (146098) in Moffat Dale to the east.

The SE aspect of Hart Fell rises above the Black Hope and forms part of a horseshoe of peaks including Swatte Fell (728m), Hartfell Rig (739m), Under Saddle Yoke (745m) and Saddle Yoke, the latter two are the steepest and most distinctive peaks in the area.

Park on the left, just beyond the second bridge at Cappelgill. Walk W back over the first bridge, go through a gate on the right and follow the burn which drains from the large cleft on the hillside. Go through the gate on the left-hand side of the field and contour steeply NE to climb the ridge above Black Craigs to gain the top of Nether Coomb Craig.

The plateau of Swatte Fell follows, with its rather ill-defined summit, then Falcon Craig, from where a fence leads up the SE ridge of Hart Fell to the summit. (5.5km; 660m; 2h 20 min). From there follow the fence NE and east to Hartfell Rig and descend east to a col, leaving the fence to skirt the upper corrie of the Whirly Gill to the broad north ridge of Under Saddle Yoke. Descend steeply to the col and climb to the steep sided summit of Saddle Yoke. Descend the south ridge to gain the track which leads back to Cappelgill.

Tom Prentice

White Coomb across Loch Skeen from Lochcraig Head

White Coomb; 821m; (OS Sheet 79; NT163150); *white corrie*

The high ground north-east of Moffat rises steeply from the glen of the Moffat Water to form an extensive area of rounded hills cut by deep and surprisingly craggy valleys. White Coomb is the most easterly and highest of these hills and forms part of a horseshoe enclosing the picturesque Loch Skeen.

The most direct route starts from the National Trust for Scotland car park below the Grey Mare's Tail waterfall on the A708 from where a well-maintained path ascends the steep NE side of the fall to the Tail Burn. If the water is low the burn can be crossed a safe distance beyond the top of the fall, at a point where the path levels off and a wall runs up the hillside towards Upper Tarnberry.

Alternatively, continue along the footpath beside the Tail Burn above the Grey Mare's Tail to the outflow of Loch Skeen where there are stepping stones. From here aim SSW across the peat to the lower slopes of the east shoulder of White Coomb and a wall. Follow the path beside the wall to the summit of White Coomb with only a short break at a rock outcrop near the top. (2km; 610m; 1h 40min).

From White Coomb descend west then north along the high ground over Firthhope Rig and Donald's Cleuch Head, then down E along the spur on the SW side of Loch Skeen to rejoin the path down the Tail Burn. It is also possible to continue the horseshoe round Loch Skeen to Lochcraig Head, descending its east ridge to a wall and a rather incipient and muddy path by the east side of Loch Skeen.

A much longer and less interesting approach can be made from the road to the north which runs between Tweedsmuir and St. Mary's Loch. The route goes over the tops of Nickies Knowe, Lochcraig Head and Firthhope Rig, returning by Moll's Cleuch Dod.

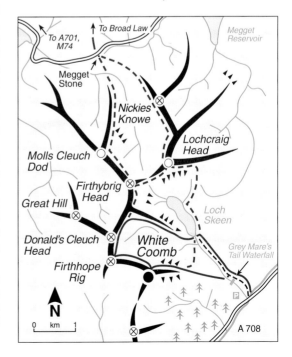

Broad Law from the north

Broad Law; 840m; (OS Sheet 72; NT146235)

This Corbett lies in the heart of the hills between Peebles and Moffat. In general they are all rounded, grassy and highly dissected into ridges and spurs so that walking along their crests is dry, with good views.

The usual starting point for the shortest ascent of Broad Law is the Megget Stone (151203) at the highest point of the minor road from Tweedsmuir in the Tweed Valley to St. Mary's Loch. It is possible to park near the cattle grid. A fence leads up the crest of the broad ridge over the minor humps of Fans Law and Cairn Law to the long gentle rise to Broad Law. (3.5km; 400m; 1h 30min).

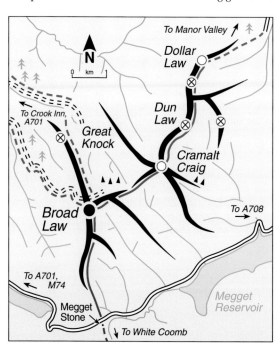

The wide crest of the hills continues NE to Cramalt Craig and from there to Dollar Law which overlooks the head of the Manor Valley.

Alternative routes of ascent are available from the west and north. The western approach is from near the Crook Inn (110260) on the A701, following a track at first beside the north bank the Hearthstane Burn and then above it, to the summit and returning via Great Knock and the Polmood Burn. From Peebles and the north it is possible to approach up the beautiful Manor Valley to Manorhead farm, from where a steep ridge leads up to Dun Law. From there the way continues over Cramalt Craig to Broad Law. If Dollar Law is included in the return, 4 hours will be needed for the round trip.

Paul Hannon

Green Lowther from Dunrig

The Lowther Hills

Lowther Hill*; 725m; (OS Sheet 71 or 78; NS890107); *canal hill*
Green Lowther*; 732m; (OS Sheet 71 or 78; NS901121)

Lowther Hill and Green Lowther are the highest points in an extensive region of high, rounded moorland flanked by Annandale to the NE and Nithsdale to the SW and which stretches from the B740, NW of the old gold and lead-mining village of Wanlockhead, to the edge of the Forest of Ae some 25km to the SE.

LOWTHER HILL*

GREEN LOWTHER*

This range is cut by deep valleys carrying the B797 and the A702, with easy access from the M74.

A long high-level ridge connects Lowther Hill and Green Lowther, the dominant feature being radar installations on their summits and a tarmaced service road.

Park in Wanlockhead and follow the track signposted Southern Upland Way and Public Footpath by the Enterkin Pass to Carronbridge which leaves the B797 at 876129. At the house continue alongside the fence on the right and follow occasional SUW markers SE to gain the service road. This can now be followed, with some grassy short-cuts, to the summit of Lowther Hill. (2km; 260m; 1h).

A more interesting route takes in the summit of East Lowther Hill. Follow the service road to the first sharp left-hand bend. Go over the crash barrier, follow the Enterkin Pass path (not now signposted) south to the col at the head of the pass, then climb to the summit of East Mount Lowther. (3.5km; 160m; 1h 10min), an odd name, as it lies to the SW of Lowther Hill. The mountain indicator covers an impressive panorama from the Lake District to the Highlands.

Return to the col and climb Lowther Hill with its summit golf ball, surrounded by a perimeter fence and a sign restricting access. Go clockwise, through a gate to meet the service road and NE along the ridge to Green Lowther, 1.5km distant. (7km; 390m; 2h 10min).

Dun Law (677m) is a possible addition, before returning to Wanlockhead by the outward route.

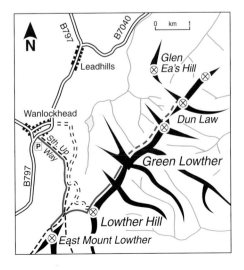

Culter Fell from Glenkirk

Culter Fell*; 748m; (OS Sheet 72; NT052291); *hill of the ploughshare*

CULTER FELL*

The Culter Hills are bounded on the west by the A702 and on the east by the A701. They are sprawling hills, gently rounded along their summits, but in many places steep-sided on their lower slopes and cut by deeply-etched valleys and streams. Culter Fell is the highest of this group.

Although it is possible to ascend Culter Fell from the west via Kings Beck or from Culter Waterhead over Knock Hill, these routes are marred by ugly tracks and an ascent from the east, starting from Glenkirk, is preferred.

The road up the Holms Water from the A701 2km south of Broughton ends at a locked gate and roadside parking just before Glenkirk. The road continues past Holms Waterhead from where tracks on the right lead up Leishfoot Hill to gain Culter Fell's south ridge at the col before Moss Law. This route can be used in ascent or descent, but makes for a short and not very interesting day.

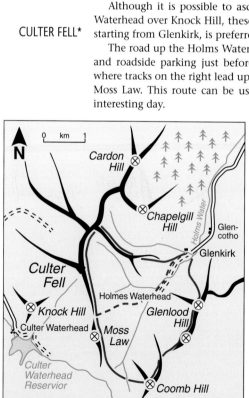

A more enjoyable round can be had by going through the gate before Glenkirk, following the road past the house and ascending Congrie Hill to gain the spur which descends from the col between King Bank Head and Culter Fell. From the col follow Culter's broad north ridge to the summit. (3.7km; 598m; 1h 40min). Tinto is prominent to the north and Lowther Hill with its radar 'golf ball' is clearly seen to the south. The rounded expanse of the Moffat hills are clear but harder to identify. From the summit follow the wall down the S ridge, go over Moss Law and descend to Holm Nick.

Once the sharp pull up to Glenwhappen Rig is over you can admire the views back to Culter Fell and distant Tinto. Continue over Coomb Hill and Broomy Law to Glenlood Hill. From here make a gradual descent first NE and then north to arrive at the small bridge over the Holms Water close to the locked gate by Glenkirk.

With their large populations of grouse and sheep, Culter Fell and its neighbouring hills should be avoided during the shooting and lambing seasons unless it is certain that no adverse effects will be caused.

Tom Prentice

Tinto and the River Clyde from the north-east

Tinto*; 707m; (OS Sheet 72; NS953343); *fiery or beacon hill*

Situated south-east of Lanark and although strictly speaking lying within the Midland Valley of Scotland, Tinto is usually regarded as the north-western outpost of the Border hills. It stands in complete isolation, with the River Clyde flowing round its base for many miles, and this makes Tinto the most prominent landmark in the upper reaches of the Clyde Valley, and also a splendid viewpoint in good weather.

The most popular ascent, although probably the least exciting, is from Fallburn to the NE of the hill, where there is a large car park. A broad track goes SW up the ridge of Totherin Hill to the summit which for some reason has one of the largest cairns on any Scottish hill. (5km; 460m; 1h 50min).

A slightly more adventurous approach is from Wiston to the south. Parking is possible at the back of Wiston Lodge YMCA (please ask permission), from where a road leads through a gate then left and past a house to a water supply building. Continue straight ahead, over a stile by a gate and into a field, bordered on the right by a wall and plantation. Follow the wall and the fields beyond to gain the path which zig-zags to the east of the Pap Craig screes and over The Dimple to the summit. (3 km; 450m; 1h 30min). The ground is fairly steep, and care should be taken in mist if using this route as a means of descent.

Another route starts to the east of the hill at a small parking space on the A73 at 985353 and ascends Wee Hill and Scaut Hill, before turning west to the summit. Access to this path has been blocked by the erection of a high fence at its start, but the route is included here in the hope that improvements in access mean it can be used easily again in the near future.

TINTO

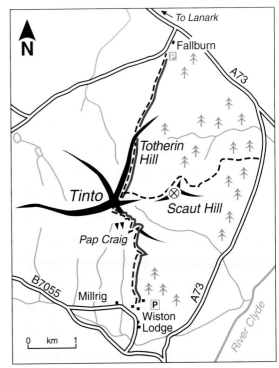

West Kip and Scald Law in the Pentland hills

Graham Little

The Pentland Hills

Scald Law*; 579m; (OS Sheet 66; NT192611); *scabby, speckled hill*

This long range of rounded hills runs SW from the outskirts of Edinburgh almost to Carnwath. The northern part of the range, lying within the Pentland Hills Regional Park, has become the playground of the capital city, providing a wide variety of outdoor opportunities.

Scald Law (579m) along with a cluster of other accessible hills gives fine hillwalking, with a variety of permutations encouraged by the paths and tracks that run east to west through the range.

The usual approach is from the east with good parking available at several places: Flotterstone visitors centre (233631), off the A702, 500 metres NE of Silverburn (211608) and at the little settlement of Nine Mile Burn (177576). The latter is, however, a bit too far south to conveniently tackle the main group of hills.

To climb Scald Law only, park NE of Silverburn and use the Kirk Road to reach the col between Carnethy Hill and Scald Law. A well-made path can then be followed to the triangulation pillar on the summit. The col also gives an easy approach to Carnethy Hill (576m), the second highest of the group.

The best and highest of the Pentland Hills can be traversed by parking at Flotterstone then following the main spine south over Turnhouse Hill (506m), Carnethy Hill (576m), Scald Law (579m), East Kip (534m) and West Kip (551m) – the most shapely of the group. From the summit of West Kip a short descent to the west leads to a col crossed by a track. A choice of three routes descend to the A702. The most westerly, a grassy path down Monks Rig, is the most interesting and passes the curious Font Stone en route to Nine Mile Burn. Transport back to Flotterstone is now required. Alternatively return by a descent north to the Logan Burn to the head of Loganlea Reservoir and thence by track and road around Glencorse Reservoir to Flotterstone.

A full circuit of the northern hills gives a challenging day and can be conveniently undertaken from Flotterstone. This involves extending the traverse described above i.e. from near the head of Loganlea Reservoir ascend Black Hill (501m) then head NE over a succession of grassy tops: Bell's Hill, Harbour Hill, Capelaw Hill to the viewpoint indicator (spot the errors!) on Allermuir Hill (493m). A deviation to pick up Caerketton Hill (452m) above the artificial ski slopes of Hillend can be made before following the obvious track over to Castlelaw Hill (488m). The south side of Castlelaw Hill is a military firing range. If in use (read flags warn) descend east of the danger area to Castlelaw and a path to the minor road to Glencorse Reservoir 800m from Flotterstone. The Flotterstone Inn is well placed to provide much needed refreshment.

SCALD LAW*

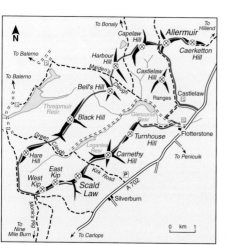

Eildon Hills from Scott's View

The Eildon Hills

Eildon Mid Hill*; 422m; (OS Sheet 73; NT548323); *fort hills*

The three tops of this compact group comprise one of the most distinctive hill views in the Borders. For all their modest height, this remnant of an ancient volcanic plug thrusts from the surrounding red clay fields with a real sense of purpose and provides a fine little hill round – perfect prior to a good Sunday lunch in Melrose!

Approaches from the west and east are available although the most satisfying route starts in Melrose – at a small sign for Eildon Walk on the east side of the B6359, just south of the A6091 overpass (547338). The path, now part of the well signed St Cuthbert's Way, slips between terraced housing, crosses a burn then turns right up a long flight of wooden steps. As height is

EILDON MID HILL*

gained the path passes through several kissing gates then winds up through mats of gorse to the wide col between the north and middle tops. A track gives easy access to Eildon North Hill (404m), which is crowned with the slight remains of a pre-historic hill fort and was also used as a Roman signal station. The great Roman camp of Trimontium (*the place of the three hills*) lies below to the NE. Returning to the col a steeper path climbs through a scattering of stunted conifers to the trig pillar and viewpoint indicator of Eildon Mid Hill, at 422m the highest top. The panoramic views over the Borders countryside are captivating and were apparently of great inspiration to Sir Walter Scott. Eildon Mid Hill is occasionally used as a military firing range when access may be restricted. A steep descent to the SW then south gains a good path leading to the lower south top (371m).

A number of return options are available but the most direct is to skirt east of Mid Hill to the main col and then to retrace the ascent route. As you descend, good views of Melrose Abbey far below contrast with the urban sprawl of Galashiels across the valley.

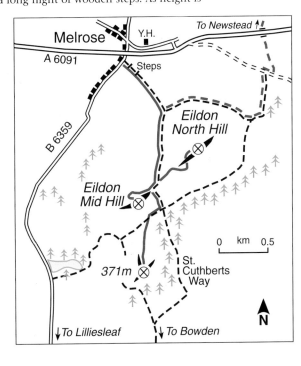

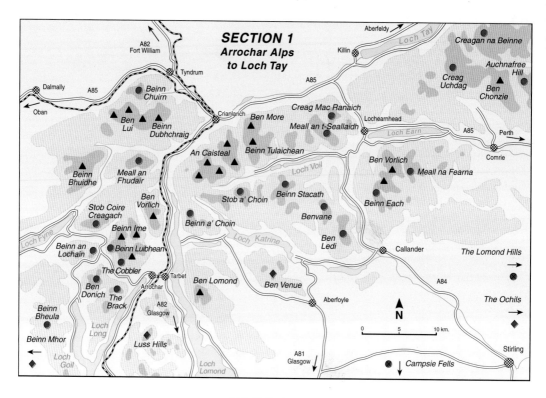

SECTION 1

Arrochar Alps to Loch Tay

The Campsie Fells

Dumgoyne*; 427m; (OS Sheet 64; NS542827); *fort of arrows*
Earl's Seat*; 578m; (OS Sheet 64; NS569838)

The Campsie Fells (*crooked seat hills*) are for the most part a featureless expanse of high moorland giving rough walking across tussocky grass and boggy hollows. Earl's Seat is the highest point, but like most of the Campsie tops (flattering the Earl of Mentieth probably) is an unremarkable hill whose best feature is the northern escarpment which overlooks the Endrick valley with a view to Ben Lomond and beyond. The best known hill of the Campsies is Dumgoyne, an old volcanic plug standing in isolation from the rest of the plateau at its western end. Dumgoyne's distinctive position and shape make it the most popular of the Campsies and its ascent is the best short walk in these hills. A large boulder has appeared on the summit, placed there by the Rotary Club of Strathendrick assisted by a helicopter.

Two ascent routes to Dumgoyne are commonly used. The shorter one starts from the A81 midway between Blanefield and Killearn at the Glengoyne distillery, there being a car park on the opposite side of the road. The other route starts from Blanefield village and goes along the Pipe Road, the line of the water supply from Loch Katrine to Glasgow. The approach from the A81 past Craigbrock farm is impracticable if you come by car as there is no space to park.

From the car park at Glengoyne distillery, cross the A81 and take the private road uphill to Blairgar cottage and continue across a field to reach the open hillside. Cross a drystone dyke to climb an obvious eroded scar on the steep west side of the hill and traverse to the SW ridge above its lowest crags. Continue up this ridge to the summit. (2km; 360m; 1h 10min).

The Pipe Road contours round the western perimeter of the Campsies from Blanefield to Killearn, passing below Dumgoyne, and offers a pleasant approach to the hill. In Blanefield there is only limited parking in the village near the start. Go along the Pipe Road for 2km to Cantywheery cottage and 100 metres beyond go through a gate on the right to follow a grassy path uphill towards a little crag. Go leftwards past this crag for a short distance, cross the burn flowing down from Graham's Cairn and head NW gradually uphill along a sheep track under the steep slopes of Dumfoyn (a minor Dumgoyne, not named; 546825). Cross another small burn below Dumgoyne and continue up a path across its south face to reach the SW ridge not far below the summit. (3.5km; 360m; 1h 30min).

To reach Earl's Seat, follow the Pipe Road route to Dumgoyne until just past the little crag, then go NE up the burn to reach Graham's Cairn. Continue in the same direction across rough boggy ground, crossing little streams and ditches which form the source of the Ballagan Burn, and finally climb more steeply to the trig point of Earl's Seat, which should be easy to find even in the thickest of weather being the meeting point of three fences. (6km; 520m; 2h 20min).

To include Dumgoyne on the return, go west then SW along the broad undulating ridge over Garloch Hill, following paths to reach the col NE of Dumgoyne. Climb steeply to the summit from there, avoiding the crags of the east face.

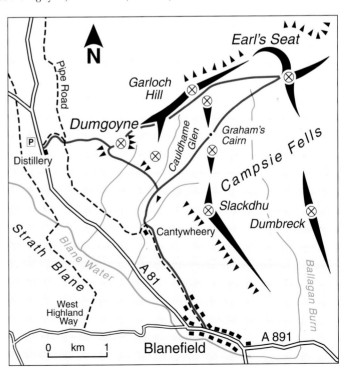

Doune Hill and distant Ben Lomond

The Luss Hills

Doune Hill*; 734m; (OS Sheet 56; NS290971); *hill of the black water* or *fort*
Beinn Chaorach*; 713m; (OS Sheet 56; NS287923); *hill of sheep*

DOUNE HILL*

BEINN
CHAORACH*

The Luss hills, bounded by Loch Lomond, Loch Long and Glen Fruin, form a compact group of rounded grassy hills which give very pleasant hillwalking within easy reach of Glasgow. Access from the west above Loch Long is not recommended, as there are forest plantations, firing ranges and other military installations. On the south, the road that was made in the 1980s to give access to naval installations in the Gareloch and Loch Long is now a public road and goes along the lower slopes of the south-western hills, parallel to and just above the narrow older Glen Fruin road. The best routes of access to the central and northern hills are from the A82 on the west side of Loch Lomond, either up Glen Luss from Luss village or up Glen Douglas from Inverbeg. A public road goes 3km up Glen Luss to end near Glenmollochan farm and gives access to the central hills, but there are only a few places at the roadside where it is possible to park a car. The Glen Douglas road goes from Loch Lomond to Loch Long and, starting from Invergroin farm half way across, the three northern hills are easily accessible.

Although none of the Luss hills have the status of Corbetts, there are four over 700m. They are steep sided and the whole group gives a wide selection of hillwalks from short half days to much longer outings. These hills are principally used for sheep-farming, so particular care should be taken not to cause disturbance, especially in the spring lambing season.

Doune Hill can be reached over the summit of Beinn Eich (703m), the prominent conical hill seen in the view west from Luss village. From the end of the public road in Glen Luss walk up the private road to Edentaggart farm, taking the signposted diversion to the west of the farm. From there climb west to cross a dry stone dyke by a stile and continue up a grassy path along the ridge to Beinn Eich. Go NW along a broad level ridge of grass and eroded peat over Beinn Lochain to the rounded summit and trig point of Doune Hill. (6.5km; 780m; 2h 50min). The return may be varied by going NE to the 701m lower top, then SE down to the head of Glen Mollochan and back to Glen Luss by a track along the north side of the burn.

The ridge on the north side of Glen Luss, consisting of Beinn Dubh (642m) and Mid Hill (657m), gives a short outing of about 4 hours. The best parking place is at the north end of Luss Village. Walk back towards Luss Primary School and follow the short no through road beside the school to steps, which lead to the large wooden footbridge over the A82. Go past the house and continue straight ahead on a path through a kissing gate. Turn immediately right and cross a stile to open fields and an intermittent path. Climb north up to the wide grassy track on the crest of the SE ridge of Beinn Dubh, from where there are good views across Loch Lomond. This track leads most of the way to the flat summit. (3.5km; 610m; 1h 50min). Continue along a very broad ridge of eroded peat to the 657m top of Mid Hill. Then go south over a slight rise and SE down a grassy ridge which leads finally through fields to the road near Glenmollochan farm, 3km up the road in Glen Luss from the starting point.

Access to the SW corner of the Luss hills is from the upper of the two roads through Glen Fruin. Just to the east of the bridge across the Auchengaich Burn there is a private road up to a small reservoir, and 20 or 30 metres up this road there is space to park a few cars. From there a steep but otherwise perfectly easy ascent up grassy slopes leads NE to Beinn Tharsuinn (656m), from where a broad and fairly level ridge continues NNW to Beinn Chaorach (713m). (3km; 580m; 1h 40min).

A longer, but very pleasant approach to Beinn Chaorach is from Luss village, starting at a car park on the east side of the A82 350 metres south of the bridge over the Luss Water at 357923. Go 250 metres north along the A82 and follow the private road to Auchengavin farm. From the shed at the end of the road go west across grazing land towards the north end of a larch plantation and continue up the bracken-covered hillside and the grassy crest called The Paps to reach a fence. Go through a gate and continue above the fence to reach the flat east end of Coille-eughain Hill. The fairly level 2km long crest of this hill, much of it eroded peat bog, ends below the steep slope up to Creag an Leinibh (657m). From there the broad grassy ridge continues to an unnamed 693m top, followed by Beinn Tharsuinn and finally Beinn Chaorach. (8km; 1000m; 3h 40min). To return by a different route, go 250 metres north from the trig point and descend east down a well defined grassy ridge on the north side of the Sheiling Burn. From the sheepfank at its foot go ENE to cross the Luss Water by a footbridge at 315933 to reach the track that leads past Edentaggart farm and down Glen Luss.

33

Beinn Eich and Doune Hill

Martin Ross

Clach Bheinn from Loch Eck

Donald Bennet

Beinn Mhor*; 741m; (OS Sheet 56; NS107908); *big hill*
Clach Bheinn*; 643m; (OS Sheet 56; NS126886); *hill of the stone*

BEINN MHOR*

CLACH BHEINN*

34

The district of Cowal is relatively unfrequented by hillwalkers despite being remarkably rugged and hilly. Possibly the extensive forests which clothe the lower hillsides in dense blankets of spruce are a deterrent to climbers. The Cowal landscape is certainly dominated by forestry and several villages, such as that in Glenbranter, have been built up round the forest industry. Loch Eck, a splendid narrow loch in the heart of the district, is surrounded by forests, some now being clear-felled, and to the west of the loch Beinn Mhor is the highest hill in Cowal. The west side of Loch Eck is a continuous series of wooded crags and corries, well seen from the A815 between Strachur and Dunoon. To the SE of Beinn Mhor is the lower but impressive looking Clach Bheinn, which has some remarkable crags and pinnacle-shaped boulders on its north side.

The traverse of Beinn Mhor and Clach Bheinn is the best hillwalk in Cowal. Two approach routes are possible. The longer one, and scenically the finer, starts at the Benmore Garden and one has to walk 6km along the forest track on the west side of Loch Eck almost to Bernice before starting the climb. A shorter, but less scenically attractive route is from secluded Glen Massan to the south of Beinn Mhor. Anyone with time to spare should also visit the Benmore Garden with its fine collection of rhododendrons and avenues of redwood trees.

The Glen Massan route starts just beyond Stonefield at the end of the public road where there is a small car park. Walk up the private road in the glen for 2km to Glenmassan cottage, and after crossing the Allt Coire Mheasan follow a forest track northwards up the lower tree-covered slopes of Sron Mhor, the SW ridge of Beinn Mhor. This track leads steadily upwards, with waymarkers at regular intervals, to reach the open grassy corrie above the forest. The continuation of the route northwards follows the ATV tracks which finally disappear just below the ridge about 500 metres SW of the summit of Beinn Mhor. The trig point is on a small rocky knoll at the south end of a flat area of grass and small rocky outcrops. (6km; 670m; 2h 30min).

On a clear day many of the well known hills of the Southern Highlands are visible, seen from a different angle: Ben Cruachan, Ben Lui, the Arrochar Alps and Ben Lomond are rather different when seen from a near neighbour.

To continue to Clach Bheinn, go SE along a wide grassy ridge towards the edge overlooking Coire an t-Sith. In places the ground is quite boggy. Continue south then SE and reach the col below Clach Bheinn, from where a short grassy slope with rock outcrops leads ENE to the summit cairn. There is another cairned point, only slightly lower, about 100 metres to the NE.

To descend to Glen Massan, return SW and cross the flat top of Creachan Mor. Continue SE along a narrowing ridge to the first col and then bear south on a descending traverse across the hillside to reach a gap in the forest above the glen at 121870. There is a narrow strip of grass and bracken which gives a short steep descent to the glen not far from the day's starting point.

The Loch Eck route starts at the Benmore Garden car park and goes north for almost 6km along the forest track on the west side of the loch. A few hundred metres before reaching Bernice, leave the track and bear SW up the grassy hillside to reach the east ridge of Beinn Mhor.

Climb this ridge, which is narrow and well-defined at first with crags on both sides, leading to flatter slopes before the summit is reached. Continue the traverse to Clach Bheinn as described above and return to the Benmore Garden car park by descending the SE ridge for 1km, then going down east steeply to the forest track along the side of Loch Eck.

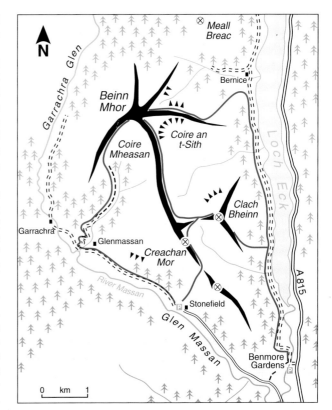

Beinn Mhor from Clach Bheinn

Donald Bennet

Ben Donich viewed down Hell's Glen

Ben Donich; 847m; (OS Sheet 56; NN218043); *brown hill*

BEN DONICH

Ben Donich occupies a commanding position in the angle between Glen Croe and Gleann Mor, 3km SSW of the Rest and be Thankful pass. Four ridges radiate from the summit, to north, south, east and west, and the hill is almost entirely surrounded by forest, some of which in Glen Croe has been felled and replanted in recent years. On the whole it is a grassy hill, and the only distinct crags are in the corrie between the west and north ridges. The most direct route of ascent is up the north ridge, starting at a height of 300m from the B828 at the head of Gleann Mor, 500 metres south of the Rest and be Thankful, the high starting point making quite a short outing.

A Forestry Commission track branches off, leading towards the foot of the north ridge and forks at the edge of the forest. Turn left and go downhill for 200 metres along the forest track (cycle route) above Glen Croe. A green post indicates the start of the route to Ben Donich through an area of forest which has been felled and replanted, but a gap has been left, up which a rough path climbs to a stile over the top fence.

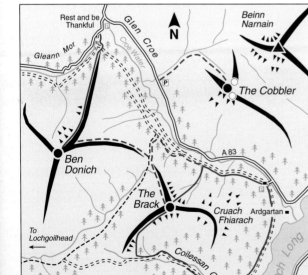

From there gain the crest of the north ridge and follow it over some grassy knolls. Higher up the first of several rock fissures is reached, and one should be careful if there is snow on the ground as some of these fissures form quite deep crevasses. There are impressive crags on the west side of the ridge and beyond a little dip at 817m the ascent continues along a broad ridge to the summit trig point. (3.5km; 550m; 1h 40min).

An alternative and longer approach, which enables Ben Donich and The Brack to be climbed together, starts from the Forestry Commission office at the foot of Glen Croe. Walk along the forest track up the glen below The Brack for almost 4km to reach the start of the waymarked path at 242047. This path leads south to the Bealach Dubh-lic (384m), the col between The Brack and Ben Donich. From the bealach both hills can be easily climbed. The east ridge of Ben Donich is broad and featureless, and not a very interesting route. (7km; 830m; 3h). This col can also be reached by a path from Lochgoilhead.

The Brack is a very rugged hill overlooking Ardgartan near the foot of Glen Croe. The north face above this glen is particularly steep and rocky, with an impressively dark and gloomy crag high up under the summit. The long and broad east ridge, Cruach Fhiarach, extends towards Ardgartan, but its flanks are extensively forested and there are no ascent routes on that part of the hill.

The most direct ascent is up the north side above Glen Croe, starting from the Forestry Commission office at the foot of the glen at 270037. Walk up the glen by the forest track on the south side of the Croe Water for 2km to a point about a hundred metres beyond a double bend in the track. A stream descending from the NE corrie of The Brack cascades down through the forest, and a few metres east of the bridge over the stream a signpost marks the start of a narrow path which strikes steeply uphill. Follow this path upwards through a clearing beside the stream to reach the open hillside. Continue up the path which higher up crosses to the west side of the stream and leads towards a large pointed boulder at the foot of the north face crags (a cave under the biggest offers dry shelter in bad weather).

Keep on directly upwards to the left of the big crag and before reaching some smaller crags and pinnacles higher up the corrie bear right up a grassy gully, climbing a steep little path to the north ridge of The Brack. Finally, turn south and go up the last hundred metres of the north ridge to the summit. (3.5km; 750m; 2h).

As an alternative to the steep climb up the grassy gully, bear south from the pointed boulder up the shallow grassy corrie, keeping below the upper crags and pinnacles to reach the east ridge at a col where there is a small lochan (247028). Turn right and climb NW to the summit.

A traverse of the hill can be made by descending the SW ridge which is broad and hummocky and calls for accurate navigation in mist. Pass below the 578m knoll at the foot of the ridge on its east side and reach the path from Lochgoilhead to Ardgartan at the point where it enters the forest. Follow this path into the forest and continue down the Coilessan Glen by the forest track to reach the lochside tarred road and the final 3km back to the Forestry Commission office in Glen Croe.

THE BRACK

37

The Brack from Coire Coinnich

Hamish Brown

Beinn Bheula across Loch Goil

Beinn Bheula; 779m; (OS Sheet 56; NS154983); *hill of mouths* or *ford*

To the west of Lochgoilhead there is an area of steep craggy hills with dense coniferous forests (some now being felled) along their lower slopes. Beinn Bheula is the highest of these hills. The east face, which is well seen from Lochgoilhead, is quite rocky, with many crags and escarpments above the forested glen of the Lettermay Burn, and the route described is on this side of the hill. The west side of Beinn Bheula is less attractive scenically, but the hill can be easily climbed from Invermoaden (1.5km north of Loch Eck) up the stream in Coire Aodainn.

38

BEINN BHEULA

Leave the road from Lochgoilhead to Carrick Castle at Lettermay. It is possible to drive a short distance further up to the edge of the forest at 188999 and start there. Walk up the forest track for just over 1km to a junction and go right for 200 metres to the Lettermay Burn. The path through the forest on the west side of the Lettermay Burn which is shown on the present map is impassible due to wind-blown trees and other obstacles, so follow the narrow path which goes along the SW bank of the burn. This path is boggy and obstructed by trees in places, but on the whole is easy to follow for just over 1km to reach open ground. Continue west more steeply uphill on the south side of the waterfalls on the burn flowing from Curra Lochain, still following an indifferent path leading to level ground near the top of the falls.

From there climb SSW then SW up the NE shoulder of Beinn Bheula. This forms a broad and indistinct ridge, with grassy knolls, small crags and traces of a path in places, but in bad visibility there are few recognisable features. Higher up, as a discontinuous line of crags is approached, make a rising traverse leftwards up a grassy gully through the crags and reach the crest of the north ridge of Beinn Bheula a few hundred metres from the summit, which is called Caisteal Dubh. The final climb to the trig point is on smooth short-cropped grass, in contrast to the rougher slopes below. (5km; 730m; 2h 30min).

A traverse of the hill can be made by continuing south along the broad grassy ridge for 750 metres to the twin humps of Creag Sgoilte (767m). From there descend SSW at first, thereby avoiding the crags due south of Creag Sgoilte. Once down onto flatter ground, bear east then NE across grassy slopes towards the outflow of Lochain nan Cnaimh. The descent path shown on the OS map has almost totally disappeared. At the outflow of the lochan a path appears and is followed down the left bank of the stream for a short distance before crossing to the right bank. Soon a firebreak is reached and followed NNE along a descending line through the forest, crossing many wet and muddy patches, until the end of the forest track is reached and followed back to the day's starting point.

Peter Hodgkiss

The Cobbler from the Narnain Boulders

The Cobbler; 884m; (OS Sheet 56; NN259058)

Three jagged rock peaks give The Cobbler distinctive character and well justifies the claim of the Corbetts to be taken as seriously as the Munros. The Cobbler has for long been one of Scotland's most popular peaks.

Despite the formidable appearance, the ascent is easy until the last few metres to the topmost point where some rock-climbing ability and a good head for heights is called for.

The traditional ascent route is from the A83 car park near the head of Loch Long. A wide path leads into the forest. Follow this steeply uphill to reach and cross a track at 100m. Continue upwards by a rough `staircase', the concrete blocks of a track from old hydro construction work. At the top of the `staircase' follow a path SW to reach the Allt a' Bhalachain (*buttermilk burn*) at a small dam. When forest harvesting begins, a new path will begin as above, but climb gradually WSW to meet the forest track at 288046. The route then contours before climbing NE to join the path at 290053.

From the dam continue up a path on the NE side of this burn to the Narnain Boulders and, a few hundred metres further, cross the burn. The path leads into the corrie below the three peaks and reaches the col between the Centre and North peaks, the last ascent being steep.

From the col a short diversion NE leads, with a little easy scrambling, to the spectacular North Peak. The route to the summit of The Cobbler goes SW from the col by a path along the broad grassy ridge to the summit rock. To reach the topmost point, scramble through a hole in the summit rock and delicately follow an exposed ledge on the south side to then climb onto this airy summit (4.5km; 890m; 2h 30min).

For those staying at Ardgartan youth hostel or camp site a convenient path starts from the A83 at the foot of Glen Croe and climbs up to reach the long SE ridge which is followed to the foot of the South Peak. From there descend slightly to cross the corrie to the path of the previous route.

The shortest route, but least attractive scenically, starts from a car park about 4km up the A83 in Glen Croe at 243060. Climb up a path on the SE of the stream to about 400m and then steeply SE to the col between the North and Centre peaks. (1h 30min from the road).

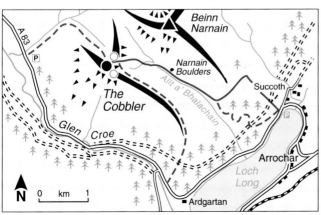

Beinn an Lochain; 901m; (OS Sheet 56; NN218079); *hill of the little loch*

Beinn an Lochain is a prominent hill at the head of Glen Croe which at one time was listed as a Munro. More recent measurements by the Ordnance Survey have placed it firmly near the top of the Corbetts. The east face rises steeply above Loch Restil for 650m in a succession of crags, mostly grassy and of no climbing interest except when snow and ice clad in winter. The summit overlooks the equally steep north face which has some impressive cliffs above Glen Kinglas with a few classic winter climbs. Between these two faces the well-defined NE ridge rises in a succession of steps and is a fine feature of the mountain. The south top (834m) is about 600 metres south of the summit and from it the southern slopes drop in long steep grassy slopes, interspersed with little crags, to Gleann Mor.

The best route of ascent is the NE ridge, which is steep and narrow enough in places to give a very fine hillwalk. The foot of the ridge near Butterbridge is planted with trees, so start about 750 metres NNE of the north end of Loch Restil at 234089, where there is ample car parking on the A83.

Cross the little burn flowing from Loch Restil at a small concrete dam and head NNW along a path to the start of the NE ridge. A well-defined path goes up the ridge, which at about 600m levels out at two little knolls (637m) and then steepens suddenly.

The path rises right, across steep grass to avoid crags on the crest of the ridge, which is regained at another level section (764m). Continue to the foot of the last rise, where the path is just on the left side of the ridge, a fairly narrow rocky crest, dropping steeply on the north side. The climb ends at the top of this section and the summit cairn is a few metres further on. (2km; 660m; 1h 40min).

An alternative ascent goes from the car park at the Rest and be Thankful pass. Climb due west up a steep slope with many little crags, all easily avoidable, to reach the 834m south top. Then continue north along the ridge past some tiny lochans to the summit. (2km; 650m; 1h 40min). This is not as interesting a route as the NE ridge, but could be combined with it as part of a fine traverse.

Beinn Luibhean; 858m; (OS Sheet 56; NN242079); *hill of the little plants*

This hill, which rises steeply above the Rest and be Thankful pass at the head of Glen Croe, is the western outlier of Beinn Ime, from which it is separated by the Bealach a' Mhargaidh, about 680m.

The most direct route, and probably the most pleasant one up the hill as it catches plenty of sun, even in the depths of winter, is the south ridge, which is also a good start for a longer traverse over Beinn Ime, Beinn Narnain and The Cobbler. Start at the car park beside the A83 at 242060, walk up the road for 50 metres and take to the steep hillside on the right, going north beside a fence for 100 metres and through a gate onto the open hill. Continue north up the broad grassy ridge which leads directly to the summit, a very short and easy ascent. (2km; 680m; 1h 40min).

The western perimeter of the hill is continuously steep and the ascent direct from the Rest and be Thankful may be short, but has little else to recommend it. Further north, the small area of forest NW of the summit has been felled and left a 'no-go' area so any ascent should be made to skirt this.

BEINN AN
LOCHAIN

BEINN LUIBHEAN

Beinn an Lochain from the east

Gordon Blyth

Stob Coire Creagach from the Rest and be Thankful

Stob Coire Creagach (Binnein an Fhidhleir); 817m; (OS Sheet 56; NN230109);
peak of the craggy corrie (fiddler's peak)

The north side of Glen Kinglas is dominated through its 10km length down to Loch Fyne by a high ridge, whose southern slopes drop in a single sweep from the summits down to the glen. There are several tops on this ridge, and the prominent western one has the name Binnein an Fhidhleir (811m), but it is not the highest point, which is 1.5km further east and unnamed on present Ordnance Survey maps. The name Stob Coire Creagach has been adopted for this 817m point as it stands at the head of Coire Creagach, the eastern corrie of the hill overlooking upper Glen Kinglas.

Any ascent of this hill from Glen Kinglas, which is the only practicable starting point, is a short and relentlessly steep climb of over 600m. This is particularly true if one starts from the glen to the west of Butterbridge. The slopes overlooking Coire Creagach and upper Glen Kinglas are more varied and very craggy.

The shortest and probably most painless ascent to the highest point starts just west of the A83 bridge over the Kinglas Water. There is a large car parking area on the south side of the road (234095) near Butterbridge (adjacent is a fine example of a stone arch bridge built in the 18th Century under the direction of Major Caulfeild, General Wade's successor). From the roadside enter the Butterbridge Plantation, a fenced area which has been planted with native species such as birch, rowan and Scots pine. Go uphill through the plantation and cross a stile over the upper fence (235099), then climb up rightwards by a grassy gully which gives an obvious way through a discontinuous line of crags. Above bear NW up the grassy hillside to the final steepening where a few little crags, easily avoidable, guard the summit. (1.5km; 640m; 1h 40min).

Anyone wanting more exercise after this short climb can either go west to Binnein an Fhidhleir and enjoy the view out to Loch Fyne, or traverse NE along the undulating ridge above Coire Creagach. The latter leads in 3km to the end of the hill from where one can descend into the head of Glen Kinglas and return by the track down the glen.

Andrew Dempster

Meall an Fhudair from Beinn Damhain

Meall an Fhudair; 764m; (OS Sheet 56; NN270192); *hill of the powder*

Meall an Fhudair and its lower and more popular neighbour Troisgeach (733m) form a large and featureless area of high ground between the head of Glen Fyne and the foot of Glen Falloch. The Corbett is not a hill of well-defined ridges and corries, but rather a shapeless lump, its eastern end being quite steep with little rock outcrops. The summit area between Troisgeach and Meall an Fhudair is a very flat, broad ridge, more like a plateau, dotted with many small lochans. The best view of the hill is from the lower reaches of Glen Fyne, from where its rounded shape is recognisable, or from Beinn Damhain across the Lairig Arnan.

The usual route of ascent is from the A82 at the foot of Glen Falloch, from where Troisgeach in particular is a popular short outing which gives good views down Loch Lomond and north to the Ben Lui group. There is space to park a few cars at the roadside opposite Glenfalloch Farm. From there walk up the private hydro track which zig-zags up the slopes of Troisgeach Bheag to join a higher road which contours round the hillside. Turn right and walk along this road for a short distance, then climb NW steeply for a short distance beside a small stream to gain the east ridge of Troisgeach. Follow the crest of this ridge for 1.5km (quite rocky in places) but higher up becomes less well defined and needs careful navigation in bad visibility. The summit with its small cairn is about 100 metres west of a little narrow lochan.

Continue WNW for almost 1km along a broad ridge towards Meall nan Caora (721m), then descend SW to a wide flat plateau which is crossed in a SW direction. The rough and featureless nature of the ground makes this a confusing exercise in bad visibility (many rocky knolls, peaty hollows and pools) but it is a perfectly easy walk otherwise. This area has a curiously large number of boulders perched precariously on embedded stones. The route gradually bears round westwards and the ridge becomes better defined as it leads upwards to the summit of Meall an Fhudair. (6km; 800m; 2h 40min). On a clear day there is a fine view across Glen Fyne to Beinn Bhuidhe, and down the glen towards Loch Fyne.

Return by the outward route or, alternatively and slightly easier, by making a long descending traverse ESE to reach the end of the hydro track in the Lairig Arnan. This track gives a pleasant walk for 3.5km down to Glen Falloch.

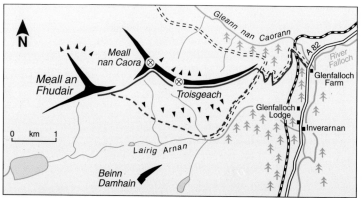

Beinn Chuirn from the Coille Coire Chuilc

Beinn Chuirn; 880m; (OS Sheet 50; NN280292); *cairn hill*

When seen from the east, looking up the glen of River Cononish, Beinn Chuirn looks rather like a small version of Ben Lui. Both hills have similar east facing corries, but Beinn Chuirn is very much overshadowed by its big neighbour. On its north side slopes drop steeply towards Glen Lochy, with a narrow strip of forestry beside the River Lochy.

Two routes of ascent may be recommended, which taken together make a good traverse. The shorter one starts in Glen Lochy 2km NW of the summit of Beinn Chuirn, the longer starts at Tyndrum and goes for 3.5km along a private road to Cononish farm before climbing the SE ridge of the hill. The slopes of Beinn Chuirn below this ridge have for several years been the site of an exploratory gold mining operation, and bulldozed tracks and other scars on the hillside have created an unsightly mess. These workings may become permanent, on the other hand uncertain economics may bring them to an end, only leaving scars on the hill.

The Glen Lochy route starts on the A85 6.5km west of Tyndrum. There is only limited space to park on the north side of the road about 500 metres west of Arrivain and about 200 metres from the bridge taking the Oban railway across the River Lochy. To stay on the right side of the law, wade across the River Lochy and go under the railway bridge, then continue along the bank of the Allt Garbh Choirean for about 500 metres. Once above the trees bear east on the north side of the northmost stream in the corrie and climb a grassy spur which steepens near its top but is not as craggy as the map indicates. This spur leads to a little lochan and the summit of Beinn Chuirn is about 400 metres (2km; 660m; 1h 40min).

The better route starts off the A82 where there is parking at the start of the private road to Cononish (343292). Continue along the track past the farm towards Ben Lui for a few hundred metres and climb west up the grassy hillside, keeping well south of the prominent Eas Anie waterfall. Once the ground becomes more level, bear NW then north across the burn above the Eas Anie and continue up the broad SE ridge of Beinn Chuirn. The ridge becomes level for a short distance past the top of a steep gully on the east face, and then continues easily for about 200 metres to the summit cairn. The remains of an old fence crosses the summit a few metres north of the cairn. (6km; 700m; 2h 30min).

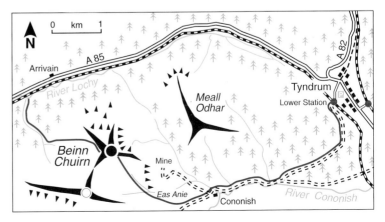

Hugh Barron

The Maol Mor Ridge of Beinn a' Choin

Beinn a' Choin; 770m; (OS Sheet 56; NN354130); *hill of the dog*

Beinn a' Choin is the highest of a group of hills enclosed within the triangle formed by Loch Lomond, Loch Arklet and the NW end of Loch Katrine. From the summit two long, broad grassy ridges enclosing the Corriearklet Burn drop southwards to Loch Arklet, and these ridges give easy ascent routes. The most direct way is up the western ridge over Stob an Fhainne (655m), and a longer circuit can be made by going up one ridge and down the other. The hill is mostly grassy, with many small rock outcrops, and easy going on the ridges.

The most direct route starts from the road on the north side of Loch Arklet about 100 metres east of the dam where there is space to park by the roadside. Go due north up the steepening grassy hillside and in just over an hour reach Stob an Fhainne, whose summit is a little rocky outcrop crossed by a fence. Continue north along a broad grassy ridge, leaving the fence which drops down on the west side of the ridge, and follow a faint path to reach the flat boggy Bealach a' Mheim (587m).

Bear NW and climb between rock outcrops towards Beinn a' Choin. The fence is reached again and followed north, but it passes to the east of the summit, which might be missed in bad visibility. In such conditions, cross the fence at a tiny lochan and go NW for 70 metres to the summit which is a flat-topped knoll with a large cairn at its north edge. (3.5km; 690m; 2h).

In clear weather there is a fine view of many of the Southern Highland mountains in an arc from the Arrochar Alps round to Ben More.

For the longer circuit of Beinn a' Choin's two southern ridges, the best starting point is at Corriearklet, where you should seek permission to park beside the farm's access road. From the farm climb NE to reach the ridge of Maol Mor, which has many ups and downs. The highest point is 694m, and is about 600 metres NW of the 684m trig point. The preceding route is joined at the Bealach a' Mheim and followed to the summit. (6km; 850m; 2h 50min). On the return, the SE ridge of Sgurr an Fhainne gives a fast descent to Corriearklet.

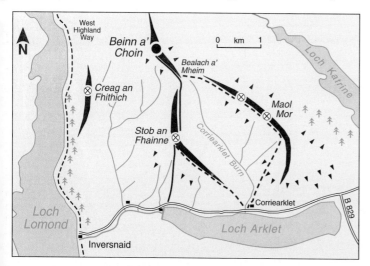

Andrew Dempster

Ben Venue from Ben A' n

Ben Venue*; 729m; (OS Sheet 57; NN474063); *hill of the caves* or *hill of the stirks*

Ben Venue is a rugged and prominent little mountain overlooking The Trossachs at the east end of Loch Katrine. The NE face above the Achray Water is steep, with crags and trees on the lower slopes which give an impression of impregnability; however, this is misleading. The eastern side of the hill is densely forested in Gleann Riabhach, and the western side, including the outlier Beinn Bhreac (703m), is wild and rough country extending for several kilometres towards the head of Loch Katrine.

A traverse of the hill from south to north, or vice versa, is recommended, provided an obliging driver is available. The south to north traverse goes from Ledard near the head of Loch Ard to the Loch Achray Hotel.

From a parking place beside the B829 500 metres east of Kinlochard, walk for 200 metres along the private road to Ledard and follow signs which indicate the path across the Ledard Burn. This path leads uphill on the west side of the burn through a fine stand of oak, then through scattered birches along the edge of a plantation, with the Ledard Burn in a deep gorge below. In about 2km the path deteriorates as it reaches a very boggy area, and crosses to the east side of the burn to continue to a pass between Beinn Bhreac and Creag a' Bhealaich.

At this point Ben Venue comes into view and the path continues NE for 1km on a level traverse to the lowest point of the ridge between Creag a' Bhealaich and Ben Venue (729m). Here another path drops SE into the head of Gleann Riabhach, but the route to Ben Venue continues NE up steepening rocky ground to the NW top of Ben Venue, which is the highest point by about two metres. (5km; 690m; 2h 20min).

The traverse continues SE for a few hundred metres, following a tortuous path to the lower SE top of the hill (727m), which has a trig point. Two descent routes are possible. The easier one goes south down grassy slopes into Gleann Riabhach to meet the path in that glen at the edge of the forest. This path has been much improved and gives a pleasant walk down through the forest, leading to the forest track beside the Achray Water, 1km from the Loch Achray Hotel.

The alternative descent goes down the little corrie to the NE of the 727m top, following a faint path to the east of the burn. At the highest scattered birches, bear north to reach the upper edge of the birch wood at a boulder where the burn plunges down a narrow rocky gully. Descend steeply through the wood by faint traces of a narrow zig-zag path on the east side of the burn to more level ground where a good path continues past the Loch Katrine sluices to join the forest track leading to the Loch Achray Hotel. If forest harvesting takes place, alternative routes will be signposted.

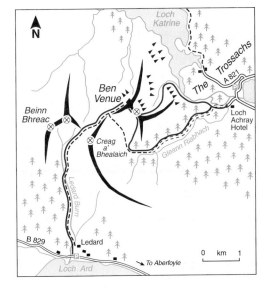

Stob a' Choin

Paul Milligan

Stob a' Choin; 869m; (OS Sheets 56 and 57; NN416159); *peak of the dog*

STOB A' CHOIN

Situated 3km SW of Inverlochlarig, Stob a' Choin is the highest point of the range of hills lying between the glacial trenches of Loch Katrine and Glen Gyle to the south and Loch Voil and the River Larig to the north. This fine hill, with its steep northern flanks and pointed summit, increasingly dominates the view as one approaches from Balquhidder along the narrow public road on the north side of Loch Voil. From the north or NW, the character of Stob a' Choin is well seen, its north face rising steeply in a single sweep from the River Larig to its castellated summit ridge of four tops, typical of the Crianlarich hills with their grassy lower slopes and knobbly ridges.

The public road ends 750 metres east of Inverlochlarig farm at a car park. From there walk west along the right of way which leads eventually to Inverarnan in Glen Falloch, and was once the coffin route for the MacGregors on their way to Balquhidder Kirk. Pass through the farm and continue for 1km to a footbridge across the River Larig. There is a choice of route, either directly and steeply SW to reach the north ridge of Stob a' Choin, or SE up easier slopes to reach the NE ridge. There is no access to the hill from Blaircreich through the forest at the foot of the NE ridge.

The direct route is a long steep pull up grassy slopes which under soft snow cover in winter might be avalanche prone, and under hard snow or ice would definitely require ice axe and crampons. From the footbridge make a rising traverse SW, crossing the stream flowing down from the Bealach Coire an Laoigh at about 400m, and continue SW below a line of broken crags to reach the north ridge at a little platform at 630m. The ridge leads to the north top, which has a cairn and finer views, but is 4m lower than the summit. (4.5km; 740m; 2h 20min).

The NE ridge is a more attractive route: less relentlessly steep and on a good winter's day receiving some sunshine, which the direct route does not. It does involve a bit more climbing over the eastern tops of Stob a' Choin, but they give a pleasant traverse along an undulating steep-sided ridge. (6km; 900m; 2h 50min).

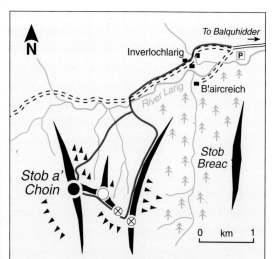

Hamish Brown

Ceann na Baintighearna and Beinn Stacath from the River Larig

Beinn Stacath; 771m; (OS Sheet 57; NN474163); *peaky hill*

BEINN STACATH

This hill is not named on maps, but is shown as a 771m trig point. This Corbett is not a distinctive hill, and when seen from Glen Buckie, which is the usual route of approach, the summit is hidden behind the upper part of the east ridge. It is possible to get a glimpse of the hill from the road on the north side of Loch Voil near Craigruie, and it is seen clearly from the end of this road near Inverlochlarig, the western slopes above the Invernenty Burn being forested and offering no obvious line of ascent.

The narrow public road which goes south from Balquhidder up Glen Buckie ends at Ballimore farm, where cars can be parked. From there cross the Calair Burn and follow the right of way westwards on the south side of the burn. The path is rather muddy after wet weather, and in 2km it turns south towards Brig o' Turk. The track on the north side of the Calair Burn may appear to be a better route, but should not be followed as it goes through an area enclosed by a high fence which may be used for deer farming.

Near the point where the right of way turns south below the crags of Bealach a' Chonnaidh, leave the path and cross the Calair Burn. This is usually quite easy, but if the burn is in spate go upstream for about 400 metres to a bridge across the Allt a' Ghlinne Dhuibh at 508165. Once on the north bank of this burn, bear NW across the rising moor to the foot of the east ridge of Beinn Stacath and follow its broad undulating crest. There is a faint path, more like a sheep track, which leads over three or four grassy knolls. Beyond the last of these climb more steeply west towards a prominent little rocky point on the main north-south ridge of the hill, and from there go NNW for about 300 metres past a lochan on the crest of this broad ridge to the summit trig point. (6km; 650m; 2h 30min).

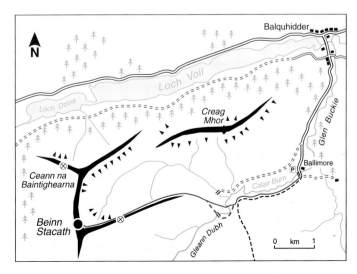

Ben Ledi from Callander

Ben Ledi; 879m; (OS Sheet 57; NN562097); *hill of the gentle slope,* or *God's hill*

Ben Ledi rises about 8km to the WNW of Callander on the southern edge of the Highlands. Like Ben Lomond to its west and Ben Vorlich and Stuc a' Chroin to its NE, it is a prominent landmark in the view from the lowlands of Central Scotland. The main spine of the hill rises from the east end of Loch Venachar to the summit as a broad grassy ridge and continues to Benvane, 4km to the north. The east side of Ben Ledi above the Pass of Leny and Loch Lubnaig, is steep and craggy and extensively forest covered. On the west, grassy slopes rise from the Glen Finglas Reservoir to the summit ridge and a new woodland of native trees has been planted on that side of the hill by the Woodland Trust.

The traditional route to Ben Ledi starts from a car park near the Corrieachrombie bridge at 586092, ascending to the broad and undulating SE ridge and thence to the summit. (4.5km 760m; 2h 20min).

An alternative goes north along the Sustrans cycle track towards Stank. Go along this track for just over 1km, then follow a forest track NW uphill and at the point where it turns left go up a path through the forest in the Stank Glen just above the burn. Continue uphill by the path to reach the open hillside at a prominent waymarker. The route continues WNW by a path through the heather to reach a fence. Go along it to a gate and stile and from there climb west up a better path to reach the Bealach nan Corp (557110) at the foot of Ben Ledi's NW ridge. Go up the ridge by a line of fence posts and finish along a fairly level crest. (5.5km; 800m; 2h 40min).

BEN LEDI

When the traditional car park is full a 'new' route to Ben Ledi starts from the car park at 608081 near Bochastle on the A821 300 metres south of Kilmahog. From there a track, not shown on the present map, goes west through the forest on the north side of Bochastle Hill, to cross the footpath through the forest near 580093 and join the existing forest track above Coireachrombie at 580095.This track will give the most direct access to Ben Ledi from the Bochastle car park, and it may even be possible to cycle some distance up the hill.

The western approach to Ben Ledi starts from Brig o'Turk. Go through the village for 1km, (cars can be parked at the end of the public road) and follow the right-hand private road which goes uphill above the Glen Finglas Reservoir to some cottages and sheds. The newly planted woodland lies on the hillside above, below the rocky knoll of Stuc Odhar. Continue NE up the track in Gleann Casaig for 1.5km to the point where the track crosses a small stream and turns north, and from there climb up grassy slopes for 2km to reach the ridge of Ben Ledi a short distance NW of the summit. (6km; 760m; 2h 40min). This western approach is now pleasanter than routes on the eastern side of Ben Ledi.

The energetic can combine Ben Ledi and Benvane in a long high level traverse.

Benvane; 821m; (OS Sheet 57; NN535137); *white hill*

Benvane is the highest point on the 8km-long ridge which goes NNW from Ben Ledi to end above Glen Buckie to the south of Balquhidder. Like Ben Ledi, the hill is forested along most of the eastern slopes above Loch Lubnaig. There are four distinct routes up Benvane: from Balquhidder by Glen Buckie and the north ridge of the hill; from Strathyre through the forest on the east side of the hill; from Brig o' Turk by the Glen Finglas Reservoir; from Ben Ledi by a high level traverse.

The route from Glen Buckie is very straightforward, starting at the end of the public road at Ballimore farm, where there is space for cars to be parked. Cross the Calair Burn and at the right of way signpost start uphill, going due south past a little plantation and up the long north ridge of Benvane directly to the summit. (4km; 620m; 2h).

The route from Strathyre (the least attractive) goes along the minor road on the west side of the River Balvag for just over 2km. One may drive to there and park at the roadside (557151). Follow the forest track which climbs to the col at the head of Glen Buckie and turns north there. 100 metres beyond the turn take a path on the left and follow it NW through the forest for 100 metres to reach a wide clearing. Continue NW following vague ATV tracks across very wet and boggy ground to a stile over a high fence. Turn SW and climb up the grassy hillside to the north ridge of Benvane, and follow to the summit. (4.5km; 670m; 2h 10min).

The Brig o' Turk route may be preferred by those driving north from Glasgow via Aberfoyle, as the driving distance is reduced. From Brig o' Turk, where cars should be left, walk up the private road on the east side of the Glen Finglas Reservoir as far as Gleann Casaig, and climb the 4.5km south ridge of Benvane, passing a knoll at 753m shortly before reaching the summit. (7km; 700m; 2h 50min).

The Ben Ledi – Benvane traverse follows the broad grassy 6km ridge between the two hills. Going north from the 650m col reached on the ascent of Ben Ledi from Stank Glen, Lochan nan Corp is soon reached and, beyond, a short ascent leads to a level section with another small lochan on the crest. The ridge to Ardnandave Hill branches eastwards thereafter and the main ridge turns NW and drops over Stuc Dhubh to its lowest point at 600m before rising, turning west for almost 1km and finally rising NNW to Benvane.

The most efficient way of traversing both hills if you have to return to your starting point is probably to start from Brig o' Turk and climb Ben Ledi from Gleann Casaig, traverse to Benvane as described above and descend its south ridge to the Glen Finglas Reservoir and back to Brig o' Turk. The total distance is about 19 km, with 1100m of ascent.

BENVANE

Benvane

Mark Gear

Creag Mac Ranaich

Meall an t-Seallaidh; 852m; (OS Sheet 51; NN542234); *hill of the view*
Creag Mac Ranaich; 809m; (OS Sheet 51; NN545255); *Mac Ranaich's rock*

**MEALL AN T-
SEALLAIDH**

**CREAG MAC
RANAICH**

These two hills lie between Balquhidder and Glen Dochart in an area of high ground bounded on the east by Glen Ogle. Meall an t-Seallaidh is a grassy hill, best seen from the south (Strathyre or Glen Buckie) and from that direction the most obvious feature is the continuously steep hillside rising directly above the road to Balquhidder, which gives the impression that any ascent of that side of the hill would require an unrelenting effort.

Creag Mac Ranaich is more remote, rising at the head of Glen Kendrum, and can be seen from the A84 midway between Kingshouse Hotel and Lochearnhead. High up just below the summit there is a big SE facing buttress which is an impressive feature of the hill, although discontinuous and intersected by grass ledges.

These two hills can be climbed together, and Lochearnhead is probably the best starting point for this traverse. The route from there starts at the south end of the village up the very narrow road past the Episcopal church, but there is virtually no space along this road for car parking and the small church car park should not be used. Use the public car park in Lochearnhead beside the Crieff road, and walk from there. Go up the narrow road past the church for 400 metres to a bridge, go under it and follow the cycle track uphill round a few zig-zags to the line of the one time Edinburgh to Oban railway, then go SW along the line for almost 1km to a bridge. Cross this bridge and go up Glen Kendrum, following a track to the head of the glen at the bealach between Creag Mac Ranaich and Meall an t-Seallaidh. Climb NE up steep grass slopes between small crags to reach the flat summit area of Creag Mac Ranaich where there are two tops about 300 metres apart, the northern one being marginally higher. (9km; 700m; 3h 10min). In thick weather the cairn on the northern top can be identified by an iron fence post.

To continue the traverse, return to the track at the bealach and go SW across rough heather and peat to the col NW of Cam Chreag, where there is a little lochan. Turn south and go over or round Cam Chreag and along the grassy ridge to Meall an t-Seallaidh. (11km; 960m; 4h 10min). To return to Glen Kendrum, descend ENE down grassy slopes, steep at the top, easier lower down. Cross the Kendrum Burn without difficulty, unless in spate, in which case cross higher up.

A much shorter ascent of Creag Mac Ranaich can be made from the A85 at the head of Glen Ogle. Park just south of the loch at the top of the pass, cross a bridge over the disused railway and climb SW beside a plantation. Continue SW up the steep rough hillside to the col just NW of Meall Sgallachd and continue up the north ridge of Creag Mac Ranaich, passing a tall cairn just before reaching the summit. (3km; 530m; 1h 40min).

Meall an t-Seallaidh can be climbed easily from Balquhidder village, going up the right of way in Kirkton Glen. Start from the Auld Kirk, where Rob Roy McGregor is buried, and follow the path up into the forest to join a forest track which leads north almost to the upper edge of the trees. Continue along a path onto the open hillside below the prominent little crag Leum an Eireannaich, then make a rising traverse east towards Cam Chreag where the route described above is joined and followed south to Meall an t-Seallaidh. (6km; 710m; 2h 40min).

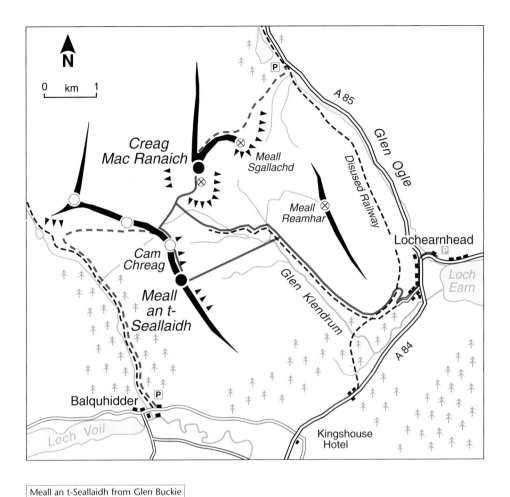

Meall an t-Seallaidh from Glen Buckie

Donald Bennet

Beinn Each

Paul Milligan

Beinn Each; 813m; (OS Sheet 57; NN601158); *horse hill*

BEINN EACH

Beinn Each stands on the southern edge of the Highlands but is hidden from the main road past Loch Lubnaig. It is the main summit on the twisting and hummocky SW ridge of popular Munro, Stuc a' Chroin, with which it could be combined.

The nearest point of access is from a lay-by on the side of the A84 (584136). Follow the right of way which climbs steeply through trees behind Ardchullarie More to join a forest track leading north through to Glen Ample. Once over the watershed turn east and climb steeply up the north side of the burn which comes down in a series of small waterfalls from below Beinn Each's summit. Follow the north branch to its source. Continue NNE over steep, undulating ground for a further 300 metres to reach a line of fence posts which are followed to the summit. (3km; 690m; 1h 50min).

Stuc a' Chroin (617174) lies 2.5km to the NE along a knobbly ridge. From Beinn Each descend steeply north to Bealack nan Cabar. Continue NE over a lower top to Bealach Glas, and climb east then NE to the summit. The route follows the line of an old fence which winds its way through many little outcrops. (5.5km; 1030m; 2h 50min). To return to the start descent NW to Creag Dubh then cross the corrie northwards for the path to Glenample and the tramp back over the watershed. Best of all, making transport arrangements, is to continue over Stuc a' Chroin to Loch Earn.

A large sign at the start gives notice of restrictions during the stalking season.

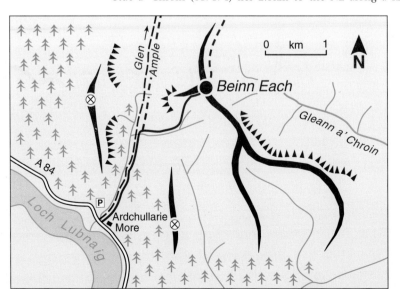

Derek Sime

Meall na Fearna

Meall na Fearna; 809m; (OS Sheets 51 and 57; NN650186); *alder hill*

Meall na Fearna stands on the western edge of a tract of rugged hill country lying to the east of Ben Vorlich between Glen Artney and Strath Earn: a grassy hill with heather and peat bog which is home for many grouse, hare and deer. From both north and south the summit is hidden by smaller outlying tops. The high undulating ground above 600m may cause route finding problems in misty weather.

The shortest approach is from the north. Park on the grass verge at Ardvorlich on the south side of Loch Earn. Go through the east gate of Ardvorlich House and follow the private road which soon becomes a rough track south into Glen Vorlich. After 1km, at a bifurcation, take the grassy east branch for 3.5km to the Glen Vorlich – Gleann an Dubh Choirein bealach. In its upper reaches the Glen Vorlich path is intermittent and boggy. The route continues steeply NE onto an unnamed outlying top and then turns SE via a shallow col of peat hags to the summit marked by a handful of stones. (6.5km; 600m; 2h 30min).

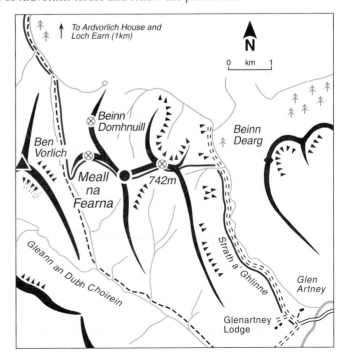

There is a longer southern approach from Glen Artney. From the car park by Glenartney Church go SW along the road to Glenartney Lodge. Continue NNW on a good track along Srath a' Ghlinne. Leave the track after 3.5km. (It is possible to cycle to this point). Strike west up the north side of the burn which leads onto point 742m. Descend to a col of peat hags and continue up the final grassy slope to Meall na Fearna. (8.5km; 650m; 3h).

Both routes have restrictions during the stalking season.

Andrew Dempster

Creag Uchdag from the south-east

Creag Uchdag; 879m; (OS Sheet 51; NN708323); *crag of the hollows/slopes*
Creagan na Beinne; 888m; (OS Sheets 51 or 52; NN744368); *little hill of the rocks/crags*
Auchnafree Hill; 789m; (OS Sheet 52; NN808308); *hill of the deer forest field*

CREAG UCHDAG

CREAGAN NA
BEINNE

AUCHNAFREE HILL

Between Loch Tay, Strath Earn and the Sma' Glen there is some surprisingly hilly country with one Munro (Ben Chonzie), these three Corbetts, and several other sprawling summits of near-Corbett height. While Auchnafree Hill can be climbed along with Ben Chonzie, the Corbetts themselves are well scattered with deep glens separating them. Historically the glens have been important through routes and various cross-country combinations are described into which one could fit the Corbetts. The hills are generally big convex domes, deeply cut by corries and often with rough peaty plateaux. The most recent maps are recommended for accurate information on the many tracks bulldozed from the glens up onto the heights.

Glen Almond and Glen Lednock give lengthy valley access from east and south, with shorter Glen Turret between. On the Loch Tay side the glens are much shorter. Glen Almond has a private road up most of its length, but is a pedestrian (and cycle) right of way through to Ardtalnaig on Loch Tay. Glen Turret has a private water authority road up to the dam and an estate track thereafter almost up to Lochan Uaine. (The public are allowed to drive up to the dam, despite the notice at the start of the road). The public road in Glen Lednock ends at the dam but it is easy to walk along the north side of the reservoir to pick up the old right of way (cut by the raised water level) which leads to the old ferry inn of Ardeonaig on Loch Tay. From Invergeldie, 2km below the Loch Lednock dam, another right of way goes over to the head of Glen Almond at Dunan and down to Ardtalnaig. There is also an interesting path from Glen Quaich (4km from Amulree) through Glen Lochan to Auchnafree in Glen Almond.

Combining Corbetts with good cross-country routes is recommended; there are many possibilities, one or two of which may be mentioned. Drive to Invergeldie and by Loch Lednock, take in Creag Uchdag on the way to Ardeonaig for the night. The next day walk to Ardtalnaig and traverse Creagan na Beinne to Dunan, then on over to Invergeldie again. Auchnafree Hill can be traversed using Glen Almond and Glen Turret. As the whole area is sheep country with plenty of grouse moors too, and some stalking, the sporting season is best avoided. There are also huge numbers of mountain hares, particularly on Auchnafree Hill and Ben Chonzie. The Strath Earn side has an unusual number of waterfalls: Monzie, Keltie, Barvick, Turret, The Deil's Cauldron and Sput Rolla below the Lednock dam.

Creag Uchdag from the south is reached by setting off from the car park at the Lednock dam and walking along the north shore to a circular stone enclosure. A steady rising traverse thereafter leads to the knobbly heights. (3.5km; 530m; 1h 50min). From the north the path can be followed up the Finglen to the watershed, then east for the summit. Minor crags on both routes, can easily be avoided. (6km; 760m; 2h 50min).

Creagan na Beinne is easiest from the north, Ardtalnaig, side. It is worth walking through Gleann a' Chilleine to Dunan (notable moraine bumps) and ascending the Corbett by the south ridge, descending by the north ridge and either down to Tullichglass or by the stalkers path beyond an intermediate bump towards Beinn Bhreac. (10km; 760m; 3h 20m). Waterfall enthusiasts could descend to the NNE and visit the Acharn Falls.

Auchnafree Hill is almost equally easy from three directions: Glen Turret, Glen Almond and Glen Lochan. Glen Turret is very attractive, starting in rich farm land and ending in utter solitude. Parking is available at the dam. The Falls of Turret are worth a diversion. At 806286 a track (not on the map) zig-zags up to the slot of the burn below Ton Eich; use this, then go up the prow of Ton Eich and round to Auchnafree's large cairn. (From dam 6km; 390m; 2h). Add an hour if walking up from the Distillery). Descend westwards to enjoy the fastness of the upper Turret.

From Newton Bridge there is an equally good walk up Glen Almond to Auchnafree. A track twists up onto Crom Chreag from which Auchnafree Hill is easily reached. (11km; 660m; 3h 20min). The same ascent would also be made if coming through Glen Lochan from Glen Quaich. (9km; 660m; 3h 20min). Glen Almond can be regained by descending any of the deep corries which are such a feature. The Allt Coire Chultrain is perhaps the most interesting. The crest eastwards is very broken and boggy in places but offers a high-level return route to Newton Bridge.

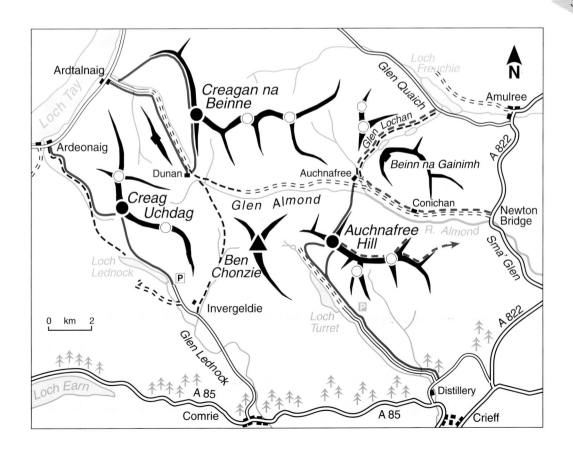

The Ochils with the Nebit above Alva

The Ochils

Ben Cleuch*; 721m; (OS Sheet 58; NN902006); *gullied hill*
Dumyat*; 418m; (OS Sheet 57 and 58; NS835977); *fort of the Maeatae*

BEN CLEUCH*

DUMYAT*

Often mistaken for Highland outliers, the Ochils are extensive and impressive lowland hills. The most enticing view is from the south, where a long frieze of 35-degree slopes rears above the Hillfoot villages stretching east from Stirling. Only two parts of the range see much human traffic: the swathe of 600m summits enclosed by the loop of the River Devon (including the highest point, Ben Cleuch) and isolated, craggy Dumyat at the western end, well seen from Stirling University.

One can take in the highest tops plus Dumyat in a long traverse, but this omits the excellent southern spurs and gorges. Ben Cleuch is often approached by The Law, north of Tillicoultry's Mill Glen, with an eventual descent via Ben Ever and the Silver Glen track. (4km; 700m; 2h). Although this is a fast circuit, it is more interesting to use the Gannel path on ascent (turn back abruptly uphill just before the end of the Mill Glen walkway), and then to descend along Millar Hill, SSE of Ben Ever. This ridge eventually drops steeply to woods and screes, but crossing the fence brings a path which re-enters the Mill Glen via steep zig-zags. Alternatively, an old path drops SW over Wood Hill to meet a woodland through-route just east of the Silver Burn.

Blairdenon Hill can be added to Ben Cleuch across Ben Buck followed by an area of hags and heather. Better, though, is to include it in another fine Hillfoots circuit, the Colsnaur-Bengengie horseshoe. Both these outliers are under 600m and illustrate how walkers who visit merely the highest Ochils miss much that is good in the range.

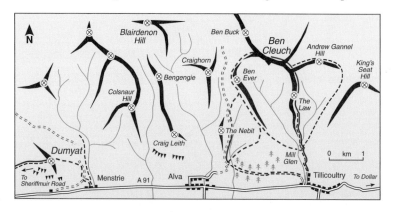

Dumyat is a Sunday stroll from lay-bys close to where pylons cross the Sheriffmuir road. Ascent of the eastern flank from Menstrie is also easy, but best of all is Warroch Glen, a cleft gained by a steep rightward traverse from the Blairlogie car park. Although cluttered with cairns and ironwork, the top of Dumyat is a great viewpoint. A full traverse of the Ochils over its 610m (2000ft) summits, from Sheriffmuir to Glendevon is a fine hillwalk.

East Lomond; West Lomond in the background

The Lomond Hills

West Lomond*; 522m; (OS Sheets 58 and 59; NO197066); *west beacon hill*
East Lomond*; 424m; (OS Sheets 58 and 59; NO244062); *east beacon hill*

Though there are many access points and local interests and strong walkers could start at Scotlandwell and take in Bishop Hill as well as the Lomonds, to reach Falkland, the popular start is the Craidmead car park (toilet) on the hill road from Leslie to Falkland (228062).

A track heads WNW to reach West Lomond, the highest of these hills, the last slope being tackled by circuiting round to the north. (3km; 230m; 1hr 10min).

Another track heads east to a car park/relay masts site below the cone of East Lomond, the summit (fort rings, view indicator) reached by steep paths. (2km; 140m; 50min). A descriptive walk round a limekiln lies off the track (237059). A steep path drops down into historic Falkland and, driver allowing, visiting both tops and descending to Falkland is recommended.

WEST LOMOND*

EAST LOMOND*

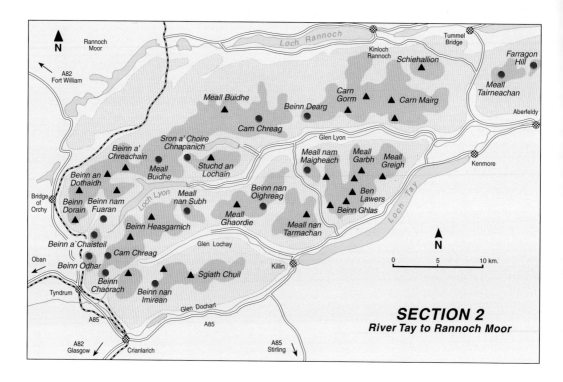

SECTION 2

River Tay to Rannoch Moor

Raymond Hay

Farragon Hill from Loch Derculich

Farragon Hill; 783m; (OS Sheet 52; NN840553); *St. Fergan's hill*
Meall Tairneachan; 787m; (OS Sheet 52; NN807543); *hill of thunder*

These hills are the highest points on the expanse of high moorland stretching west from Pitlochry towards Schiehallion. In the age of North Sea oil, this area has acquired an added commercial importance as a source of the mineral barytes, and there are several mines high up on the hills with tracks leading to them. Each hill can be ascended in a half day or evening, the combination of the two is best accomplished with a cycle.

For Meall Tarineachan, park near the junction of the B846 and the road leading to Schiehallion at a public carpark for an old limekiln (778546). Ascend directly along the edge of the forest to a small top. A short traverse north of Meall Odhar Mor leads to several interesting rocky knolls with fine views across to Schiehallion. The summit plateau lies around the horseshoe shaped ridge. Traverse this easily with only minor decent and ascent to the cylindrical trig point. (3km; 410m; 1h 20min). Return by the same route.

Farragon Hill is further removed from the road, but is accessible by a track passing only 1km east of the summit. The use of a cycle is a great advantage. From the south, use one of several private roads through the Edradynate Estate (no parking on the estate without permission) starting from the minor road on the north side of the River Tay near Edradynate. The estate requests that walkers check with them prior to walking in order to avoid stalking or mine activities. The tarmac road ends at Brae of Cluny and the relevant track branches north just past the trees. From there the track climbs past Loch Derculich to the ridge east of the summit before continuing to Loch Tummel.

From the north, start at Netherton at 870596 beside the road on the south side of Loch Tummel. From there a track leads 6km uphill past Beinn Eagagach to the ridge just east of Farragon Hill. Once on the ridge, go WSW to Farragon Hill, whose summit is fairly craggy. (7.3km; 700m; 2h 50min from the south). (7.25km; 850m; 3h from the north).

In order to ascend the hills in combination, the best approach starts from the B846 between Coshieville and Tummel Bridge at a height of just over 300m, where a track (780562) goes SE uphill through the forest. This track is for mining access and parking is not permitted where it leaves the B846. It is best to park as above and the use of a cycle is recommended. Cycle up the track until almost on the summit of Meall Tairneachan. (3.8km; 470m 1h 40min). The track is then followed past a barytes mine to its end at 826550. Cross a boggy corrie and ascend through a gap in the crags SW of the summit of Farragon Hill (8km; 700m 3h).

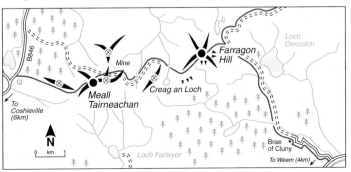

The shoulder of Beinn Dearg looking up Glen Lyon

Beinn Dearg; 830m; (OS Sheet 51; NN608497); *red hill*
Cam Chreag; 862m; (OS Sheet 51; NN536491); *crooked crag*

60

BEINN DEARG

CAM CHREAG

These two rounded hills rise on the north side of Glen Lyon above Innerwick and Bridge of Balgie. The right of way across the Lairig Ghallabhaich from Glen Lyon to Loch Rannoch passes between them. Both hills can be climbed from Innerwick, but it is better to tackle them in turn rather than attempt any high level traverse between as the intervening ground is rough and there is a great deal of descent and ascent. The approaches from the north are much longer, only the Lairig Ghallabhaich right of way giving access through the extensive Rannoch Forest.

Going to Cam Chreag, take the track from the car park on the west side of the Allt Ghallabhaich through the trees and across the Allt a' Choire Uidhre. Further west the track crosses back to the south bank of this stream and continues for 2.5km to end at a hut below the east face of Cam Chreag. The crags on this face are nowhere very big, and the ascent can best be made about 500 metres SE of the summit to reach the long level shoulder of the hill. (6km; 660m; 2h 30min).

The descent can be varied by going south down heathery slopes to reach the Glen Lyon road just above Gallin, 4.5km west of Innerwick. The walk along the road in this part of the glen is very pleasant.

For Beinn Dearg head up the east bank of the Allt Ghallabhaich, keeping by the river until the forest is reached. The pull up through the forest is quite steep and one can either continue along the right of way and turn east 500 metres after leaving the forest. Alternatively climb the zig-zag forest track to the edge of the trees and climb east from there up the long west flank of Beinn Dearg, which is a featureless dome. Hence, the summit can be hard to find in the mist. The true summit is about 100 metres south of a cairn on the fence line. Beinn Dearg is a finer hill than Cam Chreag, with good views to the Ben Lawers range. (4.5km; 630m; 2h 10min).

On the descent it is rewarding to walk out along the level shoulder of Creag Ard, from where there is a good view eastwards down the length of lower Glen Lyon. From Creag Ard the return to Innerwick goes west then SW to avoid the steepest slopes.

A longer circuit of Beinn Dearg and Creag Ard together with the Munro Carn Gorm can be

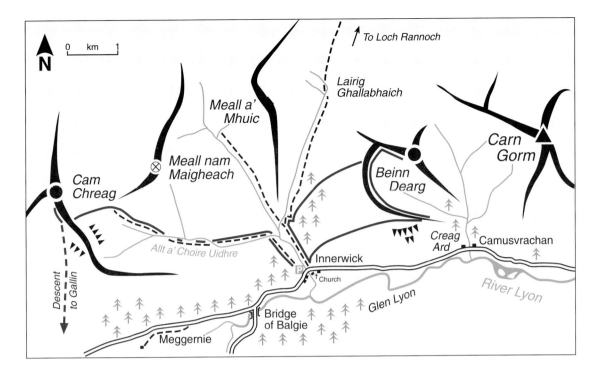

made starting and finishing at Camusvrachan.

If intending to climb Beinn Dearg and Cam Chreag in a single day, it is not necessary to return to Innerwick provided the streams at the confluence of the Allt a' Choire Uidhre and the Allt Ghallabhaich can be crossed.

Cam Chreag of Glen Lyon with Shiehallion in the distance

Peter Bailey

Meall nan Subh

Meall nan Subh; 806m; (OS Sheet 51; NN460397); *hill of the soo (raspberry)*

Meall nan Subh is characterised by a superabundance of rough lumps, crags, bogs and dubs but its position, close to the road between Glen Lyon and Glen Lochay, means that it can be climbed as a coda to larger scores in those glens.

This road crosses the pass between Meall nan Subh and its massive Munro neighbour Beinn Heasgarnich, and there is a gate just south of its highest point at 452386 which may be locked. However, one can drive as far as the gate, if not from one glen to the other, so the ascent of this hill can be started at a height of 500m. Park at any convenient point near the gate and leave the road near the highest point. There are several rocky spurs, each one a temptation to rest awhile, and it is worth wending over to the most northerly bump (459398) which is the best viewpoint and gives a reward out of all proportion to the effort needed to reach it. Beinn Heasgarnich shows its great proportions, and there is a long view down Glen Lyon.

The highest point is about 200 metres to the SE, but in thick weather it might be difficult to decide which of the three or four bumps on the flat summit is the true top. (1.5km; 310m; 1h). Descend more or less by the route of ascent. Far from having no features of interest, this small hill rewards the modest ascent.

Sron a' Choire Chnapanich; 837m; (OS Sheet 51; NN456453); *nose of the knobbly corrie*
Meall Buidhe; 910m; (OS Sheet 51; NN427449); *yellow hill*

These remote Corbetts lie above the upper reaches of Glen Lyon from where they are usually climbed together. The energetic can even incorporate the Munro of Stuchd an Lochain for a tramper's triptych. Meall Buidhe is rather lost in the jumble of hills on the north side of Loch Lyon, but has an extensive view over Rannoch Moor.

Pubil, at the head of Glen Lyon, is indicated as a dead end (but it is generally possible to drive from there over the pass to Glen Lochay and Killin). Park either at the hamlet or on/under the dam and head along the north side of Loch Lyon by a track. After 1km however, head up by one of the burns and then traverse round to reach the col at about 700m between the headwaters of the Eas nan Aighean and the Feith Thalain. A fence leads north up the bold shoulder ahead, and above it a wide upland walk leads round west to Meall Buidhe. (5km; 570m; 2h 10min). (Note the revised height). The northern slopes drop down in a great brown sweep to Rannoch Moor, with the vast Rannoch Forest and the railway adding touches of human geometry to the landscape, in contrast with the convex slopes on the Loch Lyon side.

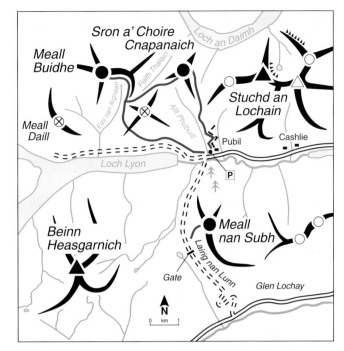

Return to the col from where the fence eventually leads on to the second Corbett however, rather than following the fence, it is easier to go down the Feith Thalain for 1km and then bear up east to reach the wide col 1km SW of Sron a' Choire Chanpanich.

The final slopes up the SW side of this hill give remarkably smooth walking on mossy turf and heather, shorn to the texture of coir matting. The summit is a grassy prow high above Loch an Daimh. (10km; 810m; 3h 40min). The true height of this hill only appeared on maps in 1987 (until then it was shown as c.686m!)

Descend the SSE ridge towards a col (whence the Meall an Odhar ridge offers the Munro temptation) and angle down to the Allt Phubuill. If returning to the dam cross to descend above field/plantings; for Pubil pick up and follow down the zig-zags of the track.

Sron a' Choire Chnapanich over Loch Daimh

Alan Hall

Beinn nan Oighreag; 909m; (OS Sheet 51; NN541412); *cloudberry hill*

In the 1930's it was suggested that Beinn nan Oighreag might just be a Munro, so it saw a flurry of activity unequalled until the present. Historically, this hill must have seen plenty of droving and other traffic on foot through the Lairig Breisleich, the most direct pass from Bridge of Balgie in Glen Lyon to Killin. Old descriptions described the pass as "a villainous bog, all peat hags and heathery hummocks". Large clusters of shielings are shown in the glen leading south from the Lairig Breisleich and this glen gives the most attractive route of ascent, starting in Glen Lochay.

In rather less than 1km, from where the two lower Glen Lochay roads meet (539353) look out for a small tarred road on the right. Park tidily here and head off up the small road with its zig-zags leading to a hill path which then circles round the open bracken hillside (superb views up Glen Lochay) to follow up the Allt Dhuin Croisg to a scattering of ruined shielings. Immediately above these shielings the south ridge of Beinn nan Oighreag rises at an easy angle and gives a straightforward ascent to the summit. (7km; 770m; 2h 50min).

If suitable transport can be arranged on the road from Loch Tay to Glen Lyon, it would be pleasant to descend the NE ridge, thus completing the traverse of the hill. It is also quite possible to combine the ascent of Beinn nan Oighreag with its neighbouring Munro, Meall Ghaordaidh, the col between them being about 640m. Otherwise, the simplest return to Glen Lochay is by the route of ascent.

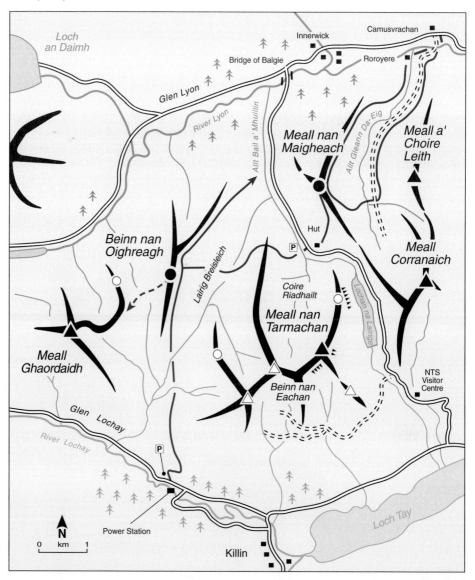

BEINN NAN OIGHREAG

64

Meall nam Maigheach

It is also possible to climb Beinn nan Oighreag from the east, starting at 500m on the road between Loch Tay and Glen Lyon at a small hut near the point 582417 where the road turns north to follow the Allt Bail a' Mhuilinn down to Glen Lyon. Bear due west across the rounded ridge (low part of the north ridge of Beinn nan Eachan) then descend to the unavoidable bogs at the summit of the Lairig Breisleich and climb directly up the east side of Beinn nan Oighreag. (4.5km; 560m; 2h). A line of fence posts across the path may be useful in misty conditions. As Meall nam Maigheach can be climbed from the same starting point they could easily be tackled in turn on the same day.

Meall nam Maigheach; 779m; (OS Sheet 51; NN585436); *hill of the hares*

The lower summit, Meall Luaidhe, means *hill of lead*, a reminder of one-time mining, well described in V.A. Firsoff's book *In the Hills of Breadalbane*. The reason for the name Gleann Da-Eig (*glen of the two eggs*) for the glen on the east side of Meall nam Maigheach is not known, but that glen offers the most pleasing route up the hill, although few walkers actually take it. The possibility of a starting point at the height of 500m on the Loch Tay to Glen Lyon road is irresistible. Beinn nan Oighreag can also be climbed from the same starting point, offering two Corbetts in one day.

The best starting point is at the roadside hut (582417) where the road turns north to follow the Allt Bail a' Mhuilinn. Parking elsewhere is not easy, and the obvious small quarry spot near the cairn at the watershed is not recommended as the natural line from there to the hill over Meall nan Eun runs into an unfriendly terrain of peat hags and heather.

Meall nam Maigheach presents a shallow corrie towards the hut, with a wall visible on the left (north) flank. Follow either flank, avoiding the worst of the hill's peaty areas; in mist the wall, which leads up onto the summit, is the surer line and following it down to the road gives the fastest way off. (2km; 290m; 1h).

Those seeking an interesting walk rather than a short exercise in bog-dodging should start in Glen Lyon at Camusvrachan. Cross the River Lyon, go west to Roroyere and follow the stalkers path up the west side of the Allt Gleann Da-Eig. Skirting the north facing crags of Creag an Eildneag climb up the fine eastern prow of this hill which so dominates the views from Glen Lyon and is, in its turn, a magnificent viewpoint up and down what many regard as the finest glen south of the Caledonian Canal. A grand walk of 3km leads SW to the rather undistinguished top of Meall nam Maigheach. (6.5km; 620m; 2h 30min). There is a bulldozed track in Gleann Da-Eig, and this can be used as an alternative route of return to Glen Lyon by first descending steeply east from the summit to reach it.

Beinn Odhar; 901m; (OS Sheet 50; NN337338); *dun-coloured hill*
Beinn Chaorach; 818m; (OS Sheet 50; NN358328); *sheep hill*
Cam Chreag; 884m; (OS Sheet 50; NN375346); *crooked crag*
Beinn nam Fuaran; 806m; (OS Sheet 50; NN361381); *hill of the springs*
Beinn a' Chaisteil; 886m; (OS Sheet 50; NN347364); *castle hill*

These steep-sided grassy hills lying to the NW of Tyndrum are bounded on the south and west by the A82, and to the north by Auch Gleann. To their east rise the Munros of Ben Challum and Creag Mhor. They form a very compact group so, despite a good deal of climbing and descent, it is quite possible to traverse all of them in a single day – a unique Corbett 'hand'. In fact, this is the only straight forward combination of Corbett to allow a hillwalker to tick five Corbetts in a day.

BEINN ODHAR

BEINN CHAORACH

CAM CHREAG

BEINN NAM
FUARAN

BEINN A'
CHAISTEIL

The best starting point is on the A82 near its summit 329331 where adequate parking is available. A short distance north of this point the West Highland Way makes use of a cattle-creep to cross under the West Highland Railway. From the east side of the railway climb steeply SE to gain the south ridge of Beinn Odhar which is followed up an old track to a long disused lead mine, beyond which a small lochan is passed before reaching the summit. (2.5km; 600m; 1h 40min).

Descend SE for 300m to reach a lochan where one comes to the remains of an electric fence. Follow this ESE to the col between Beinn Odhar and Beinn Chaorach and steeply up onto the ridge of the latter hill. The fence turns north about 200 metres north of the summit of Beinn Chaorach. (5km; 970m; 3h). Descend the smooth ridge NNE to the next col, where there are the remains of a small wind generator which once provided power for the electric fence. From there bear NE then east up more broken hillside to the top of Cam Chreag. (7.5km; 1220m; 3h 50min). The old electric fences on these hills are unusually close to ground-level.

Descend the long NNW ridge of Cam Chreag to the Abhainn Ghlas, cross this stream and climb due north to the summit of Beinn nam Fuaran. (11.5km; 1630m; 5h 20min). Follow the fence in descent steeply SW down a stony slope to a bealach of peat hags and continue along

66

in the same direction to the summit of Beinn a' Chaisteil. (13.5km; 1970m; 6h 20min).

The broken cliffs of Creagan Liatha prevent a direct descent south or SW to Glen Coralan, so head SE down the ridge to a track in the glen which can be followed down to the Auch Gleann and the meeting with the West Highland Way near Auch. Finally, walk south along the Way for almost 3km, only climbing another 100m to the day's starting point.

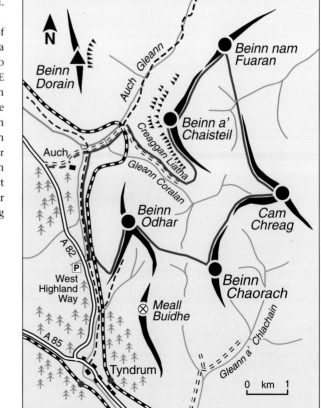

Beinn Odhar

67

Beinn a' Chaisteil and Beinn Odhar from Beinn Bhreac-liath

The Meggernie slopes of Cam Chreag from above Bridge of Balgie

Auch Glen and Beinn a' Chaisteil

Beinn nan Imirean from Glen Dochart

Hamish Brown

Beinn nan Imirean; 849m; (OS Sheet 51; NN419309); *hill of the ridge*

Beinn nan Imirean stands at the west end of the extensive tract of relatively uninteresting hills and moorland between Glen Dochart and Glen Lochay, and is a modest hill which from the A85 appears as an insignificant cone rising above the peat moors guarding Meall Glas. On its own the ascent is a half day's exercise, but as an outlier of Meall Glas, it can be the prelude to a hefty traverse of a Corbett and two Munros.

The shortest approach is from Glen Dochart across the low skirt of gentle-angled moorland of peat hags and winding streams NE of Loch Iubhair.

Parking can be found at the side of the A85 east of the private road to Auchessan. From the Auchessan estate buildings, follow a track north up the east side of the unnamed stream which flows down east of Creag nan Uan. Follow this stream towards its source over rough moorland and strike WNW to Meall Garbh and up the SE ridge of Beinn nan Imirean. (5km; 690m; 2h 20min). The summit is a small slabby outcrop of rock, the cairn not always surviving the wind. The outlying position of the summit cone provides a unique view up and down Glen Dochart, a fine reward for the rather uninteresting ascent. The route has some weekday restrictions during the stalking season and the estate is very sensitive about dogs on the hill.

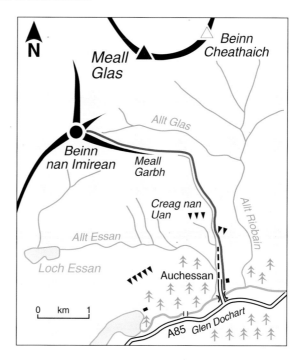

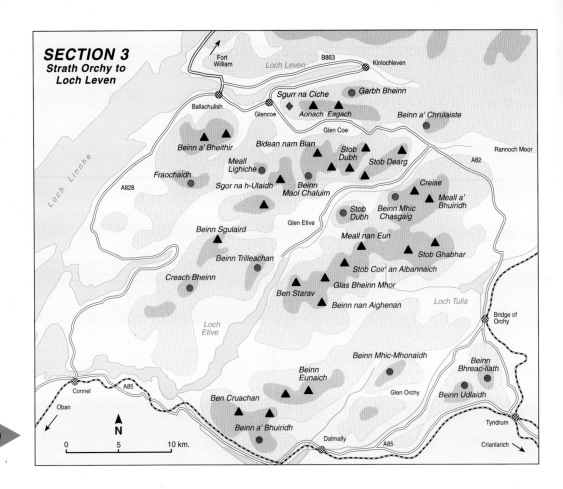

SECTION 3

Strath Orchy to Loch Leven

Hamish Brown

Beinn a' Bhuiridh from the north

Beinn a' Bhuiridh; 897m; (OS Sheet 50; NN094283); *hill of roaring (of stags)*

Those who have made the complete circuit of Ben Cruachan's huge corrie holding the pumped-storage reservoir will have discovered Beinn a' Bhuiridh to be a fine summit in its own right, jutting out southwards to command views along several glens and across Loch Awe. For those still to make an ascent of this hill, this is the finest option, while what follows is the best option for a circuit over the Corbett itself. The pumped-storage visitor centre in the Pass of Brander, St Conan's Kirk and Kilchurn Castle, as well as the delightful woodland and water scenery along the shore of Loch Awe, are additional attractions in the vicinity of Beinn a' Bhuiridh.

BEINN A' BHUIRIDH

The start is at the junction of the A85 and the old military road, now the B8077, where there is room for car parking along the edge of the B8077. Take the track, which was once part of an old mineral line to quarry workings, round to the Allt Coire Ghlais. Follow the burn up into Coire Glas, a wild place with bold crags to the south, but with an easy climb up to the Larig Torran. Cattle used to be driven across this pass to graze in the corrie with the reservoir, and Wallace led his forces this way. From the pass there is a steep pull of 270m up to the knobbly rock summit of Beinn a' Bhuiridh and a view south which comes like a revelation. (6km; 840m; 2h 50min.)

Descend the long east ridge over Monadh Driseig to return to the starting point; a treat given good evening light on the Ben Lui hills. The lowest slope at the foot of the ridge is steep and there are some crags, so it is advisable when setting out at the beginning of the day to look at this slope and note a suitable way through the crags.

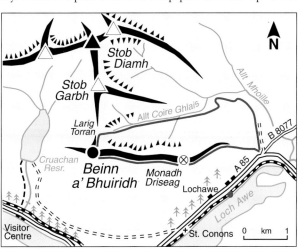

Beinn Mhic-Mhonaidh from Glen Strae

Hamish Brown

Beinn Mhic-Mhonaidh; 796m; (OS Sheet 50; NN208350); *hill of the son of the moor*

**BEINN MHIC-
MHONAIDH**

This shy hill is perhaps best seen in the view up Glen Strae where it rises in bold parabolic outline; otherwise the hill lies hidden away in country swamped with forestry plantings. Both routes suggested, from Glen Strae or Glen Orchy, have river/stream crossings which could be hazardous in spate conditions and both offer approaches where a cycle would be useful.

Glen Strae: Park on the B8077 (once the military road west) which breaks off the A85 at Dalmally and circles to rejoin the A85 at the NE corner of Loch Awe. Follow the Glen Strae track (N side of the river) for 6.5km to its end at the river. A path continues up the Glen, crossing to the east bank, where one leaves it to head uphill on a steep rising ascent (some crags to avoid) to reach the crest 1km before the final curve to the stony summit. (9.5km; 750m; 3h 30min). The summit is a great viewpoint with such giants in view as Cruachan, Starav, Stob Ghabhar and Beinn Laoigh. Descend NE to a small lochan then descend the regular-angled NW flank to the shieling ruins of Airigh Challtium where the east bank path can be picked up by the remnant oakwood.

Glen Orchy: At the Eas Urchaidh (Falls of Orchy) there is a bailly bridge from which the falls are viewed. The forestry track leads to a Forest Reserve (stands of magnificent old Scots pines) and is also the start of a cycle trail leading to Bridge of Orchy. The track climbs round for 2km to the Allt Broighleachan ending at a secretive meadow. Take the indicated cycle trail ford over the stream (230332) and immediately turn off left (W) on a trail which eventually leads up to the edge of the forest above the watershed and just south of the ruined Airigh Chailleach shielings. Note this point well for the return. Climb NW to gain the crest which is then followed to the summit. (6.5km; 730m; 1h 50min). Descend NE to the lochan and then south back down to the forest again.

Beinn Udlaidh; 840m; (OS Sheet 50; NN280332); *dark* or *gloomy hill*
Beinn Bhreac-liath; 802m; (OS Sheet 50; NN302339); *speckled grey hill*

These two hills, bounded by Glen Orchy, Glen Lochy and the A82 between Tyndrum and Bridge of Orchy, offer a short but varied day's walking. Their flanks are extensively afforested and access has to make use of the few gaps remaining. Plantings in Glen Orchy stretch from Invergaunan to Arichastlich, and Invergaunan is perhaps the best starting point for the traverse of the two hills. (Limited parking, avoid Invergaunan entrance).

Walk up the Allt Ghamhnain for about 1.5km then bear SW more steeply onto the north ridge of Beinn Udlaidh. A remarkable line of quartz rock is reached; a prominent feature of the hill, clearly seen from the main road above Loch Tulla. (It crosses the ridge to form part of the cliffs of Coire Daimh). The ascent up the north ridge to the extensive flat summit is stony, but easy. A mast has recently appeared. (4km; 710m; 2h 10min).

Continue SE, then ENE down to a broad col at about 600m and climb, steeply at first, to the fairly flat top of Beinn Bhreac-liath. (6.5km; 920m; 3h). The circuit can be completed by walking down the long easy-angled north ridge of the hill to return to the starting point at Invergaunan. If a second car is available, a descent from Beinn Bhreac-liath can be made east to the south edge of the Coille Bhreac-liath forest, which is followed down Coire Chalein to the A82. This route gives the shortest ascent of Beinn Bhreac-liath, and the traverse described above could equally well be done in reverse.

The shortest ascent of these two hills starts and finishes at Arinabea in Glen Lochy where the streams create breaks in the forest by which it is quite easy to reach the col between them.

Beinn Bhreac-liath and Beinn Udlaih seen from the north across Loch Tulla

Scott Johnstone

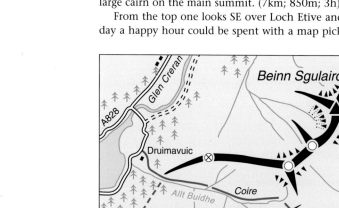

Creach Bheinn above Loch Creran

Creach Bheinn; 810m; (OS Sheet 50; NN023422); *hill of spoil*

The sprawling mass of this hill, with a great expanse of afforestation covering its west flank, is very obvious from the A828 on the north side of Loch Creran. The summit offers fine views to Loch Etive and the Firth of Lorn.

Start from the A828 just north of Druimavuic House near the head of Loch Creran where a metal gate (007451) leads to a path through the trees. Initially this path skirts the stone wall bounding the policies of the house, but it soon reaches a second gate in open ground and continues east up the north side of the Allt Buidhe, faint and intermittent in its upper reaches, to the bealach (560m) between Creach Bheinn and Beinn Sgulaird. From the bealach a well-defined ridge leads SW over Creag na Cathaig for 1km, before rising steeply due west to the NE top of Creach Bheinn (804m). From there a short descent and reascent leads SW for 1km to the large cairn on the main summit. (7km; 850m; 3h).

From the top one looks SE over Loch Etive and SW down the Firth of Lorn, and on a clear day a happy hour could be spent with a map picking out the islands and their hills. Closer to hand, Creach Bheinn has a rich crop of spring flowers, with purple saxifrage particularly evident under the hill's granite crags.

An alternative route to Creach Bheinn, shorter and steeper, but one that might be preferred by those planning to continue the traverse to Beinn Sgulaird, is to cross to the south side of the Allt Buidhe about 300 metres beyond the upper limit of the forest on that side of the stream and climb steeply through heather to gain the west ridge of the hill at Meall nan Caorach. Continue along this ridge over Meall Garbh to the NE top and so to the summit. (5km; 850m; 2h 30min).

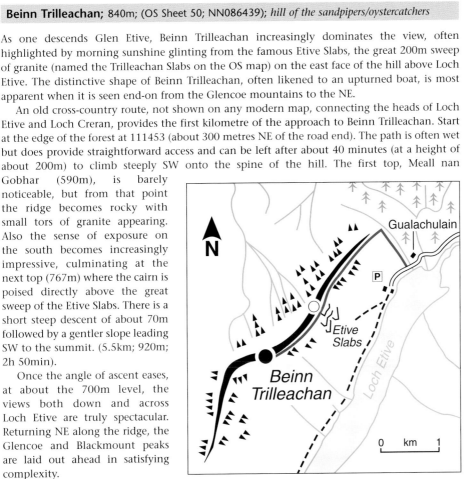

Beinn Trilleachan from Loch Etive

Andrew Dempster

75

BEINN
TRILLEACHAN

Beinn Trilleachan; 840m; (OS Sheet 50; NN086439); *hill of the sandpipers/oystercatchers*

As one descends Glen Etive, Beinn Trilleachan increasingly dominates the view, often highlighted by morning sunshine glinting from the famous Etive Slabs, the great 200m sweep of granite (named the Trilleachan Slabs on the OS map) on the east face of the hill above Loch Etive. The distinctive shape of Beinn Trilleachan, often likened to an upturned boat, is most apparent when it is seen end-on from the Glencoe mountains to the NE.

An old cross-country route, not shown on any modern map, connecting the heads of Loch Etive and Loch Creran, provides the first kilometre of the approach to Beinn Trilleachan. Start at the edge of the forest at 111453 (about 300 metres NE of the road end). The path is often wet but does provide straightforward access and can be left after about 40 minutes (at a height of about 200m) to climb steeply SW onto the spine of the hill. The first top, Meall nan Gobhar (590m), is barely noticeable, but from that point the ridge becomes rocky with small tors of granite appearing. Also the sense of exposure on the south becomes increasingly impressive, culminating at the next top (767m) where the cairn is poised directly above the great sweep of the Etive Slabs. There is a short steep descent of about 70m followed by a gentler slope leading SW to the summit. (5.5km; 920m; 2h 50min).

Once the angle of ascent eases, at about the 700m level, the views both down and across Loch Etive are truly spectacular. Returning NE along the ridge, the Glencoe and Blackmount peaks are laid out ahead in satisfying complexity.

Peter Hodgkiss

Fraochaidh from the east

Fraochaidh; 879m; (OS Sheet 41; NN029517); *heathery hill*

There is a fine view of this hill from the A828 at Duror of Appin, but any ascent from the west involves penetrating a barrier of afforestation, and is not advised. Despite the greater height and mass of its northern neighbour Beinn a' Bheithir, Fraochaidh, when climbed over its long undulating NE ridge, gives the impression of being a much larger hill than its actual height would suggest.

Start from East Laroch, Ballachulish, along the minor road on the west side of the River Laroch. The tarmac soon gives way to track and, when it dwindles, a good path continues south. After 3.5km, at a cairn, drop left from the path to make an easy crossing of the River Laroch. The right of way shown on the OS map as a path leading SSW over to Glen Creran is faint and intermittent, but a stiff climb of 170m through thick grass does end un-mistakably on the Mam Uchdaich (390m), unnamed on the OS map. Where the right of way crosses a stile into the forested slopes above Glen Creran, turn SW and follow a faint path beside the deer fence, then over the humpy crest of the first top (626m).

Descend SSW and cross a knoll to a lochan, and on to the next top (718m). Continue along the ridge, which narrows and becomes rockier, dropping 80m and turning west over two more knolls. The iron stanchions of an old fence appear before the final ridge climbs WNW for 200m, levels out and turns WSW to the cairn of Fraochaidh with a splendid view down Loch Linnhe. (10km; 1020m; 4h).

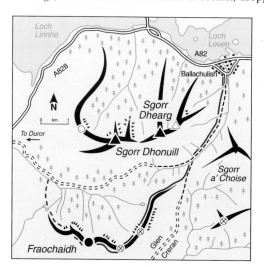

If transport is available at Duror, Fraochaidh can be traversed, provided one is willing to engage a short section of old and trackless forest. Descend the main ridge WNW, then west and finally NW to a lochan at 013529. Drop steeply due north to the forest edge. There is no firebreak, but 15 minutes of struggle through trees and drainage ditches bring one to a forest track, and a right turn leads down by zig-zags to a footbridge at 014541. From there a forest track leads to Duror.

Peter Hodgkiss

Meall Lighiche from Gleann-leac-na-muidhe

Meall Lighiche; 772m; (OS Sheet 41; NN094528); *doctor's hill*

Truly retiring, Meall Lighiche is hemmed in on all sides by other hills, but it can be seen in the view up Gleann-leac-na-muidhe from the main road through Glen Coe. The western slopes are rounded, dropping to the forests of Glen Creran, but the eastern flank falls precipitously from the outlying top Creag Bhan (719m) to the head of Gleann-leac-na-muidhe. Because of the encircling hills and the western afforestation, the only reasonable approach is from Glen Coe, a route which follows a fine narrow glen.

There is parking by the A82 (119564) and a track runs south on the west bank of the Allt na Muidhe. Follow it to a bridge across the burn and through the farm, Gleann-leac-na-muidhe. The track continues further than shown on the map and ends after 2.5km at a confluence of streams.

Cross to the west bank of the Allt na Muidhe and follow a faint path west for 300 metres. Turn south and climb the steep, terraced grass slope for 450m to the small cairn on Creag Bhan From there, there is a particularly fine view of the northern arc of Beinn a' Bheithir and Ben Nevis. Level ground continues SSW for 200 metres before the final ridge climbs west along a line of old iron fence posts. The summit cairn of Meall Lighiche sits on a slab of quartz-embedded schist. There is a magnificent view down Glen Creran and out to Mull. (5km; 730m; 2h 20min).

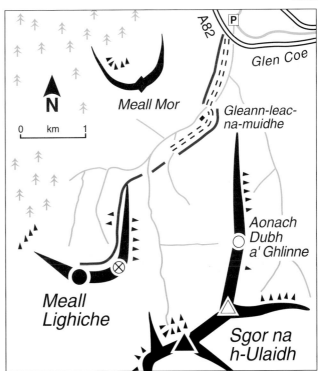

Beinn Maol Chaluim from Glen Etive

BEINN MAOL CHALUIM

Beinn Maol Chaluim; 907m; (OS Sheets 41 and 50; NN135526); *Malcolm's bare hill*

Beinn Maol Chaluim, like Meall Lighiche, is a retiring hill, hidden behind the greater Glen Coe peaks.

Approaches to the hill can be made either from Glen Coe to the north or from Glen Etive to the SE, but the former involves some heavy going in the wild Fionn Ghleann, while the route from Glen Etive gives a high ridge walk in splendid surroundings.

Leave the Glen Etive road at 149496 at the south end of the Gleann Fhaolain afforestation. The small area of open hillside below Creag na Caillich is the only gap in the trees on the NW side of the Glen Etive road. Climb steeply by a faint path up the side of the forest to its upper edge (about 200m) and then NW up the steep hillside to the broad crest of the south ridge of Beinn Maol Chaluim. Continue north across a slight drop to reach a line of crags straddling the ridge above 600m. Bypass these either by a faint path to the left or a long rising traverse to the right, to reach the SE top of Beinn Maol Chaluim (847m).

The easy ridge stretches NE for 1km (with a splendid backcloth of Bidean nam Bian) to reach the summit of this fine hill. (4km; 820m; 2h 20min).

STOB DUBH, BEINN CEITLEIN

Stob Dubh, Beinn Ceitlein; 883m; (OS Sheet 50; NN166488); *black peak*

From anywhere in Glen Etive this hill appears steep, dark and intimidating. The SW facet is deeply scored by a gorge making the hill instantly recognisable. Stob Dubh is almost completely encircled by the greater peaks of the Blackmount and Glencoe, and lies at the hub of a huge wheel of ridges with the only break provided by Glen Etive. An outlier, Beinn Ceitlein, is included in this description, and the traverse of the two peaks makes a good round.

Leave the Glen Etive road at 137468, the same starting point as for Ben Starav. Walk down a private track, not easily seen from above when driving down the glen. After crossing the River Etive on a bridge high above deep pools, take the track NE for just over 1km to another smaller bridge over the Allt Ceitlein. Above looms the uncompromisingly steep SW ridge of Stob Dubh, rising 850m in 2km. Underfoot the going is excellent on short grass, and the minor crags at roughly half height are easily turned, mainly on the right. Once above the last of these bluffs, the angle eases and the cairn is soon reached. (4.5km; 900m; 2h 30min).

To continue to Beinn Ceitlein, there is a steep descent ESE for 120m before a broad ridge curls up NE to the first and higher of two tops (845m). The descent can be made SE down steep, rough ground for a few hundred metres, then bear south across the eastward-flowing stream in Coire Dubh-mor to reach the headwaters of the Allt Ceitlein. Follow the north bank, along which a path soon appears that leads back to the start.

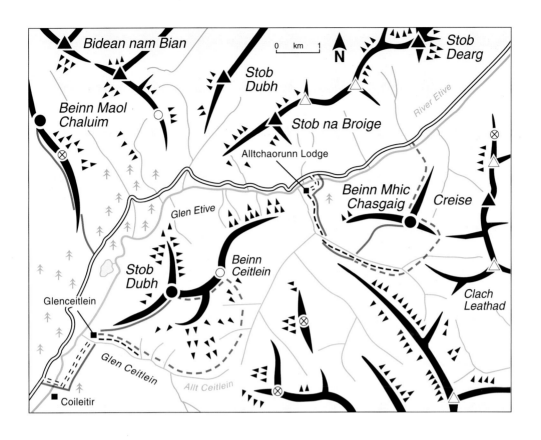

Stob Dubh from the head of Loch Etive

Hamish Brown

Beinn Mhic Chasgaig and Stob Dearg (Buachaille Etive Mor) behind

Beinn Mhic Chasgaig; 864m; (OS Sheets 41 and 50; NN221501); *MacChasgaig's hill*

BEINN MHIC
CHASGAIG

Beinn Mhic Chasgaig is hemmed in to the north, south and east by the larger mountain ridges of Buachaille Etive Mor and the Blackmount, but presents a bold front to Glen Etive, above which its NW wall extends for 3km. From Alltchaorunn one sees a shapely cone, apparently ringed high up by crags, with a strangely isolated little patch of forest on its north flank. A direct route can be made up this west ridge and the crags can be turned but a more circuitous and easier-angled route passing through a spectacular ravine is described below.

Start at the bridge over the River Etive at 198513. This bridge has a corrugated iron gate with barbed wire some 2m high, and is normally locked. If bridge access is not possible, the only alternative approach is to wade the river, which may pose a problem.

From the bridge a track goes to Alltchaorunn and, beyond, a good path follows the east bank of the Allt a' Chaorainn. (There are some wide, deep pools worn from the granite bedrock that are ideal for swimming). In 1km a junction of burns is reached; follow the Allt Coire Ghiubhasan, keeping to the north bank for 100 metres, then hunting carefully downhill for a wire-rope aiding the descent to a single-plank bridge. Roughly 30 metres above the bridge on the south bank, a stalkers path follows the burn through a glen so narrow and steep-sided as to have the atmosphere, if not the scale, of a Himalayan defile.

Follow the path for 1km until it drops almost to the burn, and an open gorge on the SW flank of Beinn Mhic Chasgaig appears. Cross the burn and climb steeply up the east side of this gorge, veering east once the angle eases, to reach the summit plateau with the cairn at its north end. (4.5km; 750m; 2h 20min).

An alternative route follows the path beside the Allt Coire Ghiubhasan for a further 1.5km until SW of the col between Beinn Mhic Chasgaig and Clach Leathad. Climb easily to this col, from where a last pull leads to the summit.

A shorter, but very steep ascent can be made from about 2km further up the River Etive. Choose a suitable river crossing near 221520 then traverse left to the north ridge which can be easily followed to the summit. (1.75km; 685m; 1h 50min).

Hamish Brown

Beinn na Chrulaiste

Beinn a' Chrulaiste; 857m; (OS Sheet 41; NN246566); *rocky hill*

Although Beinn a' Chrulaiste appears as a great lump of a hill compared with its more elegant and majestic neighbours, the ascent is most rewarding for the views from the summit.

The most convenient starting place is at the Kingshouse Hotel where there is car parking space and the assurance of refreshment upon return. Go north up the Allt a' Bhalaich for 1.5km to a height of about 350m, and then bear WNW up a broad ridge. This is more rugged than the map indicates, with some rocky outcrops, and leads directly to the summit. (3km; 600m; 1h 40min). There is a remarkable view of the Buachaille Etive Mor.

The return to the Kingshouse can be varied by descending WNW at first, then NE and east to traverse the broad range over the twin tops of Meall Bhalach.

The west ridge of Beinn a' Chrulaiste, starting from Altnafeadh, is a pleasant route, particularly on the descent, for there is a splendid view of the Glen Coe peaks. Begin up the right of way to the Devil's Staircase, but leave the main path after about 200 metres, even with the edge of the forest. Follow a small path to cross a narrow gorge by an even narrower bridge. Faint paths lead to the west ridge, which is ascended to the summit.

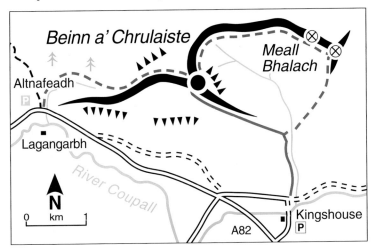

BEINN A'
CHRULAISTE

Garbh Bheinn

Chris Townsend

Garbh Bheinn; 867m; (OS Sheet 41; NN169601); *rough hill*

GARBH BHEINN

Garbh Bheinn is an isolated peak between the Aonach Eagach ridge to the south and Loch Leven to the north. The West Highland Way contours the east end of the hill as it descends towards Kinlochleven. This fine hill has been largely neglected, being surrounded by higher and better known peaks, and is to some extent hidden by them. The best roadside viewpoint for the hill is from the highest point on the B863 along the south side of Loch Leven, a view looking directly up the west ridge.

The west ridge provides a good route of ascent for Garbh Bheinn. Cars can be left at two small lay-bys near the bridge over the Allt Gleann a' Chaolais, 300 metres east of the Caolasnacon caravan site. From the east side of the bridge follow a prominent path up the Allt Gleann a' Chaolais for 60 metres and then a faint path which leads onto the ridge and continues between rocky outcrops. The crest of the ridge can be followed throughout over a succession of false tops. During the ascent there are views back across Loch Linnhe to the Ardgour hills and over to the little seen north face of the Aonach Eagach.

Alternatively, a slightly easier ascent can be made by continuing along the path beside the Allt Gleann a' Chaolais for a further 1km before ascending north to the first col on the west ridge, which is followed to the top. (3km; 850m; 2h 10min).

The top has two cairns. The first of red igneous rock appears to be the higher, though the second of white stones gives the better view over the Glen Coe hills, the Mamores and Ben Nevis, and east along the length of the Blackwater Reservoir. The return can be made back down the west ridge, or by a steeper descent south from the first col on the ridge to the path beside the Allt Gleann a' Chaolais. Another possibility is to complete the traverse down the NE ridge to join the West Highland Way near Kinlochleven.

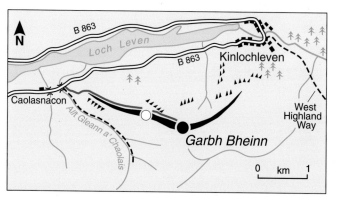

Sgorr na Ciche (Pap of Glencoe)

Hamish Brown

Sgorr na Ciche (Pap of Glencoe)*; 742m; (OS Sheet 41; NN125594); *peak of the breast*

The very prominent peak above Glencoe village is Sgorr na Ciche, more commonly known by its anglicised name, the Pap of Glencoe. The peak forms the true western end of the long ridge which extends for 11km to the Devil's Staircase along the north side of Glen Coe, the central and highest part of this ridge being the Aonach Eagach.

Sgorr na Ciche may readily be included in a traverse of the Aonach Eagach, the route to Sgorr nam Fiannaidh involving about 2km of rough ridge walking. The Pap, on its own, gives a very pleasant half day climb from the road between Glencoe village and the Clachaig Hotel.

The nearest public parking is at the edge of Glen Coe village. Walk 1km east up the road to 111586 where a track leads up the hill. The track turns right and traverses the hill to a stream. The main path is met here. Follow the path up the south side of the second, more southerly of two parallel streams which flow down from the col between Sgorr na Ciche and Sgorr nam Fiannaidh. At 300m the path makes a long upward traverse to the right (east) followed by a longer leftward rising traverse to reach the col.

From there easy scrambling leads directly to the summit of Sgorr na Ciche, or alternatively there is a cairned path which avoids all difficulties up the NE ridge. (2.5km; 720m; 1h 50min).

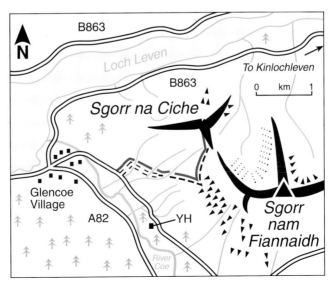

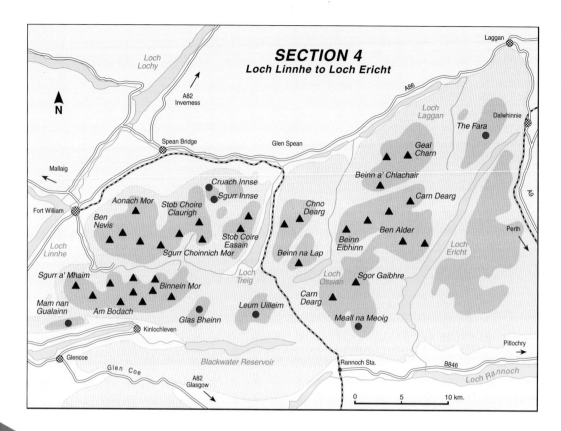

SECTION 4

Loch Linnhe to Loch Ericht

Mam na Gualainn from above Kinlochleven

Mam na Gualainn; 796m; (OS Sheet 41; NN115625); *rise of the shoulder*

This hill is situated between Loch Leven and the western end of the Mamore Forest hills, and although it is dwarfed by near neighbours, offers magnificent views, particularly of the Beinn a' Bheithir massif beyond Ballachulish.

The shortest ascent of this hill is from near Callert on the B863 on the north side of Loch Leven. There is a right of way to Lairigmor which starts some distance east of Callert House at 097604. Parking can be found near the trees just to the east. The path is occasionally confusing, but is clear after the telecommunications mast. The right of way is followed for about 2km, almost to its highest point, and then one climbs the WSW ridge of Mam na Gualainn direct to the summit. (4km; 790m; 2h 20min). The cylindrical trig point has a memorial plaque to a fallen Marine.

A much more enjoyable walk can be had by traversing the whole ridge between Kinlochleven and Callert, thus including, Beinn na Caillich (764m). This entails the use of two cars. The traverse from east to west will give the best views.

Follow the West Highland Way from the western edge of Kinlochleven for about 2km to the point at about 250m where a path branches off to the left to cross the Allt Nathrach. Follow this path across the stream and up the steep nose of the east ridge of Beinn na Caillich, and continue along the ridge to the summit. A delightful 2.5km ridge walk follows which ends at Mam na Gualainn. (7km; 950m; 3h 10min). Mamore Lodge is an alternative start but there may be a parking charge.

From the summit of Mam na Gualainn descend the WSW ridge to reach the right of way leading down to Callert.

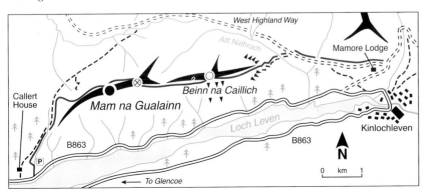

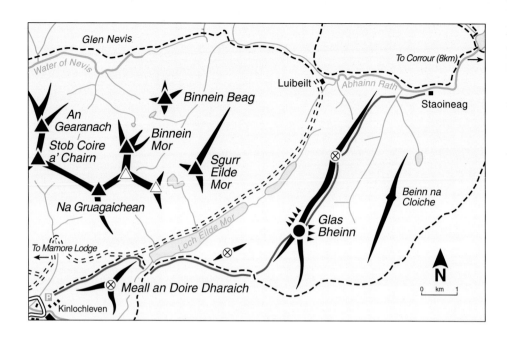

Glas Bheinn; 792m; (OS Sheet 41; NN258641); *grey hill*

This rather undistinguished hill is situated in the seldom visited hill country to the east of the Mamores, midway between Kinlochleven and the head of Loch Treig. Its isolated position above the Blackwater Reservoir provides fine views however.

The only route to Glas Bheinn which is readily accessible from a public road starts in Kinlochleven. From the Grey Mare Waterfall car park a good path (marked with red markers) leads steeply up through fine oak and birch woods to skirt the NW flank of Meall an Doire Dharaich. The track from Mamore Lodge to Loch Eilde Mor is reached and followed for 500 metres before taking another path going east round the end of the loch to the outlet dam. Cross the top of the dam and continue along the path for 2.5km to the Meall na Cruaidhe shoulder on the broad SW ridge of Glas Bheinn, and climb this ridge to the summit. (8.5km; 790m; 3h 20min).

An alternative and more attractive ascent can be made from Staoineag bothy on the south side of the Abhainn Rath, 2km SW of the head of Loch Treig, but the approach to the bothy itself involves a long walk. From the bothy cross the Allt Gleann na Giubhsachan and climb the long NE ridge past the tiny Lochan a' Chuirn Dheirg. (5.5km; 500m; 2h 10min).Energetic cyclists may opt for the steep, short ascent from between Loch Eilde Mor and Loch Eilde Beag.

Glas Bheinn from the west end of Loch Eilde Mor

Hamish Brown

Leum Uilleim

Leum Uilleim; 909m; (OS Sheet 41; NN330641); *William's leap*

Lying to the SW of Corrour Station on the West Highland Line, Leum Uilleim can provide a short yet attractive expedition on the north edge of Rannoch Moor. An isolated position in the heart of the Central Highlands makes the hill a splendid viewpoint, and the walking on the hill is good almost everywhere. The big NE facing Coire a' Bhric Beag is the most prominent feature of the hill, and the traverse of the ridges round this corrie makes a good circuit.

From Corrour station go west along a stalkers path to its end in 1.5km at the 500m contour. Continue west more steeply for 1.5km to reach the ridge which leads pleasantly over Tom an Eoin for 2km to Beinn a' Bhric (876m), which is the west top of Leum Uilleim. Descend steeply east, avoiding incipient crags, and climb the uniform slope to the main summit. (6km; 580m; 2h 20min). The return to Corrour goes along the NE ridge, steeply down the rocky nose of Sron an Lagain Ghairbh, and then across increasingly boggy ground to the station, or use the early part of the outward track.

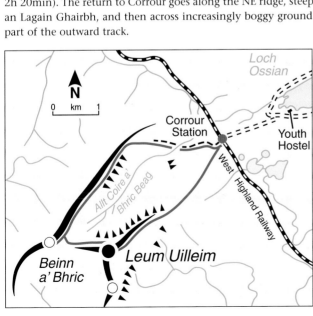

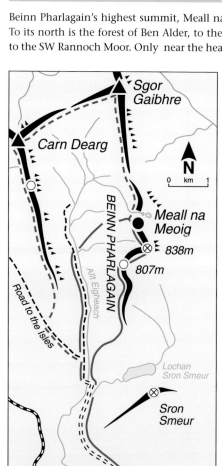

Meall na Meoig and Beinn Pharlagain from Carn Dearg

Iain Robertson

Meall na Meoig, Beinn Pharlagain; 868m; (OS Sheet 42; NN448642); *hill of whey,* pharlagain perhaps *grassy hollow*

Beinn Pharlagain's highest summit, Meall na Meoig, lies on the remote rim of Rannoch Moor. To its north is the forest of Ben Alder, to the west the hills of Loch Ossian and Loch Treig, and to the SW Rannoch Moor. Only near the head of Loch Rannoch, is there any human habitation within 7 or 8km of this hill. Access to it is either by road along Loch Rannoch, or by train to Rannoch station.

The historic Road to the Isles, leaves the B846 2.5km east of Rannoch Station. Follow this track NW then north for 3km to the bridge over the Allt Eigheach. Bear NNE on the east side of the stream up open slopes and then NE up the ridge to Leacann nan Giomach, the southern end of Beinn Pharlagain. Grass and heather slopes lead north up the undulating ridge, first to an unnamed top of 807m then NE, down and up to Pt.838m. Meall na Meoig is a further 750 metres NW, the summit being a small outcrop. (7.5km; 660m; 2h 50min). The last part of the ridge is quite broad and featureless, but two lochans on the NE side may be guides in mist.

One can either return by retracing one's steps, or, alternatively, by descending WSW to reach and follow the path down the west side of the Allt Eigheach. The slabby stream bed provides many nice places to cool off on a hot day. To extend the walk by a considerable distance one can continue north for 3.5km along the broad ridge to Sgor Gaibhre and return by Carn Dearg and its undulating south ridge, which also leads to The Road to the Isles. This gives a round trip of about 23km along broad grassy ridges, easy walking for a Corbett and two Munros.

Map labels:
Sgor Gaibhre
Carn Dearg
N
0 km 1
BEINN PHARLAGAIN
Meall na Meoig
838m
807m
Allt Eigheach
Road to the Isles
Lochan Sron Smeur
Sron Smeur
Rannoch Station P
B846
Loch Eigheach

Derek Sime

Sgurr Innse

Cruach Innse (left) and Sgurr Innse above the Lairig Leachach

Douglas Scott

Cruach Innse; 857m; (OS Sheet 41; NN279763); *hill of the meadow* or *island hill*
Sgurr Innse; 809m; (OS Sheet 41; NN290748); *peak of the meadow* or *island peak*

CRUACH INNSE

SGURR INNSE

These two peaks are well named, the massive Cruach rising above the Insh flats on the south side of the River Spean, with the shapely Sgurr appearing over its east flank. They are particularly well seen from the area around Roy Bridge. Both are steep and craggy and look well above the Lairig Leacach. The only rock of any note is on the Sgurr, but although sound is too discontinuous to give anything more than scrambling.

The best route traverses both these tops. Take the narrow public road from Spean Bridge along the south side of the River Spean to its end just below Corriechoille where the right of way to Rannoch is indicated. A private track goes south for 3km to the site of the old railway built by the British Aluminium Company for the construction of the tunnel from Loch Treig to the factory at Fort William. Vehicles can normally be left there. Continue on foot up the track through the forest and over the Allt Leachdach. A short distance beyond the bridge leave the track and climb steepening grass and heather to the NW ridge of Cruach Innse, and continue up this ridge to the flat stony summit of the hill. (4.5km; 660m; 2h 10min).

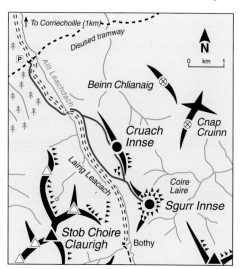

Descend SW along the broad stony ridge for 500 metres, then bear south as the ridge steepens and becomes more rocky above the broad col. Cross the col (589m) and climb SE to the steep upper rocks of Sgurr Innse. A narrow path makes a rising traverse leftwards across scree and boulders, with some optional mild scrambling, to the north shoulder of the hill and an easy walk up to the summit. (6.5km; 890m; 3h). Descend by the same route to the 589m col and slant down west to rejoin the track in the Lairig Leacach. Alternatively, one can descend to the bothy. The direct descent west to the bothy is blocked by a line of crags, so begin by descending a short distance SE and then following a terrace west between the crags.

The Fara above Loch Ericht

The Fara; 911m; (OS Sheet 42; NN598843); *ladder hill*

There can be few people driving along the A9 who have not cast a glance towards The Fara as they passed by the head of Loch Ericht, but fewer will be aware of the fine hillwalk that this long ridge offers. Although the summit is at the NE end of this ridge, and gives a round trip of only 3 hours from Dalwhinnie, to confine activity only to this part of The Fara is to miss a longer and more rewarding expedition.

The most direct approach is from Dalwhinnie, and as the slopes above Loch Ericht are now extensively forested, route-finding is a matter of avoiding the forests. From Dalwhinnie station go south across the level crossing (where there is limited parking) and follow the private track along the side of Loch Ericht for about 2km to a point (615835) where there is a gap between newer and older sections of the forest. From there climb NW up the slope through this gap. At the top of the forest follow a broken fence and a dry-stane dyke directly to the massive summit cairn. (4.5km; 550m; 2h).

The walk can be extended by traversing the ridge of The Fara to Meall Cruaidh (897m), descending SW then south to the track near Ben Alder Lodge and returning to Dalwhinnie along Loch Ericht. The Direc Mhor, 2km NNW, is a notable feature and could be taken in, returning by Allt an t-Sluic.

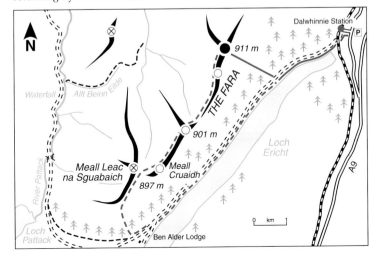

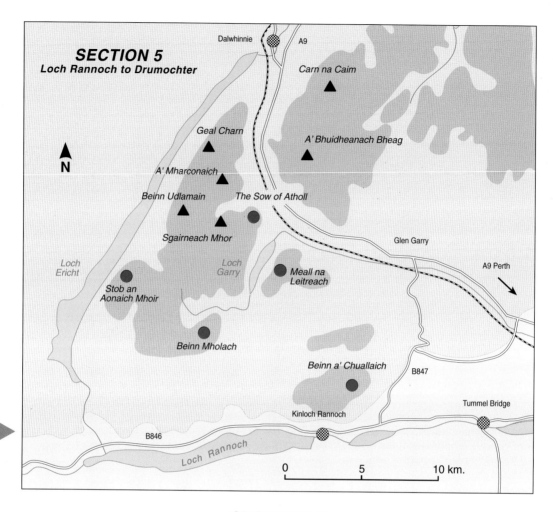

SECTION 5

Loch Rannoch to Drumochter

These two rather elusive hills are described together largely because they share a desolate and neglected corner of the Central Highlands. Access routes to them are long and climbing them together might be regarded as advantageous but an option which should only be adopted by strong walkers on long summer days.

Stob an Aonaich Mhoir is the highest point of the long ridge that encloses the east side of lower Loch Ericht. The ascent may be easy, but the approach from the south is long and uninteresting, a 12km tramp along a tarred road that has to be retraced on the return journey. (A cycle is a great advantage). This road starts at Bridge of Ericht on the north shore of Loch Rannoch and leads to Corrievarkie Lodge and a power station on the side of Loch Ericht. From the highest point of the road bear NW directly up slopes of grass and heather to the summit of Stob an Aonaich Mhoir, which is a splendid perch with views up and down Loch Ericht. (13.5km; 650m; 4h 10min).

Beinn Mholach's big cairn crowns a craggy hill which must be among the least visited summits in Scotland. The vast expanse of moor between it and Loch Rannoch has a great atmosphere of space. From Annat on the north side of Loch Rannoch a right of way goes north to Duinish and Loch Garry, and this is the easy route from the south, particularly if a cycle is used for the first 4 or 5km of the way. The alternative track starting at Craiganour is not a right of way, but it joins the Annat route after 2km. Beyond this meeting of the two tracks bear NW across the moor on the north side of the stream (Caochan an Leathaid Bhain), passing NE of Sgurran Dearg to reach and climb the steeper SE slopes of Beinn Mholach. (9km; 650m; 3h 10min).

Dalnaspidal Lodge and the right of way along the west side of Loch Garry also provides a possible approach to Beinn Mholach, and a cycle might be used for 5km to the south end of the loch. Walk on to Duinish (in spate there is a bridge upstream) and climb the NE ridge of Beinn Mholach over Creag nan Gabhar. (From Dalnaspidal: 10km; 440m; 3h).

A traverse of both hills is something of a marathon. From Beinn Mholach wend over or round the intervening hills WNW towards Stob an Aonaich Mhoir. The return journey by the Allt Feith Gharuiareagan and the Allt Shallainn is long and demanding, crossing trackless country that gives heavy going.

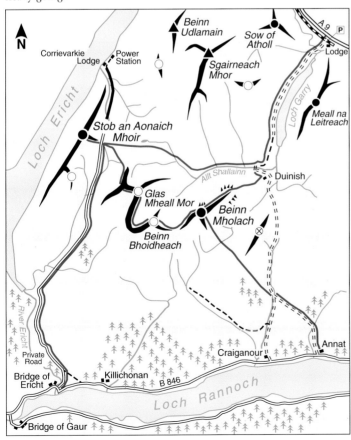

Hamish Brown

Stob an Aonaich Mhoir across Loch Ericht

94

Beinn Mholach from Meall Doire to the north-east

Andrew Dempster

Raymond Hay

Beinn a' Chuallaich

Beinn a' Chuallaich; 892m; (OS Sheet 42; NN684617); *hill of the herding*

This is a rather self-effacing hill occupying the ground between Loch Rannoch, Dunalastair Water and Loch Errochty, but it gives a pleasant short ascent, and a rewarding summit view. In winter there is often good skiing on the east facing side of the hill, which holds snow well. The traverse of the hill is particularly worthwhile provided one has suitable transport arrangements.

BEINN A'
CHUALLAICH

The shortest ascent is from the east, and although there are forestry plantings, they can be avoided. Start at a bend on the B847 (707616) where a stalkers path leads west to a small bothy. Climb WNW to reach the col between Meall a' Chuallaich and its north top, Meall nan Eun, and finish with a short climb up the NW ridge to the summit where there is a large cairn and a trig point. (3km; 590m; 1h 40min).

A pleasant traverse continues with splendid views to the west, by descending west from the summit, avoiding some small crags, to reach a stalkers path in 500 metres. This leads down south to the road beside Dunalastair Water. A longer traverse continues SW down the open hillside to the Allt Mor which is followed south, crossing to its west bank by a bridge just above the trees and finally descending a steep path beside the dramatic waterslide of the burn to reach Kinloch Rannoch.

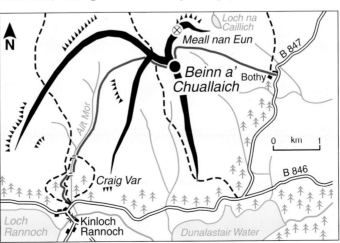

Meall na Leitreach

Gill Nisbet

96

Sow of Atholl from Meall na Leitreach

Alan O'Brien

Jim Teesdale

Meall na Leitreach

Meall na Leitreach; 775m; (OS Sheet 42; NN639703); *hill of slopes*
The Sow of Atholl; 803m; (OS Sheet 42; NN624741)

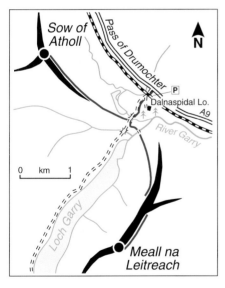

MEALL NA
LEITREACH

THE SOW OF
ATHOLL

The Pass of Drumochter, with the A9 and railway using its deep trench to break through the Grampians, is a famous travellers' route. The first proper road through the pass was constructed by General Wade in the early 18th century. If the many route improvements since then, the line of electricity pylons, a cycle way and the noise, bustle and fumes of traffic now give the pass the impression of being a major line of communication, a climb up the hills at its sides shrinks man's work into perspective. Seen from the hillsides high above, the moraine-filled pass appears as if the scouring work of the glaciers had been only yesterday.

The Sow of Atholl is the fanciful name given to balance its near neighbour to the north, An Torc, better known as the Boar of Badenoch. Originally The Sow was Meall an Dobhrachan (*watercress hill*). Both The Sow and Meall na Leitreach can be easily climbed from Dalnaspidal, in a single day if one wants, for the ascent to each one is less than 400m. Their slopes are easy grass and heather, which in winter can give delightful skiing. The flat ground surrounding Dalnaspidal Lodge is apt to flood, particularly in winter and spring so follow the track towards Loch Garry, and use the bridges shown on the map.

As one climbs south up Meall na Leitreach there is quite a dramatic view northwards through the Pass of Drumochter, with the Sow rising steeply on its west side. The summit of Meall na Leitreach is reached almost 1km across an undulating plateau. (3km; 370m; 1h 20min).

The Sow of Atholl is best climbed by its broad SE ridge, which gives a less spectacular view eastwards towards the lower country of Atholl. (3km; 400m; 1h 20min). The Sow can conveniently be climbed as the first stage in a longer traverse of the Munros west of Drumochter Pass or traversed, transport allowing, to/from the north, laybys on the A9, facing Coire Dhomhain.

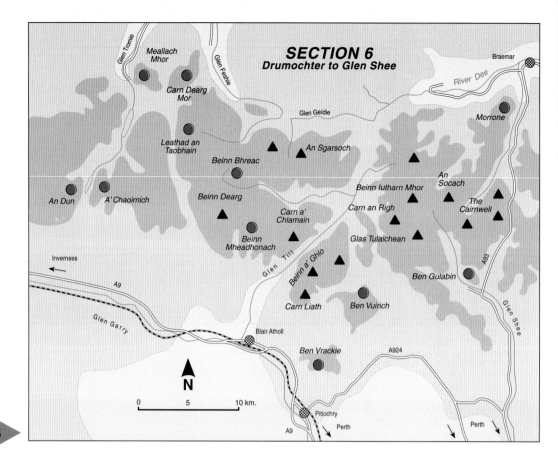

SECTION 6

Drumochter to Glen Shee

An Dun from Sronphadruig

A' Chaoirnich; 875m; (OS Sheet 42; NN735807
An Dun; 827m; (OS Sheet 42; NN717805); *the fort*

An Dun is in Section 5 of this guidebook, but is included with A' Chaoirnich in Section 6 because the two hills are conveniently climbed together.

These two naked hills, flat plateaux on top, are walled about by some of the steepest and most unrelenting hill slopes in Scotland. Wedged between them is bleak Loch an Duin and the path of the historic Gaick Pass which links Atholl and Badenoch. The approaches to the pass and the hills above are all long and lonely, but time can be saved by using a cycle. From the head of Glen Tromie it is possible to cycle to the north end of Loch an Duin on a bulldozed track. The deep gash between the two Corbetts at Loch an Duin is only traversed by a footpath.

A' CHAOIRNICH

AN DUN

The road northwards from Dalnacardoch Lodge on the A9 is the shortest and most popular approach, and leads in 9km to the neglected lodge of Sronphadruig at the southern entrance to the narrows of the Gaick Pass.

A circuit of the two hills can be made by first ascending the south ridge of An Dun or the slopes further west connecting it to Vinegar Hill. An Dun rises like some gigantic motte, very much reflecting its Gaelic name. The summit is the northerly of two small rises on the plateau. (11km; 500m; 3hr 20min). (From Sronphadruig Lodge 2.25km; 480m; 1h 20min). To continue the traverse, descend the north ridge and then steep grassy slopes to the outlet of Loch an Duin. Ascend the right side of the obvious stream/gully, steep in places and when the slopes open out, ascend north to the summit of A' Chaoirnich. (13.5km; 900m; 4hr 30min). (From the lodge: 4.75km; 880m; 2h 40min). The eroded tableland so characteristic of the Grampians is strikingly seen from this top. Descend south and then SW along the ridge to regain the track above the Lodge.

The summit areas of both hills have cairns which are not on the true summit.

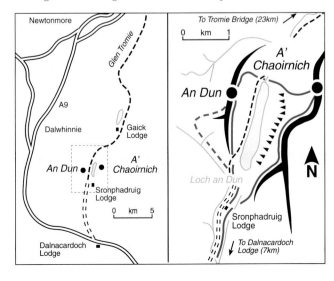

Carn Dearg Mor from Leathan an Taobhain

Leathad an Taobhain; 912m; (OS Sheet 43; NN822858); *slope of the rafters*
Carn Dearg Mor; 857m; (OS Sheet 43; NN824912); *big red cairn*

LEATHAD AN
TAOBHAIN

CARN DEARG
MOR

These two rounded hills are situated far up Glen Feshie, Carn Dearg Mor overlooking Glenfeshie Lodge, and Leathad an Taobhain 5.5km to the south in the vast tract of featureless hills and undulating plateaux between the headwaters of the River Feshie and the Minigaig Pass. The name of the latter on the OS map appears to be given to the west top which is 10m lower than the summit. The Minigaig Pass is an ancient right of way much used in the past by drovers taking their beasts from Strathspey to Atholl.

Starting from the car park 1km north of Achlean in Glen Feshie, follow the east bank of the river south for just over 1km and cross a wooden bridge to the private road on the west bank. Continue along this road to a point just before Glenfeshie Lodge where a rough track continues south for 2km to two solitary trees on the flat floor of the glen. (One can cycle to this point, but the last part of the track is not a right of way.)

Continue SW along the track which climbs steadily up the steep-sided glen to Lochan an t-Sluic. Beyond the loch the track forks, and the left branch is followed south on a gradually rising line round a series of heathery corries. This track ends at 847m on the summit of Meall an Uillt Chreagaich. A path continues SSW downhill to cross a col just west of the source of the River Feshie. There are the ruins of a small stone-built bothy on the south facing slope just west of the col. The ascent of the final 150m south to the summit of Leathad an Taobhain is straightforward, following a faint path. (15km; 680m; 4h 30min). The west top is 1km away across an expanse of tussocky grass.

Retrace the outward route as far as the junction of the tracks 500 metres SW of Lochan an t-Sluic, and take the other track which climbs steeply NNW towards the SW ridge of Carn Dearg Mor. A zig-zag path reaches this ridge which is followed for 500 metres NE to the summit. (21km; 1070m; 6h 20min). Return to Achlean along the route of ascent by Lochan an t-Sluic and Glen Feshie. An alternative is to descend NNE from Carn Dearg Mor along a broad ridge over Carn Dearg Beag to reach a track which goes down to Glen Feshie at Carnachuin.

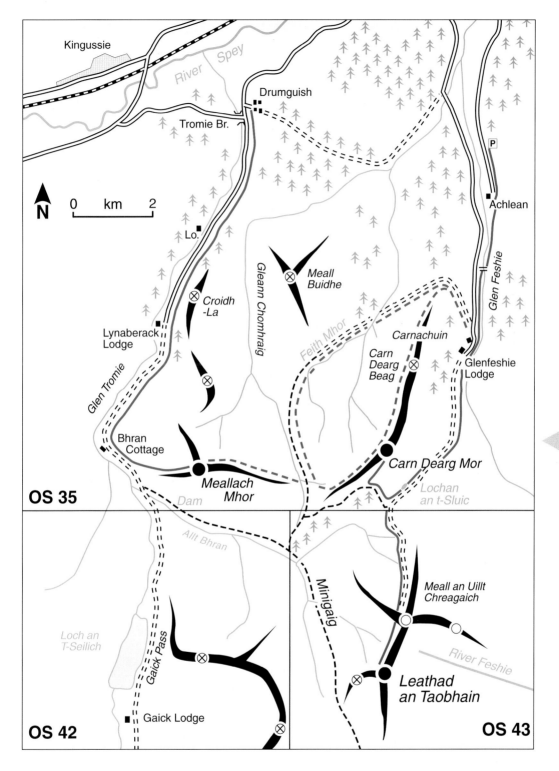

Kingussie

River Spey

Drumguish

Tromie Br.

N

0   km   2

Lo.

Meall
Buidhe

Croidh
-La

Gleann Chomhraig

Lynaberack
Lodge

Glen Tromie

Feith Mhor

Carnachuin

Carn
Dearg
Beag

Glenfeshie
Lodge

Glen Feshie

Achlean

P

Bhran
Cottage

Meallach
Mhor

Dam

Carn Dearg Mor

Lochan
an t-Sluic

OS 35

101

Allt Bhran

Loch an
T-Seilich

Gaick Pass

Minigaig

Meall an Uillt
Chreagaich

River Feshie

Gaick Lodge

Leathad
an Taobhain

OS 42

OS 43

Meallach Mhor from Glen Tromie

Alan O'Brien

Meallach Mhor; 769m; (OS Sheet 35; NN776908); *big hump*

This hill, lying between the upper Feshie and Tromie glens, is very much off the beaten track, and is seldom climbed. From any direction it involves a long walk in, but with the private road (which is a right of way) up Glen Tromie tarred for much of its length the easy option is to cycle the 10km from Tromie Bridge right to the foot of the hill.

Glen Tromie is attractively wooded in its lower reaches as far as the lodge at Lynaberack, (which resembles a council house) then bleaker landscape as far as Bhran Cottage and the confluence of the Allt Bhran and the River Tromie, which is also the junction of the historic drover roads over the Gaick and Minigaig passes.

Leave the road at the bridge over the Allt Bhran (764903) and climb the west ridge of Meallach Mhor directly to the summit. (From Tromie Bridge: 12km; 520m; 3h 40min).

One can traverse east from Meallach Mhor for 5km to reach Carn Dearg Mor, the lowest point of the broad intervening ridge being about 540m. However, the best way to combine the ascent of these two hills is to walk (or cycle) up Glen Feshie to Carnachuin and continue up the hill track of the Feith Mhor towards the col between them.

102

MEALLACH MHOR

Carn Dearg Mor from the west

Trevor Littlewood

Scott Johnstone

Beinn Bhreac from the approach up Glen Bruar

Beinn Bhreac; 912m; (OS Sheet 43; NN868820); *speckled hill*

This is a very inaccessible hill right in the heart of the expanse of featureless country at the headwaters of the Tarf Water and the River Feshie. Most hillwalkers will find this a rather taxing expedition because of the distance to the hill from the nearest point on any public road. One can walk in from Achlean in Glen Feshie, but this is even longer than from Bruar, so the latter is recommended.

Leaving the Falls of Bruar car park, follow the path which is signposted to the upper bridge. Cross the bridge and climb up through open forest to join an overgrown forest track which is followed north until it ends at a deer fence. Continue up this fence crossing an overgrown forest track to reach the main forest track which is followed until it turns east at the highest northern apex of the forest. An estate track (marked as a single dotted line on the OS map) leads NW to cross the River Bruar below Cuilltemhuc to join the right of way track to Bruar Lodge at the southern end of the Minigaig Pass.

Continue 5km to Bruar Lodge. One can also reach the lodge by the right of way/estate track from Calvine on the A9. The distance is nearly the same, and one could cycle along this rough and in places steep track.

Beyond the lodge continue along the track for a further 1km beside the Bruar Water and then follow a good stalkers path NE up the steep slope on the north side of the Allt Beinn Losgarnaich. There is no path over the very rough and boggy watershed, but once on the north side there is a faint path for over 1km on the east of the stream.

This path disappears before reaching the next very flat and featureless watershed between the Allt a' Chuil and the Tarf Water. There are some small cairns on the north side of the watershed, but they appear to have no particular significance. The ascent of the final 220m up Beinn Bhreac is then straightforward. (18km; 870m; 5h 30min).

The only feasible return is by the route of ascent, unless one wishes to descend north to the headwaters of the River Feshie and continue for a further 20km down Glen Feshie to Achlean, thus completing a long and arduous crossing of one of the wildest tracts of hill country in the Scottish Highlands. A return over Beinn Dearg is the pleasantest option and Munroists would be advised to include the Corbett when doing Beinn Dearg. Beinn Bhreac could also be combined with the Corbett Beinn Mheadhonach.

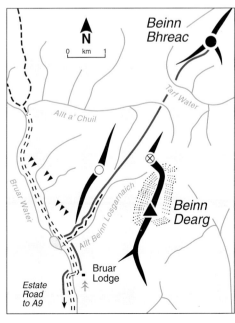

Beinn Mheadhonach from the South

Beinn Mheadhonach; 901m; (OS Sheet 43; NN880758); *middle hill*

BEINN
MHEADHONACH

This hill, which forms a narrow ridge on the NW side of Glen Tilt, is best seen from the A9 to the south of Blair Atholl. From there, looking north, the Corbett is the prominent conical hill sharply contained by two deep glens on either side.

Starting from the public car park at Old Bridge of Tilt, the route follows the private road up Glen Tilt, first on the west side of the river, then on the east side to reach Gilberts Bridge. A cylce can be used as far as Gilbert's bridge. Alternatively, one can follow the old right of way along a very pleasant footpath high on the east side of the glen; this path drops down to the river at Gilberts Bridge.

Cross the bridge to the west bank and follow the bank of the River Tilt. The forest track doesn't save time as it descends back to the river level shortly after climbing the hillside. Join a path and follow this to a stone bridge across the Allt Mhairc which rushes through a dramatic narrow linn under the bridge. Cross and follow the path above the Allt Mhairc to another fine old stone bridge 200 metres above its confluence with the Allt Diridh.

Climb NW to reach the south ridge of Beinn Mheadhonach. A rough path climbs through deep heather on the lower slopes, but higher up the heather becomes shorter and finally gives way to moss on the narrow plateau. Pass a large cairn on the east side of the ridge about half way up, and reach the small summit cairn at the north end of the narrow plateau. (10km; 750m; 4h 30min). The summit ridge has several tops of nearly equal height so beware of cairns not on the correct summit. The views of the extensive empty moorland to the north is a contrast to the civilisation at the starting point.

Andrew Dempster

Ben Vuirich from Glen Loch

Ben Vuirich; 903m; (OS Sheet 43; NN997700); *hill of roaring (of stags)*

This hill may be ascended either from Glen Brerachan on the A924 between Pitlochry and Kirkmichael, or from Loch Moraig above Blair Atholl. As the former route requires traversing much trackless peat bog, the latter is recommended.

From Blair Atholl drive to Loch Moraig, then walk ENE along an estate track across the south slopes of Carn Liath before descending SE to a bridge across the Allt Coire Lagain. The abandoned steading at Shinagag is 300 metres further on, but turn left before reaching it and head up a rough estate track across the south slopes of Meall Breac. The track ends at some butts. The following 2km heading east to the south ridge of Ben Vuirich is trackless peat bog and heavy going; however, once the ridge is reached, the last 1.5km north to the rather flat summit is pleasant walking. (11km; 720m; 3h 40min).

As an alternative, descend west from the summit and cross the low ridge north of Stac nam Bodach to the estate track coming up from Glen Loch. Follow this track SW over the watershed, but leave it where it descends steeply towards some old shielings. Continue traversing SW until the hillside becomes less steep, and descend to cross the Allt Coire Lagain. Follow the track back to Loch Moraig. If the crossing is not possible, detour to the bridge at Shinagag.

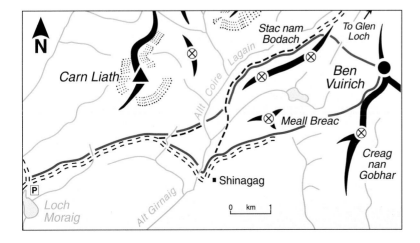

105

BEN VUIRICH

Hamish Brown

Ben Vrackie; 841m; (OS Sheets 43 and 52; NN950632); *speckled hill*

On a good day this hill must be one of the best viewpoints in the Southern Highlands, commanding views south down Strath Tay, west beyond Loch Tummel to Schiehallion and north to Beinn a' Ghlo and many other hills. Being close to Pitlochry, it is also a very popular hill with a well-constructed path most of the way to the summit.

The path starts at a small car park reached from the centre of Pitlochry by following the road to Moulin. Turn left straight after the Moulin Hotel, then take the first right, and continue to the car park, keeping right at all junctions. From the car park follow the path ascending through pleasant mixed woodland to a gate which gives access to the open hillside. The obvious path goes NNE to a shallow col to the NW of Creag Bhreac from where it traverses to the dam of Loch a' Choire. The final 320m to the summit are up the steep slopes to the east of the craggy SW face of Ben Vrackie. The view is rewarding, with the added bonus of an indicator for those who are not familiar with all the surrounding hills. (4km; 640m; 2h 10min).

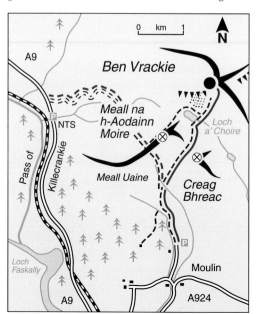

A less-frequented alternative route of ascent is to start from the north end of the Pass of Killiecrankie. It is best to park on the old A9 at the National Trust for Scotland Visitor Centre and walk up the private road for Druid (which goes under the new A9). Turn off to follow a track up by a waterworks and on up towards the dip between Meall Uaine and Meall na h'Aodainn Moire. Skirt the latter to Loch a' Choire and join the usual route to the summit. (5km; 700m; 2h 20min). A combination of the routes is recommended.

107

Ben Vrackie and Loch a' Choire

Ben Gulabin from the Spittal of Glenshee

Hamish Brown

Ben Gulabin; 806m; (OS Sheet 43; NO100722); *hill of the curlew (whimbrel)* or *hill of the beak*

BEN GULABIN

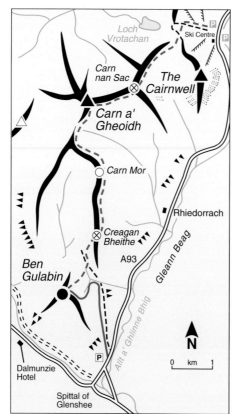

Ben Gulabin lies between Gleann Beag and the glen which comes down from Dalmunzie Hotel to the Spittal of Glenshee. North of the Spittal on the A93 there are two signs at 114714 warning southbound traffic of bends in the road ahead. At the more northerly of those signs there is a parking space with a gate giving access to Ben Gulabin. From the gate a very good track leads up to the col between Gulabin and Creagan Beithe. On the slopes of the latter hill are an old pylon and a ruined hut which are the remains of an early ski development. An ATV track up a strip of grass provides a route to the top of Ben Gulabin free from the heather which covers this side of the hill. (2.5km; 450m; 1h 20min). Return by the same way.

Ben Gulabin can also be the end point of a long traverse of the hills on the west side of Gleann Beag, starting at the Ski Centre at the Cairnwell Pass, but suitable transport arrangements would have to be made.

Leaving the Ski Centre, head WNW up Butchart's Corrie towards the col at its head and then go south along the ridge in the direction of The Cairnwell for 300 metres. Turn SW along the broad ridge which rises and falls over Carn an Sac to Carn a' Gheoidh. There go south and follow the ridge to Carn Mor. Continue south to Creagan Bheithe and descend the SW side of this ridge to join the track from Gleann Beag. Follow this to the col at 107728 and climb SW to Ben Gulabin. (9.5km; 600m; 3h 10min). Descend by returning to the col and down the track to Gleann Beag.

Hamish Brown

Morrone across the Dee

Morrone; 859m; (OS Sheet 43; NO132886); *big nose*

Morrone lies on the west side of the Clunie Water a few kilometres SW of Braemar, a featureless hill, taking away much of the sun from the village during the winter, but it is highly accessible and well worth walking up for the very fine view from the summit. Unfortunately, the broad summit is cluttered with several huts and a telecommunications tower.

Drive up Chapel Brae to the car park by the duck pond. Walk up the private track through the Morrone Birkwoods Natural Nature Reserve with its fine trees to an indicator. Originally it was intended to site this 17m higher, and not all the points shown are visible from its present position. Head a short distance east along the track and turn uphill to follow a path slanting upwards round the knoll where the indicator should have stood. A good path then leads all the way to the summit of Morrone. (2.5km; 430m; 1h 20min).

Return by the same way, or alternatively walk on SW to the top of a Landrover track heading south (used for access to the summit huts). Follow the track down to Glen Clunie opposite Auchallater farm, 3.5km south of Braemar and return to the village by the minor road on the west side of the river.

The north slopes of Morrone have fine birch and juniper woods, offering interesting ways back off the hill by an upper and lower track going along a level wide shelf back to Chapel Brae.

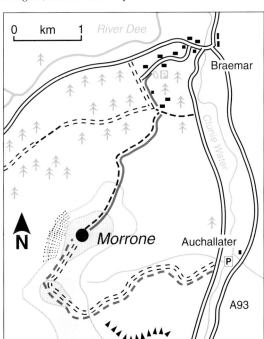

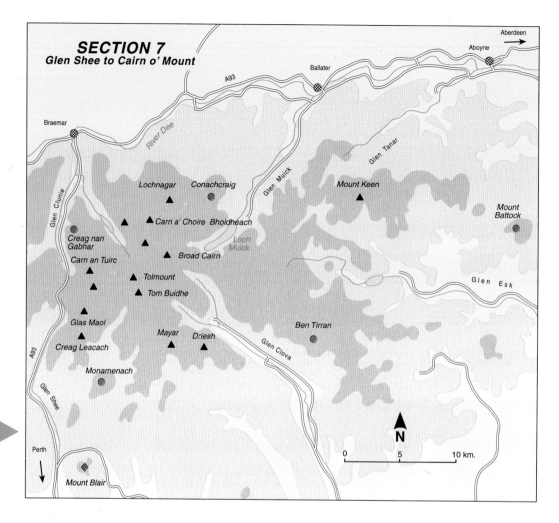

SECTION 7

Glen Shee to Cairn o'Mount

Hamish Brown

Monamenach from Glenshee

Monamenach; 807m; (OS Sheet 43; NO176706); *middle hill*

Where the Angus glens run up into the bigger domes of the Cairngorms lie some attractive landscapes and gentler hills, with Monamenach the most defined summit on the glen's western side, the undulating watershed between Glen Isla and Glen Shee.

Although a rounded heathery hill, Monamenach is quite steep and craggy in places on the east side above Glen Isla. Glen Isla however is the most favoured starting point for climbing the hill.

Start at Auchavan at the end of the public road (park cars east of the farm, by the river) and follow a track NW to a col at about 610m. From there the summit rises steeply to the NW. (2km; 450m; 1h 20min). There are good views from Monamenach into the glens on either side, and up to the higher hills to the north.

While most people descend by the same route is is also possible to take in Craigenloch Hill and descend by Glen Beanie or even to head SW out to the A93 near the Spittal of Glen Shee, but arranging transport would be called for.

A longer, more challenging day can be had by continuing from Monamenach NW to circle by Creag Leacach and Glas Maol and descend by the Monega path, the historic route from Braemar to the eastern lowlands. The head of Glen Isla is the spectacular Caenlochan Glen, a National Nature Reserve.

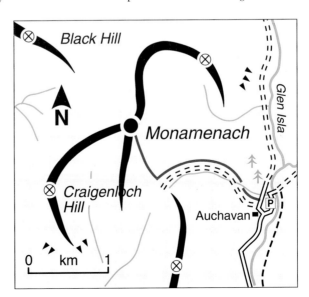

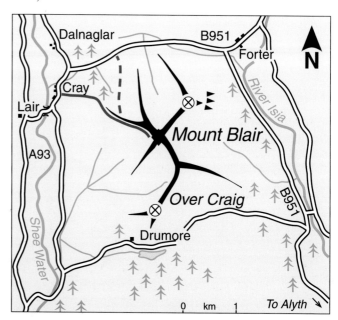

Mount Blair

Hamish Brown

Mount Blair*; 744m; (OS Sheet 43; NO167629); *hill of the moor*

MOUNT BLAIR

The sweeping, symmetrical cone of Mount Blair is well seen from Glen Shee and Glen Isla. Standing boldly between those two glens, the hill is a heathery sprawl typical of the lower Grampians, but is redeemed by excellent walking and by being a notable viewpoint. Some lower slopes are rough, with crags and scree, but these are easily avoided and ascents and traverses can be made almost at will. The hill has a long history, with prehistoric sites, some famous wells, and even a suicide's grave under the summit cairn. A large communications tower is a less welcome addition. The trig point is in Angus, the cairn in Perthshire.

Cray in Glen Shee offers two straightforward options, off the B951 leading north of the hill to Glen Isla. From the hamlet head up from the first gate north of the old church buildings. (2.2km; 425m; 1h 20min). Alternatively, 1.5km further on (158643), head up the path to the summit. (1.5km; 385m; 1h 10min).

Creag nan Gabhar from Sgor Mor

Creag nan Gabhar; 834m; (OS Sheet 43; NO154841); *goat crag*

Creag nan Gabhar lies between Glen Callater and Glen Clunie. The narrower, northern end of its ridge rises steeply from Auchallater farm (4km south of Braemar) to Sron Dubh and continues south over Sron nan Gabhar for 3km, rising gradually to the summit. At Auchallater the ridge is closely hemmed in by Clunie Water and the Callater Burn, but is 3km wide at its southern end. The walk between Sron Dubh and Creag nan Gabhar gives good views in all directions.

There is a car park at the foot of Glen Callater up which one route starts. Walk up the track for about 1.75km to the point where the track to Sron Dubh leaves on the right. Follow this track as it winds up to the Sron and then along the broad crest to Sron nan Gabhar, where it fades out. Beyond this point the going is good over dry ground with short heather. Turn SW for the final 400 metres to the summit of Creag nan Gabhar. (6km; 490m; 2h 10min). Descend SE to pick up the path of the Bealach Buidhe and follow it down Glen Callater. The fork to Lochcallater Lodge is best.

One can traverse the hill from south to north, but unless two cars are used, this will involve walking back along 5km of road at the end of the day.

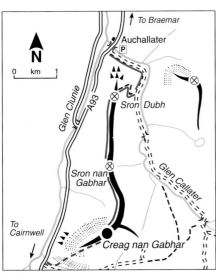

At the south end of the traverse cars can be parked beside the A93 near the bridge at 140834 in Glen Clunie. Cross the grassy stretch of land on the east side of the road and follow a path, intermittent at first, up an unnamed glen. The path goes on the south side of the glen, after 1.5km then drops to the burn. Cross, and continue east up the path, which becomes very indistinct, for a further 1.5km until a line of stones (marking the path to Lochcallater Lodge) becomes prominent. Follow the path until crossed by a Landrover track, and take this track uphill, finishing just below the shoulder of Creag nan Gabhar about 1.25km ESE of the summit. Beyond this there is a short flat stretch which is boggy, but the going is good thereafter for the final 1km to the summit. (4km; 440m; 1h 40min). Complete the traverse by reversing the route of ascent described in the second paragraph.

Andrew Dempster

Adam Watson

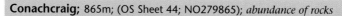
Conachraig from Glen Muick

Conachcraig; 865m; (OS Sheet 44; NO279865); *abundance of rocks*

114

CONACHCRAIG

Conachcraig is a big, rough, bouldery hill of three summits and some small cliffs, rising a few kilometres east of Lochnagar on the west side of Glen Muick. The hill stands prominently in a number of well-known views of Lochnagar from Deeside, and looks especially fine when seen from above the Linn of Muick. Note that the name Conachcraig on the OS map is marked at Pt.850m, 1km NE of the true summit.

Start at the Pay and Display car park at the end of the public road in Glen Muick, a few hundred metres NE of Spittal of Glenmuick. Take the track for 1.5km to Allt-na-giubhsaich, and follow the signposted route to Lochnagar, joining a vehicle track first on the south side of the burn, then on the north side. This track rises above the rocky gorge of Clais Rathadan and reaches a col at 700m where the Lochnagar path branches off to the left, and a grand view opens down Glen Gelder. Leave the track at a large boulder at the high point. A short climb NE from the col leads to the highest point of Conachcraig. (5km; 470m; 2h). The summit area has several slabby tors of similar height.

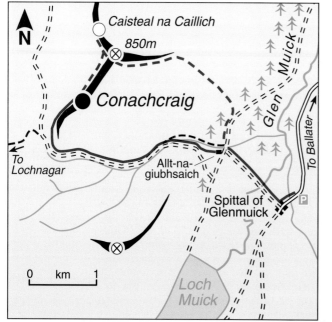

The shortest return is by the route of ascent. However, a good traverse of the tops of Conachcraig can be made by going NE for 1km along a broad ridge skirting Pt.850m, and then NW for 500 metres to the bouldery summit of Caisteal na Caillich (862m). Return to Pt.850m and descend the east ridge to the little col at Carn an Daimh, and from there go SE down heathery slopes to the pine wood of Glen Muick where a track leads back to Allt-na-giubhsaich and Spittal of Glenmuick.

The Craigs of Loch Wharral, Ben Tirran

Ben Tirran (The Goet); 896m; (OS Sheet 44; NO373746); possibly *hill of hillocks (the goat)*

The hill generally known as Ben Tirran is the highest point of the great undulating plateau between Glen Esk and Glen Clova. The map shows Ben Tirran as the lower top to the SW of the summit named The Goet (*the goat*). The best approach is above the magnificent corrie enclosing Loch Wharral.

Start just past Wheen at 353715 on the B955 up the east side of Glen Clova. From there a path, initially along the edge of a wood, leads north up the moor, eventually climbing up the side of the corrie above Loch Wharral. The point where the path crosses the burn at the top of the corrie offers a very fine view down past the loch and into Glen Clova. The path peters out shortly after, the gradient eases and an easy walk east leads to the summit. (4.5km; 650m; 2h 10min). A short detour of 500 metres to the SW leads to a cairn, from where there is a grand view along Glen Clova.

A good return route is round the top of the Craigs of Loch Wharral and then down a path west of Loch Wharral. For an even better, but longer, alternative go along the top of the Craigs of Loch Wharral to Green Hill (870m), and then descend by a path down the east side of Loch Brandy to the public road beside the hotel at Clova, 3.5km from the starting point.

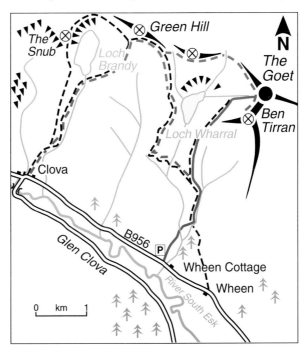

Mount Battock

116

Clachnaben

Mount Battock from near Tarfside

Mount Battock; 778m; (OS Sheets 44 and 45; NO549844)

Mount Battock, the most easterly of the higher hills of the Mounth, and the most easterly Corbett, carries short arctic-alpine vegetation on its upper slopes. As it stands between Deeside and the Mearns, there are spacious views over the lowlands of NE Scotland as well as the Cairngorms and the higher Mounth hills to the west.

The shortest route is from the south. Immediately on the west side of the bridge past Millden Lodge in Glen Esk, turn right on a minor public road to Mill of Aucheen and park behind the steading north of the house, Fernybank. Then take the road forking right past Muir Cottage and through fields beside the Burn of Turret, continuing as a track slanting east of Allrey and then NE to the summit. (7km; 640m; 2h 30min). For a longer alternative (8.5km) offering better views, take the left fork up from the bridge, to Blackcraigs farm and then by a path NW by Mount Een to Bennygray and Wester Cairn to reach Mount Battock.

An interesting route approaches from the east and can include Clachnaben, one of the most outstanding of Scotland's lower hills. Start near Spital Cottage on the B974 in Glen Dye. Follow the gravel track across the bridge over the Water of Dye, and up the river to Charr and beyond. At the point where the Burn of Badymicks joins the Water of Dye, take the right fork (NW) up a track and later branch off left (W) by a path to climb up to the broad east slope of Mount Battock. After a short useful section of track continue SW to the summit. (11km; 560m; 3h 30min).

Return by the track eastwards by the Hill of Badymicks over the plateau to the Hill of Edendocher. From there the striking granite tor and top of Clachnaben (589m) rise about 1km to the NE. Clachnaben gives a very fine view of the lowlands of NE Scotland, featuring in the old rhyme:

"Clochnaben and Bennachie
Are twa landmarks fae the sea".

From Clachnaben a path goes east down to a mature wood where a rough vehicle track follows the south side of the burn past Miller's Bog. Take the right (S) branch at a T junction to follow the Water of Dye to Spital Cottage and the B974. (From Mount Battock 13km; 3h. From Clachnaben 5.5km; 1h 20min).

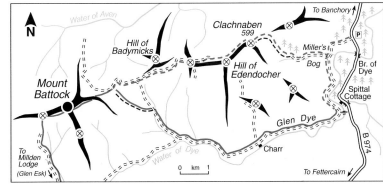

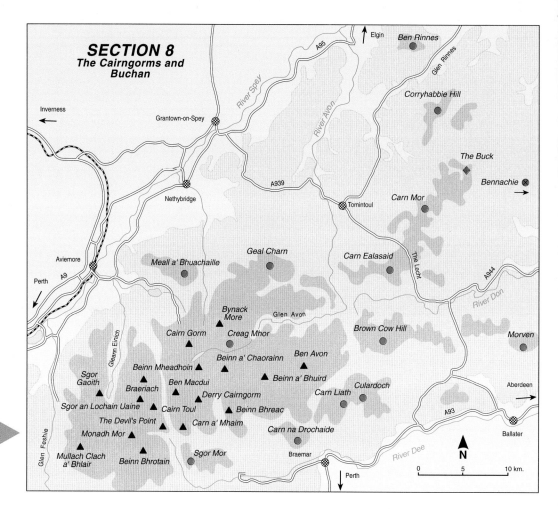

SECTION 8

The Cairngorms and Buchan

Hamish Brown

Sgor Mor with its setting looking to the Lairig Ghru

Sgor Mor; 813m; (OS Sheet 43; NO007914); *big peak*

Sgor Mor is the highest top of the hill which extends westwards from the Linn of Dee between Glen Lui and Glen Dee. A traverse gives a much more interesting walk than might be expected.

From the Linn of Dee car park (063897) follow the estate track west along the north side of the Dee for almost 5km. This runs below fragmentary schistose outcrops scattered among Caledonian pines and passes ruined settlements on the river flats before reaching White Bridge. A path continues along the north bank past Chest of Dee where the river cascades splendidly over a series of rock ledges.

Leave the footpath at the next side stream and slant up the steepening hillside to ascend the southern spur of Sgor Mor. The underlying rock changes from Moine schist to Cairngorm granite, and you clamber up broken granite blocks and then walk easily across swelling ice-polished slabs to the summit cairn. (9km; 470m; 2h 50min). Nearby is a slab with a fine circular pothole scoured out by wind blast.

A broad ridge of ice-worn granite, interspersed with patches of gravel, leads ENE for about 3km to Sgor Dubh (741m). This offers pleasant high level walking against the imposing backcloth of the main Cairngorm massif. From Sgor Dubh drop SE down the widening shoulder of the hill, eventually trending south down steeper slopes amid broken rock, long heather and Caledonian pines to rejoin the track leading back to the Linn of Dee. (16km; 4h 50min).

This hill might easily be traversed en route by anyone walking SE from the Lairig Ghru to the Linn of Dee

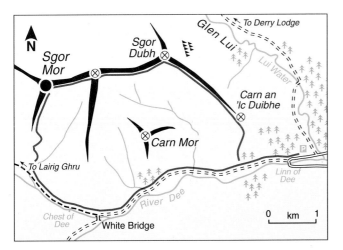

Carn an Drochaide across the River Dee

Hamish Brown

Carn na Drochaide; 818m; (OS Sheets 43; NO127938); *cairn of the bridge*

CARN NA
DROCHAIDE

Carn na Drochaide rises from the floor of the Dee valley opposite Braemar where it stands proud and isolated. On three sides, the slopes drop to near the level of the river Dee, hence it is a splendid viewpoint. The panorama includes the Dee valley, Braemar, Glen Shee, the upper Dee, the Cairngorms and a grandstand view of Beinn a' Bhuird and Ben Avon.

Start from the end of the public road near Linn of Quoich, where cars may be parked. The original parking area has been moved to stop damage to an ancient and now buried mill.

Although not the shortest way, an interesting route is to begin up the east side of the stream past the Linn of Quoich to the footbridge near the Punch Bowl. From behind the nearby cottage pass through the trees to reach the track then path leading NW. Follow this for 3km, gaining height gradually. As the path fades strike right up the hillside by its SW flank to Carn na Criche (737m). A faint track leads all the way from there along a broad heathery ridge to Carn na Drochaide. (6.5km; 490m; 2h 20min).

The large summit cairn is complemented by several cairns around the rim of the summit area. Each marks a viewpoint to the valleys below .

A shorter, but steeper route is to follow the estate track east to a gap in the trees near Allanaquoich farm. Turn up a faint track until a diagonal path is met. This traverses the lower slopes and provides easy access to the short heathery slopes above. Continue, following faint paths to the knoll of Carn Dearg. The terrain becomes more stony exhibiting an interesting style of erosion and one arrives on the summit plateau all to quickly. (3km; 500m; 1h 30min).

Either route can be used in descent, or combined for a fine traverse.

Culardoch from the west

Carn Liath; 862m; (OS Sheets 36 and 43; NO165977); *grey cairn*
Culardoch; 900m; (OS Sheets 36 and 43; NO193988); *back of the high place*

These two hills form the divide between the upper Gairn and the Dee valley. They are separated by the 650m Bealach Dearg, an old route connecting Braemar and Tomintoul by Loch Builg and now a popular mountain bike route. These are smooth sided hills, without crags or significant corries, but they enjoy settings of great charm and offer magnificent views across the Gairn to Ben Avon. Cycles are useful for access. Grouse shooting and deer stalking are actively conducted on these hills in season.

Leave cars before reaching the sawmill at Keiloch near the Invercauld Bridge. Take the gravel estate track leading NW, to the first track on the right, signposted Loch Builg. For 3km this winds uphill past mature firs, an iron gate, scattered birches and a conifer plantation. Emerging onto the open hillside the track rounds a shoulder to enter the Glen Feardar basin, enclosed on the NW by Carn Liath and on the north by Culardoch. The track dips to a wooden bridge over the Allt Cul; 400 metres on, leave the track and follow the headstream of the Allt Cul to its source in a shallow corrie. Ascend west and cross a conspicuous but ruined stone wall to reach the summit ridge of Cairn Liath, where there is a prominent cairn at 860m. The named summit is about 250 metres north of the abrupt termination of the wall and has no significant cairn. (8km; 570m; 2h 50min). Carn Liath has some half dozen tops of similar altitude on a bumpy summit ridge shaped like a wide H. The two highest are both shown as 862m and lie 1km apart but only count as one Corbett. An hour is sufficient time to visit the other tops (recommended for the prudent hillwalker) and descend to the Bealach Dearg. To continue to Culardoch follow the track NE for 1km to a shoulder at 730m, and leave it at a sharp bend to ascend east up the heathery slope to the summit. (13.5km; 890m; 4h 30min). Return via the Bealach Dearg, or else descend south more steeply to intersect a track leading back to the Allt Cul bridge.

If only Culardoch is being climbed an alternative approach is from Knockan (220936) near Inver on the A93, via the old farms of Ratlich and Achtavan, and then by the head of Glen Feardar. (9km; 590m; 3h).

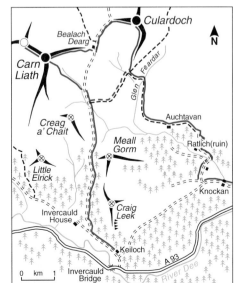

Cairn Sawvie and Brown Cow Hill beyond the River Gairn

Don Green

Brown Cow Hill; 829m; (OS Sheets 36 and 37; NOJ221044)

This smoothly contoured mass lies on the watershed between Glen Gairn and the upper reach of the Don valley, its physical form is about as exciting as the name suggests and it is separated from the more interesting massif of Ben Avon by the deep narrow trough of Glen Builg.

122

Leave the A939 at 258087 by a gateway, leaving the gate closed. A grassy track curves west for about 200 metres to meet the gravel track leading SW from Cockbridge Farm along the Cock Burn. Cross the burn by a footbridge and follow the track on the west side of the Cock Burn, gaining height and passing through a scattered plantation of mixed conifers

BROWN COW
HILL

Veering to the west, ascend more steeply by a small stream to end at about 600m beside the wide boggy saddle which separates Brown Cow Hill from Carn Oighreag. A line of grouse butts leads south up the slope to the gently rising brow of the hill. Pass through a zone of peat hags and then swing to the SW up another gentle slope to the summit area. This forms a broad ridge almost 3km long at just over 800m altitude, clad in a rich tundra of short heather, blaeberry, crowberry and cloudberry, interspersed with sphagnum and occasional mossy puddles. This provides easy walking in dry conditions, but wide convex slopes make for testing navigation in thick mist. The named top of Brown Cow Hill is the first small cairn, but the true summit is the middle top of 829m, a further kilometre to the west. (7km; 430m; 2h).

The ridge continues over Meikle Geal Charn (named for the white quartz stonefield on its crown) and Little Geal Charn, and then curves back NE past the Well of Don to Cairn Culchavie, a pleasant walk with attractive views across Glen Builg to Ben Avon. Descend from almost any point on this horseshoe to join one of the tracks which lead down to the valley floor and reach Inchmore. The main estate track continues past the site of the former Delnadamph Lodge down the upper Don valley to Cockbridge. (Complete circuit: 19km; 560m; 5h 10min).

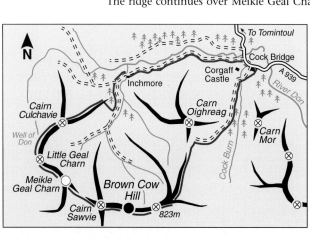

A shorter but less attractive route to Brown Cow Hill is from Corndavon Lodge in Glen Gairn, going directly up the steep south side of the hill. A cycle can be used from the B976. (6km; 430m; 2h).

Hamish Brown

Morven from the east

Morven; 872m; (OS Sheet 37; NJ376040); *big hill*

Morven is the prominent hill which rises abruptly from the farmlands of Cromar and, as an outlier of higher hills, often carries patches of snow and is well seen from Deeside. There are several obvious routes of ascent, the two described are representative and popular.

The shortest and most direct route is by the east side to a level shoulder from which a ridge leads to the top. One kilometre south of Logie Coldstone on the A97 a minor road is signposted to Groddie. In 3km a fork (410044) provides parking space and a gate gives access to a track leading west across undulating pastureland toward the lower slopes of Morven. Pass the deserted farmhouse of Balhennie by a gate on its south side and in another 100 metres reach the open hillside beyond the end of a drystone dyke. Ascend steeply for 300m by a heathery slope with small cairns marking a faint path in its upper part. At the 600m contour the angle

MORVEN

falls back to a broad platform with a cairn and an old fence line leading uphill to join the east ridge at a spur. Follow the fenceposts by a straggle of animal tracks leading west along the wide ridge, past a rock outcrop to the summit (with summit book in a tin box by the cairn). (4km; 660m; 2h).

Another longer route ascends from the south. About 2km east of Ballater leave the A93 at 389976 near Tullich old church. Pass farm buildings and go through a gate to join a track among birches and young pines to enter the glen on the east side of Crannach Hill. Continue up this track to reach the wide upland basin of the Rashy Burn. Beyond the burn the steepening southern slopes of Morven lead to the summit. (7.5km; 2h 50min).

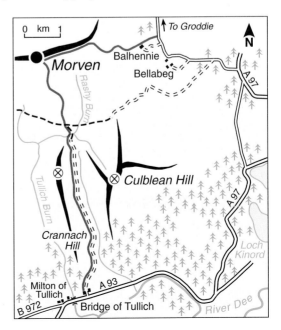

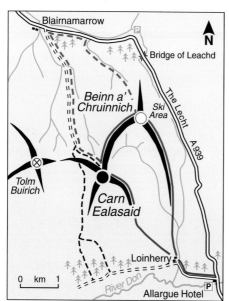

Carn Ealasaid from the Gairn

Hamish Brown

Carn Ealasaid; 792m; (OS Sheets 36 and 37; NJ227117); *Elizabeth's hill*
Carn Mor; 804m; (OS Sheet 37; NJ265183); *big cairn*

Carn Mor is the highest point on the Ladder Hills which form a dividing line between Donside and Glen Livet. Carn Ealasaid and its westerly neighbours Tolm Buirich and Craig Veann are an extension of the Ladder Hills SW from the notorious Lecht road (A939) with its ski centre.

CARN EALASAID

The two hills can be done easily in a day from the summit of the Lecht road, but this is not the most attractive way so the following descriptions give slightly longer, but more attractive routes.

CARN MOR

For Carn Ealasaid park at the Allargue Hotel (257092) and take the old track behind the hotel to the uninhabited farmhouse of Loinherry. From there climb NW towards Carn Vaich and continue pleasantly up the ridge over short heather to Carn Ealasaid. (3.5km; 390m; 1h 30min). The outing can be extended by going north to Beinn a' Chruinnich (776m) and then SE to Carn

Mhic an Toisich, passing ski pylons on the way to Carn Meadhonach. Descend a short distance west to join a track down to Loinherry (2h from Carn Ealasaid).

For Carn Mor the best approach from the east is by the Water of Nochty, which is about 3km from Bellabeg on the A944 in Strathdon. Leave the Glen Buchat road just before Torrancroy (cars can be parked at the nearby bridge over the Nochty) and take what is known as the Ladder route to the farm of Aldachuie and on to the ruin of Duffdefiance. The name is said to date back to a time when a crofter, Lucky Thain, came over the hills from Glen Livet and squatted there. He was able to build a house and have the lum 'reekin' before he was challenged by the local laird, Duff, and so sat there in defiance.

At this point a steep ascent of 190m leads to a wide ridge with a final pull up another 150m to the highest point of the path on the ridge just NE of Dun Muir. Carn Mor lies about 1.5km SW across grassy, sometimes boggy ground. (7km; 480m; 2h 30min).

If approaching from Glen Livet, park near the church at Chapeltown and take the track south of Tom a Voan to Ladderfoot. The route then follows the path up the Ladder Burn into a lovely grassy corrie and on to the ridge near Dun Muir to join the route from Donside.

To climb both hills in a single day from the A939 Lecht road, park at 223152 and walk down the road to Blairnamarrow. Follow a track south up a grassy glen and heather slopes to the NW shoulder of Carn Ealasaid, and up to the summit. (5km; 400m; 1h 50min). The descent can be made along the line of the district boundary to Beinn a' Chruinnich and then north down to the track back to the car, which can be re-parked at the Well of the Lecht car park (235152) 1km east on the A939 (2h 30min for the circuit).

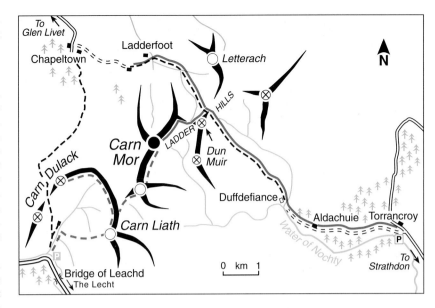

From the car park, walk north up the path towards the large building at the site of an 18th century ironstone and manganese mine. Just before reaching this take a track right up to shooting butts, and then straight up to Carn Liath (792m). Follow the district boundary over Monadh an t-Sluichd Leith (800m) to Carn Mor (4.5km; 450m; 1h 50min from the road). A pleasant alternative route back to the road is to traverse the ridge to Carn Dulack (664m) (232164) and descend east there to join the path which leads down to the car park on the A939. (3h 30min for the circuit).

Carn Mor from Carn Liath

Mark Gear

Ben Rinnes; 840m; (OS Sheet 28; NJ255354); *headland hill*

This fine hill is the second-highest summit entirely in Banffshire, Creag Mhor (895m) being the highest, and Ben Rinnes commands a glorious view over the Laich of Moray and across the Moray Firth to the hills of Ross, Sutherland and Caithness. The hill has a bold and well-defined outline which makes it a prominent landmark, easily identified from all quarters.

Ben Rinnes can be climbed from any side, but the easiest route is undoubtedly from the NE. From the B9009, about 5km SW of Dufftown, turn NW up the minor road to Milltown of Edinvillie and after 500 metres park at a track which is used to ascend Round Hill, thereafter rising to Roy's Hill. A fairly flat area is crossed before climbing more steeply up a well-worn path to the summit by the ridge resonantly named Scurran of Lochterlandoch. (3km; 550m; 1h 40min).

An enjoyable traverse, if one's transport arrangements make it possible, is to head west from Ben Rinnes down the broad west ridge to a track near the Burn of Lyneriach, and continue down to Bridge of Avon.

Corryhabbie Hill; 781m; (OS Sheet 37; NJ280288)

The rounded mass of Corryhabbie Hill is the highest ground in the area enclosed by Glen Livet, Glen Rinnes and Glen Fiddich. The best approach is from the B9009 between Dufftown and Tomintoul. At 267329 turn off and head for Ellivreid farm where cars can be left. Opposite the farm take the track towards Sheandow but after 500 metres swing SW and climb straight up the Hill of Achmore (510m). Easy walking on grass and short heather takes one gently up to Muckle Lapprach (729m) and then on to the summit of Corryhabbie Hill. (5km; 450m; 2h).

An alternative descent can be made by walking for about 200 metres NE from the summit and joining Morton's Way - a shooting road built by a one-time laird at Glenfiddich Lodge. Follow the Way NE for about 1km and then descend NW to The Saddling, making for the ruin at 275308, on the Corryhabbie Burn. Cross the bridge and walk up past Sheandow to rejoin the track to Ellivreid.

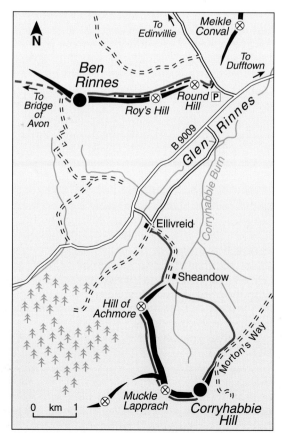

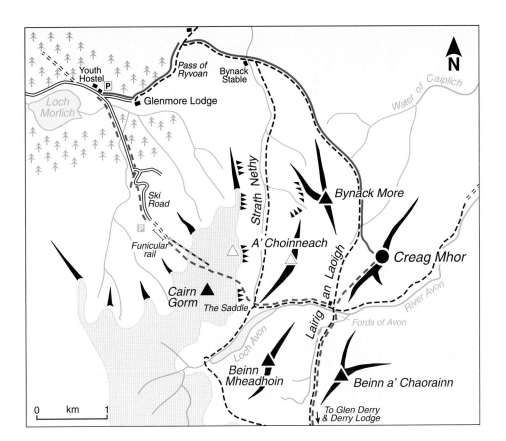

Creag Mhor; 895m; (OS Sheet 36; NJ057047); *big crag*

Creag Mhor is geographically an inaccessible Corbett, although otherwise an easy hill to climb, lying hidden away above the crossroads of the River Avon and the Lairig an Laoigh, 12km from both Glenmore Lodge and Derry Lodge.

CREAG MHOR

Many hillwalkers have skirted past Creag Mhor, bent on other ploys, but if any hill exemplifies the wisdom of climbing Corbetts along with Munros, rather than after them, it is this one. The hill can also be readily fitted in to all manner of expeditions, such as walking through the Lairig an Laoigh, visiting Loch Avon, climbing Bynack More or heading for Faindouran Lodge. The easiest approach is from Glenmore Lodge, as Derry Lodge is itself an additional 4.5km from the public road at Linn of Dee.

From the end of the public road 150 metres past Glenmore Lodge, walk through the Pass of Ryvoan and, on leaving the pass, take the right fork in the track round to Bynack Stable. The Lairig an Laoigh path rises steadily up the ridge to the SE, dips into Coire Odhar, then crosses another ridge to drop to the Glasath before pulling up again to the top of the pass at Lochan a' Bhainne between the Bynacks and Creag Mhor. From the pass turn east and climb 160m to the summit of Creag Mhor, which is a granite barn (tor), so cannot be missed. (12km; 760m; 4h).

A possible alternative (or to make a circuit) is to get a lift to the car park in Coire Cas and on up to the plateau. Head SE to the col between Cairn Gorm and Cnap Coire na Spreidhe, and then descend the steep slope SE to The Saddle (807m), the col at the head of Strath Nethy. From there descend to the path along the shore of Loch Avon and go down the river to the Fords of Avon, leaving only 200m of ascent up the broad SW ridge of Creag Mhor. (From the car park: 7.5km; 605m; 3h 45min).

Creag Mhor may be only a minor summit in the context of the Cairngorms, but these mountains, with their long distances and empty spaces, should never be treated casually. The Lairig an Laoigh path is broad and clear, but careless navigation in poor visibility has seen walkers go astray, down the Water of Caiplich for example, so allow plenty of time for this Corbett at the cross-roads of the Cairngorms.

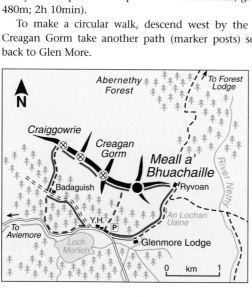

Meall a' Bhuachaille from Tullochgrue

Meall a' Bhuachaille; 810m; (OS Sheet 36; NH990115); *shepherd's hill*

MEALL A'
BHUACHAILLE

Meall a' Bhuachaille is the highest of the three rolling hills which overlook the north side of Loch Morlich in the Glen More Forest Park. They give grandstand views of the northern corries of the Cairngorms, and are themselves a fine profile when seen from afar. The Queen's Forest rises high on their southern slopes, and Abernethy Forest lies to their north, so access to these hills is rather restricted. Meall a' Bhuachaille can be easily climbed up its treeless eastern flank above Ryvoan Pass, and this can be combined with a walk through the pass from Glen More to Nethy Bridge.

The usual start is from Glen More, passing Reindeer House and walking along the road past Glenmore Lodge to the Ryvoan Pass. (Cars can be taken to a parking place 150 metres beyond the Lodge). The V-gap of Ryvoan is an old outflow channel for the glacier that once occupied Glen More; steep and craggy on the east and covered with Scots pine and heather on the west. Set in the depths of the pass is An Lochan Uaine, a little jewel of a loch which lives up to its name, the *little green loch*. Soon after leaving the pass, the road forks; keep left to Ryvoan Bothy. From there a waymarked path leads up Meall a' Bhuachaille, giving an easy ascent to the summit. (5.5km; 480m; 2h 10min).

To make a circular walk, descend west by the path and just before reaching the col to Creagan Gorm take another path (marker posts) south into the forest and down by a burn back to Glen More.

The traverse can be extended, however, to Creagan Gorm and Craiggowrie, an enjoyable 3km high level walk. Unfortunately the effects of erosion along the paths is very obvious, especially at the peaty cols. From Craiggowrie a marked path (posts) leads down to the forest and through to Badaguish. The return to Glen More can be made by one of two forest tracks: either direct to the west end of Loch Morlich and back along the main road, or along a rising traverse in the forest to drop down to the main road opposite the Glen More shop.

Donald Bennet

Geal Charn from Abernethy Forest

Geal Charn; 821m; (OS Sheet 36; NJ090126); *white cairn*

This unobtrusive, unpretentious hill stands in an area which has excellent cross-country walking, and it could well be included in (for example) a long walk from Nethy Bridge to Tomintoul. Starting from Dorback Lodge, however, the ascent of the hill by itself is barely half a day's walk.

The minor road to Dorback Lodge turns off the link road between Nethy Bridge and the A939 and goes SE for 4.5km towards the Braes of Abernethy: dark, rolling, heathery hills which are typical of the lower Cairngorms. The road ends at a turning place, but one can park in a nearby quarry. Descend and cross the Dorback Burn (which downstream cuts through fluvial deposits) to reach Upper Dell. Take the track up past a series of kettle lochs, ignoring a right fork, until the track ends on the skirts of Geal Charn.

Continue up the broad ridge, with green-rimmed Coire an Uillt Mhoir on the left, and the summit is soon reached. (4.5km; 450m; 1h 50min). The views northwards are pleasing: the Hills of Cromdale, Ben Rinnes and distant Morven in Caithness.

The Dorback Burn may well involve a paddle to start the day. In wet weather it and even the streams crossed by the track may prove impracticable to cross. In this case go round the back of Dorback Lodge and follow the estate track up the Allt Mor as far as the watershed, then climb SW to reach Geal Charn.

The approach to Geal Charn from the NE can be lengthened and improved by starting at Bridge of Brown and using the paths to the east or west of Tom an t-Suidhe Mhoir to reach Dorback. Another long approach to the hill starts at Forest Lodge in the Abernethy Forest (accessible by car from Nethy Bridge or Boat of Garten), and follows a forest track round the south side of Carn a' Chnuic to a point high on the west side of Geal Charn, 2km from the summit.

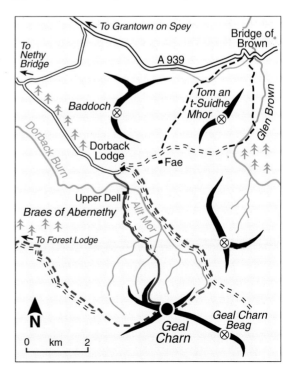

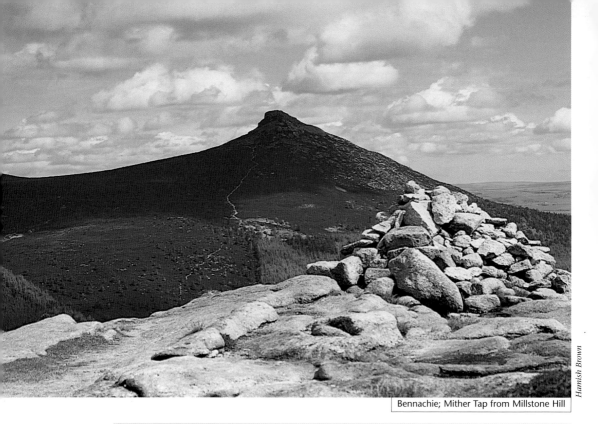

Bennachie; Mither Tap from Millstone Hill

Hamish Brown

Bennachie*; 528m; (OS Sheet 38; NJ663227); *hill of the pap*

Bennachie is the best known and probably the most popular hill in Aberdeenshire. The shapely outline can be seen from most parts of the north-east. Unsurprisingly, the rural population holds the hill in great affection and many legends are told about Bennachie.

Bennachie is not a single peak, but a ridge 5km long with several tops, the highest of which is Oxen Craig. This summit is, however, far exceeded in prominence by the Mither Tap, 518m (682224) with its large granite tor. The Tap affords excellent views, not only of the rich agricultural flatlands of the north-east, but also of the Upper Donside hills, with the eye being drawn to the not-too-distant Cairngorms.

BENNACHIE

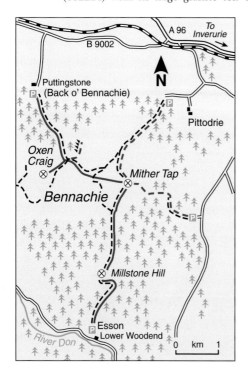

There are four car parks around the hill, from which paths lead to the various tops. The most northerly is the Back o'Bennachie car park at Puttingstone (660245). About 3km east is Pittodrie farm car park (692244), and 2km south is another (with a visitor centre) near Tullos (698216). On the south side of the hill there is Esson's car park near Lower Woodend (673190). An hour from any of these points is sufficient to reach the Mither Tap.

The Tap itself is a granite tor with its north and west faces reaching a height of about 25m, affording a few climbs in the grooves and on the pancake-like formation of the slabs. The summit can be easily reached by the broken rocks on the east side, below which can be seen a circular wall, the remains of a prehistoric fort.

Various combinations of ascents and traverses can be done using two cars, or even by leaving bikes at the foot of the planned descent route. The best traverse is from the Back o'Bennachie car park over all the tops, including Millstone Hill, 408m (676202) and down to Esson's car park. (8km; 550m; 2h 40min).

Adam Watson

The Buck of Cabrach

The Buck of Cabrach*; 721m; (OS Sheet 37; NJ413233); *Cabrach's pimple*

The Buck of Cabrach, with its markedly pointed shape, is a very conspicuous landmark in the north-east. Local people usually call it "the Buck i' the Cabrach". On the west side of the summit there are small granite outcrops of a similar formation to those on Bennachie. From the summit good views can be had across the Moray Firth, and on a clear day the Caithness hills can be seen.

The easiest access to the hill is from the B9002 just over 1km SE of its junction with the A941, where there is space for parking at 422252. From there a path follows a fence to the summit which can be reached without difficulty in about an hour. The summit, atop a surprising rock outcrop, is just large enough for the trig point. (2km; 310m; 1h).

If a longer day is desired, a traverse using two cars can be made by continuing south from the Buck to Bridge of Buchat. From the summit of the Buck follow the line of the district boundary in a generally southerly direction over Mount Meddin, Dun Mount, Creag an Eunan, Meikle Firbriggs Hill and Millhuie Hill, from which a descent south leads to Bridge of Buchat (401149). This traverse gives a 4 hour walk from the B9002.

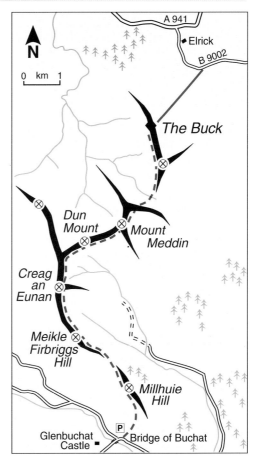

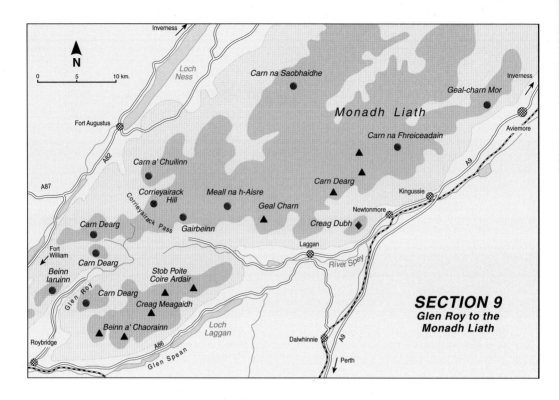

SECTION 9

Glen Roy to the Monadh Liath

Beinn Iaruinn up Glen Roy

Beinn Iaruinn; 805m; (OS Sheet 34; NN297900); *iron hill*
Carn Dearg (East of Glen Roy); 834m; (OS Sheet 34; NN345887); *red cairn*

Glen Roy has a unique feature, the Parallel Roads, which have given it an international geological fame. These parallel lines scored horizontally along the steep hillsides are the old shore-lines of natural lochs created by dams of ice as big glaciers periodically blocked the foot of the glen during the Ice Ages.

After 5km of twisting road up the glen, the farmland and woods are left behind and there is a car park and view-point from which the character of the upper glen can be seen, with the Parallel Roads prominent. The narrow public road continues for a further 8km to end at Brae Roy Lodge. There are three Carn Deargs in Glen Roy, the southmost rising opposite Beinn Iaruinn. These two hills are described together as each by itself is only half a day's climb and it is quite possible to do both in a single visit.

Beinn Iaruinn is most easily climbed by the ridge bounding Coire nan Eun. Start from the road bridge (308891) over the burn draining the corrie. Follow the ridge in a clockwise direction up and round this craggy little corrie, quite rough going, with almost 1km of bleak plateau before gaining the summit. (2km; 600m; 1h 30min). The hills to the west of Loch Lochy spring into view as the plateau is reached. The descent can be made by continuing round the corrie to drop down steep slopes on its north side.

The Carn Dearg on the opposite side of the glen is the most attractive of the three hills of this name in Glen Roy. A pleasant circuit can be made by the corries on either side of Carn Brunachain, as the NW spur of the hill is called. Start at the footbridge 1km down from Brae Roy Lodge (330909) and walk downstream to Brunachan (where quern stones were once quarried), then follow the burn steeply up into Coire Dubh. The crags and gullies can be avoided and the angle eases for gentle walking to the summit, the sudden view this time being to the Creag Meagaidh hills. (5km; 630m; 2h 10min). Return north to descend Coire na Reinich, keeping to the right bank of the burn once down into the corrie.

BEINN IARUINN

CARN DEARG

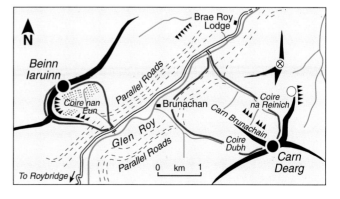

The unique character of Glen Roy has been noted in the proceeding description. The two Carn Deargs at the head of the glen, on either side of subsidiary Gleann Eachach, dominate the rather desolate country to the north of the junction of Glen Turret with Glen Roy.

The public road ends 350 metres before Brae Roy Lodge at a cattle grid, where there is parking available. A private road continues up Glen Roy, but just after crossing Turret Bridge take the left fork to its end at a sheep fank in Glen Turret. Sheep tracks and footpaths continue up the glen. Cross the Allt Eachach via a small bridge (332940) and traverse the slopes up the glen using the upper path to the watershed at 570m. The two Corbetts lie roughly north and south of this col, each one only about 1km distant, both appearing as rather featureless lumps in a neglected corner of the country. The ascent of both is easy from the col. It is suggested to ascend Carn Dearg (north) first. (7km; 600m; 2h 40min). Return the same way to the col and easily ascend to Carn Dearg (south). (9km; 800m; 3h 20min).

Instead of returning by Gleann Eachach, the descent can be made down the SW ridge of either hill, depending on which one has been climbed first. If the south peak is climbed second, an easy descent avoiding steep ground can be made by a traverse SW to join a path at 352942. Then traverse SSW to the track in Glen Roy.

A longer, but more interesting return is to go east from the col between the hills down the north bank of the Allt Dubh. A path is reached on the east side Creag a' Chail (which may be difficult in spate), and 500 metres further on there is a footbridge across the Allt Chonnal. Cross this and descend to the track in Glen Roy for a 6km walk back to Brae Roy Lodge.

134

CARN DEARG

Meal na h-Aisre from above Garva Bridge

Hamish Brown

Gairbeinn from near Melgarve

Gairbeinn; 896m; (OS Sheet 34; NN460985); *rough hill*
Corrieyairack Hill*; 891m; (OS Sheet 34; NN429988); *hill of the rising glen*

The Corrieyairack (*red corrie*) is a very ancient pass, used by drovers and travellers before being finally made into a military road by General Wade's soldiers in 1731. The Jacobite army crossed it in 1745. The two hills described here, which are of nearly equal height and both nearly Munros, lie to the north and east of the pass above the Allt Yairack. The starting point is near Melgarve, which is the furthest point up the River Spey to which one can drive, 15km from Laggan.

For a time, it wasn't known which peak was highest and both were considered Corbetts. A more recent 1:10,000 OS map showed that Gairbeinn is higher and because the drop between the two hills is not great enough for both to be Corbetts, Corrieyairack Hill was 'demoted' in 1997. However the high traverse between the two hills and the descent down the Corrieyairack Pass makes it well worth a visit.

GAIRBEINN

CORRIEYAIRACK HILL*

MEALL NA H-AISRE

From a small parking area where the tarmac road ends (468959), walk past the Melgarve buildings and leave the track at 460961. A faint path leads up the left side of a small stream until one reaches the open col. Ascend the steep slope to the SSW ridge which is followed to the summit. (3.5km; 560m; 1h 50min).

The traverse to Corrieyairack Hill is undulating, with an intermediate hill, Geal Charn (876m) to be crossed. The march line is a fence along the district boundary, a useful navigational aid in misty conditions. (7.25km; 800m; 3h). The view from the summit is better than might be expected, particularly west to Ben Tee and the Glen Garry hills. Descend 1.5 km south then SW to the pass. Follow Wade's road, now spoiled by the passing of vehicles, down the headwall of Corrie Yairack in a series of zig-zags and finally 5km back to Melgarve. Electricity transmission pylons marching alongside the road detract from any feeling of wilderness in this remote corrie.

Meall na h-Aisre; 862m; (OS Sheet 35; NH515000); *hill of the defile*

This featureless hill stands in the remote country of the Monadh Liath near the Corrieyairack Pass. There is an easy ascent from the south, starting from the upper reaches of the River Spey.

From Laggan take the public road west to Garva Bridge, a fine old bridge built by General Wade. There is a large car park by the bridge. Cross the Grava bridge and go north up the track on the west side of the stream and cross the footbridge over the Allt Coire Iain Oig at 523958. Don't cross an earlier, larger bridge, as this leads to the Munro Geal Charn, although it does

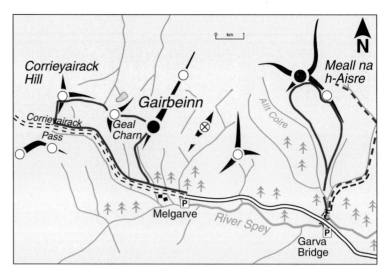

provide an alternative ascent or descent route. From the footbridge, follow the track initially, which soon becomes faint as it crosses low angled grassy ground. Aim for the SE ridge of the peak, passing a small rock outcrop on the way. Climb north up the open hillside to the broad crest called Leathad Gaothach. Continue NW over a rocky top (844m) and reach the summit of Meall na h-Aisre across shallow Coire Gorm. (6km; 630m; 2h 30min). The summit area around the trig point is flat with a broad ridge leading to a small sub-top to the NE.

Descend directly into Coire Iain Oig and follow the Allt Coire Iain Oig back to the bridge. Initially the descent is steep, but grassy ramps provide an easier angled traverse to the upper part of the Allt Coire Iain Oig. A path along the stream can then be followed back to the footbridge.

The route can be done in reverse, but the slopes south of summit are very steep. The time saved from a more direct attack will probably be lost making the steep climb. An alternative descent can be made SE to reach the stalkers path on the east side of the Feith Talagain.

The round trip is short and one can drive to the road end at Melgarve for an ascent of Garbeinn and Corrieyariack Hill to complete the day.

Meal na h-Aisre from the Allt Coire Iain Oig

Don Green

Richard Wood

Carn a' Chuilinn from Loch Tarff

CARN
A' CHUILINN

Carn a' Chuilinn; 817m; (OS Sheet 34; NH416034); *cairn of holly*

This is an isolated summit in the Glendoe Forest SE of Fort Augustus. The obvious line of approach is by the private estate road which leaves the A862 at 403090, but this may cause antagonism locally. It is better to park about 1km further east, near the cattle grid just above the bridge over the Allt Doe (408087) where there is adequate off road parking. From there an easy ascent up a grassy field leads to the track as it emerges from the wood at 404086. Continue south along the private track into Glen Doe. When this track makes a tortuous change of direction SE, continue up a stalkers path south to the steeper upper slopes of Carn a' Chuilinn. Climb directly to the craggy summit, which overlooks a maze of lochans on the east side. (6km; 620m; 2h 30min).

If the area is to be savoured for its exceptional roughness and isolation, it may be more interesting to make the ascent from Loch Tarff along the stalkers path from there to the Dubh Lochan, followed by 4km of very rough walking to Carn a' Chuilinn. The route described above can then be used for the descent.

The simplest route in many ways is to cycle or walk up the Corrieyairack Pass road from its start near Fort Augustus until opposite Creagan na Cailliche. Drop down and cross the River Tarff and climb the hill from the SW. (9.5km; 850m; 3h 30min). In spate conditions this route is not practicable for there is no bridge across the river.

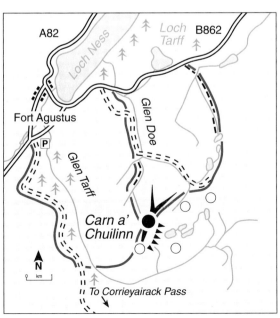

Carn na Saobhaidhe is the northernmost Corbett in the Monadh Liath and forms part of a large featureless plateau which offers a navigational challenge in bad weather. The mountain can be approached from Tomatin on the A9 by going down the splendid glen of Strath Dearn, through which the upper river Findhorn runs. Carn na Saobhaidhe is on the watershed between the Findhorn and the streams draining NW into Loch Mhor on the B862.

Till 1981 Carn na Saobhaidhe was twinned with Carn na Laraiche Maoile (584112). Not surprisingly the Corbett has the greatest surface area of all, i.e. ground encircled by the 150m contour below the summit. It is also unusually remote from any centre of population.

Leave the A9 just after the Slochd summit if going north, or before Tomatin if going south and follow the old A9 road to Findhorn Bridge. From there a public road goes up Strath Dearn as far as Coignafearn Old Lodge, where there is a locked barrier and limited parking space on the south side of the road. A private estate road continues for a further 7km past Coignafearn Lodge to the cottage of Dalbeg. A cycle can be used with advantage as far as Dalbeg.

Strike west up the track that follows the Allt Creagach. Follow the track for about 2.5km to where it forks. Follow the west fork past the waterfalls along the Allt Odhar for a further 1km. Continue up the Allt Odhar to the next tributary that joins from the NW, which is then followed towards the summit of Carn na Saobhaidhe. (14km; 420m; 3h 50min). The going on the plateau is extremely tedious because of extensive peat hags. To avoid the difficulties and greatly assist navigation outwith the landrover track it is recommended to follow the burn which has worn through the layers of peat and provides reasonable walking on its banks. There is little evidence of the summit position but the presence of a very small cairn in the flat summit local is the most likely possibility. A GPS is useful for confirming the summit position and it should be noted that the adjoining summit of Carn Mhic Lamhair sports a more substantial cairn. The view to the north takes in a wind turbine on the plateau to the summit of Beinn Dubhcharaidh.

An alternative route is from Strath Nairn to the north. Leave the B851 at 605246 where there is limited parking by the telephone kiosk. Follow the private road to Drumnaglass Lodge for 2.5km and then take the track through fields and over the River Farigaig at 596222. Continue along the track up the Allt Uisg an t-Sidhein, then take the right fork at 604187 which crosses to the Aberchalder Burn. This is followed to its source, from where the summit lies about 500 metres west. (13km; 570m; 3h 50min). These two routes can be combined in a long and interesting traverse. Substantial recent activity involves tracks being constructed to give access to the wind turbine and these may assist progress to the summit from the Dunmaglass start point.

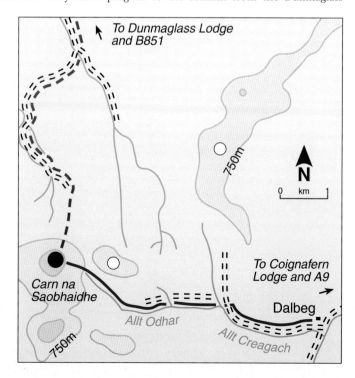

Alan O'Brien

Carn an Fhreiceadain

Carn an Fhreiceadain; 878m; (OS Sheet 35; NH725071); *watcher's (lookout) cairn*

This extensive flat hill is situated on the edge of the Monadh Liath mountains behind Kingussie, and the position makes it an excellent viewpoint across the River Spey to the glens of Tromie and Truim.

Take the road to the golf course on the north side of Kingussie, and park just before the caravan site and club house. Walk behind the club house and cross the Allt Mor by a footbridge to reach the road on the east side of this stream. Follow the track to a bridge just before Pitmain Lodge. Do not cross the bridge, but take the track going right and pass an old building. Follow the track north then NW to Beinn Bhreac.

The map indicates that the track finishes at about 750m on the south shoulder of this hill, but it continues to Carn an Fhreiceadain. (8km; 630m; 2h 50min).

On the descent, go SW from the summit past a large cairn and then south down a broad ridge, Meall Unaig, to reach a track which is followed down the Allt Mor to Pitmain Lodge and so back to Kingussie by the road through the golf course.

Creag Bheag, 487m, would make an interesting addition, descending by a path on the SE ridge.

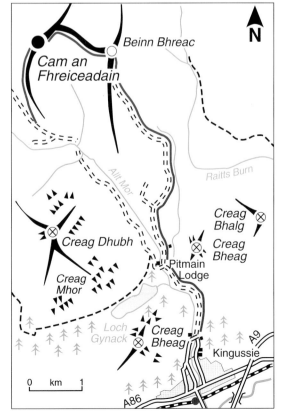

CARN AN
FHREICEADAIN

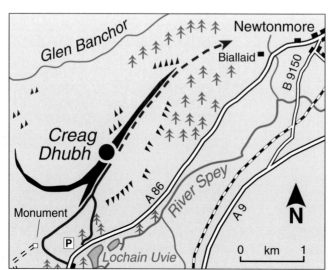

Creag Dhubh

Hamish Brown

Creag Dhubh*; 756m; (OS Sheet 35; NH678972); *black crag*

CREAG DHUBH*

Creag Dhubh, rising abruptly from flat Strathspey, is a hill of dominant character, well seen from many directions and giving a summit view which is unrivalled in the region. Along its SE side steep crags and scree slopes rise above the A86. To its north Glen Banchor separates the hill from the main Monadh Liath range. "Creag Dhubh!" is the war cry of the Clan MacPherson, and Cluny's Cave, a hide-out for clansmen and their chiefs in the terror after Culloden, is situated in the cliffs to the SW of the hill. Creag Dhubh is popular for rock climbing, the crags above Lochain Uvie rising in tiers of intimidating steepness.

Beside the A86 (just above the north end of Lochain Uvie) is a climbers car park (675958). From here make a rough rising traverse NE, below the cliffs and the worst of the screes then follow up by the edge of a plantation to gain the craggy, heathery slopes above the treeline. Break left to gain the crest of the ridge, after about 30 min, where there is a fence/stile. Several false tops lead to the summit cairn. (2km; 500m; 1h 20min). The hill is rugged and calls for careful route finding so should not be underestimated.

Descend well down the SW ridge to avoid the crags then, instead of continuing on and up to the monument turn down, ESE, by a small glen to follow a track to a gate on the A86 facing the entrance to Creagdhubh Lodge. If transport can be arranged the most pleasing traverse is to ascend by the complex NE ridge from Biallaid, just west of Newtonmore, and descend as described.

Hamish Brown

Geal-charn Mor from Speyside

Geal-charn Mor; 824m; (OS Sheet 35; NH836123); *big white hill*

This hill, the highest point of the Kinveachy Forest, between the River Spey and the River Dulnain is a superb viewpoint for the Cairngorms on the opposite side of Strathspey.

There is ample space for car parking off the main A9 at Lynwilg (882107) beside the bridge over the Allt na Criche. Follow the track NW up the finely wooded An Gleannan, climbing gradually in 2km onto the open hillside. Continue along the track until it reaches the watershed near a memorial. From there climb SW up a broad ridge which gives pleasant walking to the summit of Geal-charn Mor. (6km; 600m; 2h 20min).

GEAL-CHARN
MOR

The descent may be made by the same route, but a good circuit can be completed by descending east to reach a path to Ballinluig farm, from where there is a 1.5km walk along tracks and paths back to Lynwilg.

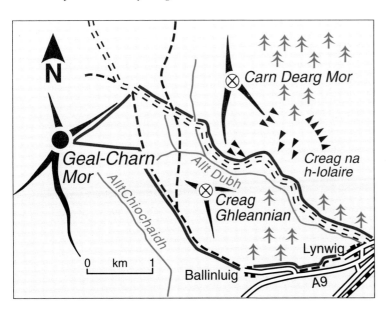

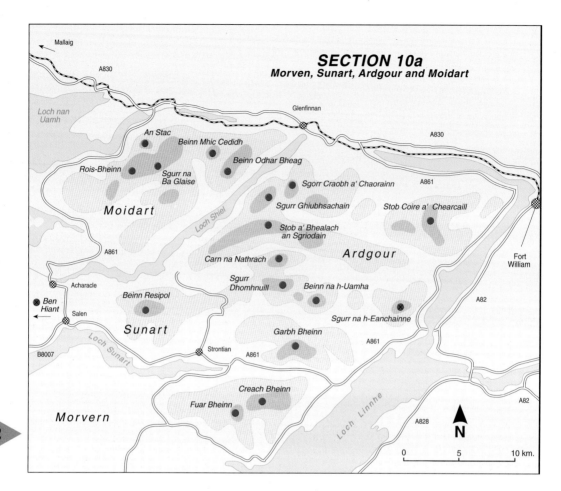

SECTION 10a

Morvern, Sunart, Ardgour and Moidart

Andrew Dempster

Beinn Resipol

Beinn Resipol; 845m; (OS Sheet 40; NM766654); from old Norse *homestead*

Situated 4.5km north of Loch Sunart about midway between Strontian and Salen, Beinn Resipol is a very prominent and isolated mountain. The hill gives a fairly short and easy climb which is rewarded by one of the finest views along the West Highland coastline, extending to the Cuillin of Skye, Ben Nevis and Ben More in Mull. Two routes to Beinn Resipol are described, which if one's transport can be arranged make an excellent traverse. From Strontian one can start 2km north of the village near Ariundle and follow the old miners' track NW towards the old mines in Coire an t-Suidhe (Corrantee). From the highest point of the path go west over Meall an t-Slugain and up the east ridge of Beinn Resipol. (7km; 750m; 3h).

The other route starts at Resipole farm and caravan site, 4km WSW of Beinn Resipol on the A861. Follow a track, which in less than 1km becomes a good footpath, up the SE side of the Allt Mhic Chiarain. For 1.5km this path goes through very pleasant woodland high on the steep side of the burn, then emerges onto the open hillside. The path tends to disappear, but continue due east along the burn to finally climb the hill's west ridge to the summit. (5km; 850m; 2h 40min). Resipol is stalked during the last week in September on to mid-October.

Ben Hiant*; 528m; (OS Sheet 47; NM537632); *holy hill*

This hill lies within the great volcanic ring complex which forms the western part of Ardnamurchan, a world renowned place of study for geologists. For hillwalkers the attraction of Ben Hiant is almost as great, for the hill is a superb viewpoint. The best ascent is from the NE, leaving the narrow B8007 near its high point 500 metres south of Loch Mudle at 551641. Climb steeply towards the lower part of the NE ridge and follow along a path round to the steeper slopes below the summit. Just below the final steep rise to the summit the path branches. The right hand path traverses up across a rocky and somewhat exposed slope which can be slippery when wet, and leads to a short grassy ascent to the summit. The left hand path is less obvious, but leads round to avoid steep ground and approach the summit from the south. (2km; 370m; 1h 10min).

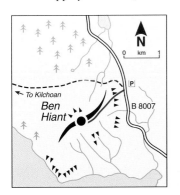

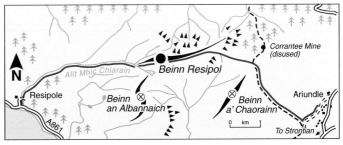

These two hills are the highest in the district of Morvern. With their lower outliers they form a well-defined horseshoe ridge round Glen Galmadale above Loch Linnhe. The complete traverse of this ridge is a good hillwalk and the best way to climb both hills, although the drops between successive tops give a lot of up and down work. A much shorter approach to Creach Bheinn is from Glen Tarbert to the north, climbing the NW ridge above the cliffs of Coire Dhuibh, but this is not a particularly good way if one wants to include Fuar Bheinn.

The west side of the horseshoe has a succession of craggy corries overlooking Glen Galmadale, but they are not very impressive when seen at close quarters. More impressive is the east side of Druim na Maodalaich, the eastern arm of the horseshoe. This falls steeply in a long line of broken cliffs of red granite, cut by many dykes which form tree-filled gullies above the narrow B8043. This steep hillside is home to feral goats.

The best starting point for the traverse is near the bridge over the Galmadale River. Walk SW along the B8043 for a few hundred metres and climb steeply beside a plantation to gain the SE ridge of Beinn na Cille (652m). The ridge is grassy, with many outcrops of granite, for this hill is within the area of Strontian granite which extends further south to the huge Glen Sanda quarry.

From Beinn na Cille continue NNW down to the col at 460m and climb the broad ridge to Fuar Bheinn. (4km; 960m; 2h 30min). Only by keeping well to the east side of the ridge does one get any impression of the corries above Glen Galmadale. From Fuar Bheinn descend NW then north to the broad featureless col, the Chuil Mhaim. From there climb just over 300m up a broad stony ridge to Creach Bheinn. Just north of the summit there is a dry stone walled enclosure that may have been built as a look-out at the time of the Napoleonic wars (marked on the map as 'camp'). It must have been a very cold one! (8km; 1260m; 4h).

Descend NE down a narrower rocky ridge and then bear east and SE across the col at the head of Coire Dhuibh and up the rounded Maol Odhar (794m). From there it is possible to descend directly SSW on a grassy spur to the head of Glen Galmadale, but the traverse continues SE then south over Meall nan Each (591m) and along the knolly ridge of Druim na Maodalaich, with fine views across Loch Linnhe, to return to the foot of Glen Galmadale.

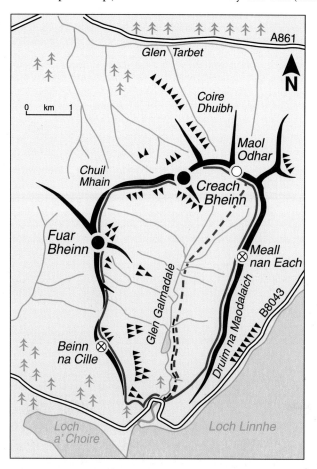

Hamish Brown

From Castle Stalker to Fuar Bheinn and Creach Bheinn

Creach Bheinn from Fuar Bheinn

Mark Gear

Garbh Bheinn of Ardgour

Garbh Bheinn; 885m; (OS Sheet 40; NM904622); *rough mountain*

Garbh Bheinn of Ardgour is one of the finest mountains in the western Highlands, and certainly the finest and most precipitous mountain in Ardgour. The best view of it is from the east, looking across Loch Linnhe from Glen Coe or Ballachulish from where the jagged outline of the mountain is very obvious. From closer at hand, the full extent of the crags on its NE face above Coire an Iubhair is best seen from the ridges on either side of that corrie. Despite its steep and rocky character, Garbh Bheinn is relatively easy of access, although the hill should be treated with respect in adverse weather conditions.

Of three or four possible routes of ascent, probably the best starts at the foot of Coire an Iubhair, where cars can be parked off the A861 at the old bridge over the Abhainn Coire an Iubhair (On OS Sheet 49). Cross to the west side of the stream and climb the long, but easy angled ridge of Sron a' Gharbh Choire Bhig. There is a good deal of bare rock, but are traces of paths up the ridge through and between the many rock outcrops, and the going is easy to the cairn at the top of the Sron, 823m, (906617).

From that point there is a superb view of the east face of Garbh Bheinn across the head of Coire an Iubhair, as well as eastwards to the Glen Coe mountains. Descend the broad rocky ridge NW to a col (748m) and climb north up steep and rocky, but perfectly easy slopes to reach the west ridge of Garbh Bheinn a short distance west of the summit, which is perched right on the edge of the precipitous east face. (5km; 880m; 2h 40min).

The return may be varied by descending the route of ascent to the 748m col, and going steeply down from there NE into the head of Coire an Iubhair. There is a path of sorts which leads down between crags and boulders to the more level floor of the corrie where the path on the east side of the stream leads back to the day's starting point.

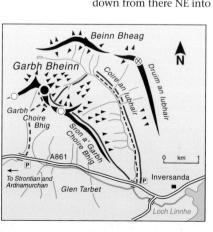

The shortest route of ascent is up Coire a' Chrothruim from a point on the A861 through Glen Tarbert (897604). The climb to the 748m col is a toilsome mixture of steep heather, scree and gravelly waterslides and, while not particularly difficult, is not recommended.

A very fine, but rather long traverse can be made round Coire an Iubhair; starting on the east side of the corrie up the ridge of Druim an Iubhair to Sgorr Mhic Eacharna (650m). Continue over Beinn Bheag (736m) and steeply down to the pass on the north side of Garbh Bheinn, Lochan Coire an Iubhair. The ascent from this pass up the north ridge of Garbh Bheinn is quite steep and the upper section of the ridge is rocky, but easy, leading over the tops of the buttresses on the hill's NE face. The descent of the Sron a' Gharbh Choire Bhig completes a fine traverse.

Jim Teesdale

Sgurr na h-Eanchainne across Loch Linnhe

Sgurr na h-Eanchainne*; 730m; (OS Sheets 40 and 41; NM996658); *peak of the brains*

Sgurr na h-Eanchainne is a very shapely peak which is well seen from the A82 between Fort William and Ballachulish. The summit rises very steeply above Loch Linnhe at Corran Ferry, so is conspicuous in views up and down the Great Glen. For the same reason it commands a superb prospect up and down Loch Linnhe and across to Glen Coe. An ascent in good weather is, therefore, highly recommended, despite the fact that it is not quite the highest hill, being just overtopped by the flat mass of unnamed Druim na Sgriodain, 734m, (978656) 2km to the west.

On the NW side of Ardgour village there is an extensive fluvio-glacial sand and gravel terrace, pock-marked here and there by 'kettle-hole' lochans. (These are the melt-out holes where large masses of glacier ice were embedded in the gravels at the time of the last Ice Age). Go north along the A861 for about 2km from the ferry to a cattle grid (014658) just beyond the Clan Maclean burial ground. Access to the open hillside can be gained on the north side of the stream below Beinn na Cille (a name often wrongly attributed to Sgurr na h-Eanchainne).

Cross to the south bank of the stream and climb steeply beside it, but before the col between the two hills is reached, turn west then south and climb up to the sharp summit of Sgurr na h-Eanchainne. (2km; 730m; 1h 50min).

The descent can be varied if desired by going to the highest point of the massif, Druim na Sgriodain, round the rim of the well formed Coire Dubh. Although a Graham, the top is of no great interest, and the view inferior. Descend steeply down a rough hillside to Loch nan Gabhar and Sallachan, keeping east of cliffs shown on the map.

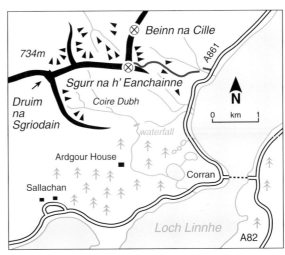

Sgurr Dhomhnuill; 888m; (OS Sheet 40; NM889678); *Donald's peak*

Sgurr Dhomhnuill is the highest peak in Ardgour, and because of its height and pointed appearance is a conspicuous landmark from many distant viewpoints. The peak stands at the head of the Strontian Glen, and is one of several peaks surrounding the headwaters of the River Scaddle.

Although one can climb Sgurr Dhomhnuill from Glen Scaddle, the walk up that glen is very long. The best approach to the mountain is from Strontian to the SW, and two routes are described.

The most scenically attractive route is up the Strontian Glen from the car park at the entrance to the Ariundle Nature Reserve (829634). Walk up the glen through a fine natural forest of oak and take the upper path leading to the disused Feith Dhomhnuill mines. Cross the stream to the east and climb onto the Druim Leac a' Sgiathain, a narrow ridge leading to Sgurr na h-lghinn (766m). Descend NE to a col at 682m and climb the south ridge of Sgurr Dhomhnuill in two steps to the summit. (8.5km; 970m; 3h 30min).

The alternative route starts at the highest point of the road from Strontian to Loch Doilet at 342m. Go ENE along a broad, featureless ridge studded with little lochans to Druim Garbh, and from its highest point (803m) descend SE and climb the NW ridge of Sgurr Dhomhnuill which gives a good scramble almost all the way to the top. (6km; 750m; 2h 40min). Although this route is shorter than the one described above, the terrain on the Druim Garbh ridge (particularly the lower part) is likely to be very confusing in bad visibility. The two routes described can be combined to give a fine traverse.

SGURR
DHOMHNUILL

BEINN NA H-
UAMHA

Beinn na h-Uamha; 762m; (OS Sheet 40; NM917664); *hill of the cave*

Beinn na h-Uamha is a remarkably rocky hill on the north side of Glen Gour several kilometres NW of Sallachan. With a twin peak, Sgurr a' Chaorainn (761m) 2.5km to the west, it forms a high ridge to the SE of Sgurr Dhomhnuill on the north side of the watershed between Glen Gour and the Strontian Glen. The traverse of this ridge from Sallachan to Strontian is a very good day's walk, and use can be made of the bus service between Ardgour village and Strontian.

Starting at Sallachan, a good track is followed on the south side of Glen Gour (Loch nan Gabhar) and the ruined cottage of Tigh Ghlinnegabhar. About 4km up the glen a crossing of the River Gour must be made and the SE ridge of Beinn na h-Uamha climbed. There is a conspicuous knoll about half way up the ridge, which is rocky for much of its length, and leads directly to the summit. (7.5km; 770m; 3h).

Continue west down a broad ridge to the col at 556m and climb more steeply to Sgurr a' Chaorainn. From there descend steeply west to the Strontian Glen and on to reach the path and track which leads very pleasantly through the oakwoods of the Ariundle Nature Reserve to the road 2km north of Strontian. One can also descend south, steeply down to Glen Gour to return to the start.

Beinn na h-Uamha from Sgurr Dhomhnuill

Carn na Nathrach*; 786m; (OS Sheet 40; NM886699); *cairn of the adders*

This hill is situated right in the heart of the wilds of Ardgour, and is the highest point of a long ridge (to which the name Beinn Mheadhoin is given) which extends from the lower reaches of Glen Hurich near Loch Doilet to Glen Scaddle. Glen Hurich and Gleann an Dubh Choirean, flanking Beinn Mheadhoin are extensively forested, and some of this forest is now being felled so access to the hills may be impeded.

The closest approach to Carn na Nathrach is from Glen Hurich as one can drive the narrow, steep public road from Strontian to Loch Doilet, and the little forestry village of Polloch. From Kinlochan, near the east end of Loch Doilet, walk (or cycle) up the forestry track in Glen Hurich for 2km and cross the River Hurich. Turn left, cross the Allt au Dubh Choirein, then take the first fork right to angle up and back onto the SW end of the Beinn Mheadhoin ridge. Strike uphill through the remains of the forest and gain the open ridge which is followed for 4km over a few knolls and a final narrow section to Carn na Nathrach. (8km; 800m; 3h 20min).

It is possible to continue the traverse east along the Beinn Mheadhoin ridge, descend to Glen Scaddle and walk for many kilometres down this glen to the road beside Loch Linnhe. If returning to Kinlochan, one can return along the ridge to the 602m knoll and descend north from there down a steep ridge on the west side of the prominent gully west of Creag Bheag. This leads to a forest track on the south side of Glen Hurich 6.5km from Kinlochan. (On ascent one could cycle up this track, thus minimising the walking distance to the hill).

CARN NA
NATHRACH

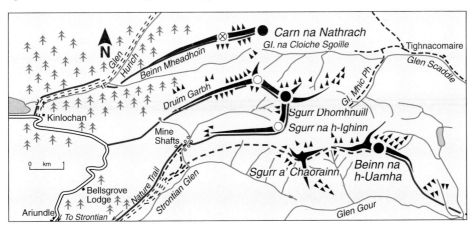

Donald Bennet

Sgurr Ghiubhsachain and Loch Shiel from Glenfinnan

Stob a' Bhealach an Sgriodain; 770m; (OS Sheet 40; NM874727); *peak of the pass of screes*
Sgurr Ghiubhsachain; 849m; (OS Sheet 40; NM875751); *peak of the fir-wood*
Sgorr Craobh a' Chaorainn; 775m; (OS Sheet 40; NM895758); *rowantree peak*

150

STOB A'
BHEALACH AN
SGRIODAIN

SGURR
GHIUBHSACHAIN

SGORR CRAOBH A'
CHAORAINN

These three mountains lie in the NW corner of Ardgour, almost isolated from the neighbouring parts of the western Highlands by the long Lochs Shiel and Eil. The heads of these two lochs are separated by about 5km over a col which is only 15m above sea level. Especially near Loch Shiel the hills are steep sided and rocky, with Sgurr Ghiubhsachain being one of the finest peaks, not only in this area, but in the whole of the west and is not to be treated lightly, especially in winter. The most convenient access to these hills is from the A830 from Fort William to Glenfinnan at a point about 2km east of Glenfinnan.

The name Druim Tarsuinn has been applied to the 770m top which is obviously incorrect, as the name is not apposite and is shown by the OS as applying to the ridge to the NW of the Bealach an Sgriodain over which the old path from Glenfinnan to Glen Hurich passes. The 770m summit is well defined and equally separate from Meall Mor so the name Stob a' Bhealach an Sgriodain has been applied to it.

This is an enticingly remote hill 14km up the Cona Glen from Loch Linnhe, 11km up Glen Hurich from Loch Doilet, which is itself not altogether easy of access from Strontian with the additional complexity of felling and reafforestation in Glen Hurich near Resourie bothy. The best route to the hill is from Callop, 2km east of Glenfinnan just off the A830. Even this route involves some descent and reascent to cross the head of the Cona Glen.

Leave the A830 at 925794 and park near the locked gate at the bridge over the Callop River. From the bridge follow the path south past Callop and up the west side of the Allt na Cruaiche. In spate conditions the Allt Coire na Leacaich is surprisingly difficult to cross, but is easy in dry weather. The path continues to a pass overlooking the head of the Cona Glen, where it divides. Go straight downhill to cross the Cona River at a prominent meander loop. (If this river is in spate, crossing will be very difficult, and an easier point will have to be found upstream). Climb SW up the west side of the stream which comes down from the col west of Meall Mor on pleasantly low angled rock and grass to reach the col itself. From there the ridge west to Druim Tarsuinn is rocky and knolly. (9km; 890m; 3h 30min).

The easiest descent is WNW to the Bealach an Sgriodain, then down to the Cona Glen and up the path to the col at the head of the Allt na Cruaiche. The path between the Cona

River and the col is none too distinct, but beyond the col the going is easy back to the day's starting point.

The traverse of Sgurr Ghiubhsachain and Sgorr na Craobh Chaorainn also starts at the bridge over the Callop River. Follow the forest track NW then SW along the shore of Loch Shiel for 5km to Guesachan cottage. Climb Sgurr Ghiubhsachain by its very fine NNE ridge, best reached by going up the Allt Coire Ghiubhsachain for some way and then traversing onto the ridge above its steep and rocky lowest part. After reaching the ridge climb steeply through rocky outcrops where care is needed in misty weather. Some scrambling can be found. Cross the shoulder of Meall a' Choire Chruinn and climb the final steep slopes to the apparent summit, from where a horizontal ridge leads to the large cairn on the true summit. (7.5km; 850m; 3h 10min).

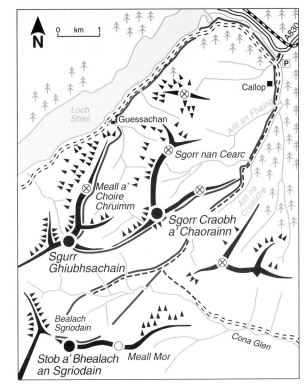

Descend steeply ESE down awkward slabs and grass, then easily along the ridge round the head of Coire Ghiubhsachain to Sgorr Craobh a' Chaorainn. This peak has a steep west face and a rocky summit where any slight difficulty can be circumvented on the east. (10km; 1040m; 4h). Continue downhill NE over Meall na Cuartaige to join the path in the Allt na Cruaiche glen, which leads back to the bridge over the Callop River. The energetic could add these two peaks after doing Stob a' Bhealach an Sgriodain.

151

Sgorr Craobh a' Chaorainn from Sgurr Ghiubhsachan

Beinn Odhar Bheag from Beinn Odhar Mor

Derek Sime

STOB COIRE A'
CHEARCAILL

Stob Coire a' Chearcaill; 771m; (OS Sheet 41; NN016726); *peak of the circular corrie*

Stob Coire a' Chearcaill is the highest hill in the NE corner of Ardgour and presents a uniformly featureless appearance towards Loch Eil, but from a point 2km south of Fort William the view of the summit across Loch Linnhe is a much more impressive sight, with crags rising above Coire a' Chearcaill at the head of Gleann Sron a' Chreagain.

The shortest route to the top, by 1km, is by the north flank, starting from a point (024769) just over 1km east of Duisky on the A861 beside Loch Eil. At that point (near a cattle grid on the east side of a large plantation) a gate gives access to open hillside. Go through open woodland for a short distance and then head straight uphill. A ruined fence and a broken path appear intermittently and lead onto the ridge a short distance east of Braigh Bhlaich. Follow the crest SW round the corrie and up to the summit where a huge cairn lies a few metres back from, and apparently higher than, the triangulation pillar. (4.5km; 770m; 2h 20min).

A slightly longer, but more attractive approach, is by Gleann Sron a' Chreagain. Unfortunately parking near the foot of this glen is very restricted as access to steadings and fields must not be blocked. From the road a track leads west through fenced, stock-grazing land for about 2km to a point about 150 metres before the last fence. A gate, slightly above the path, leads to open country from which the Braigh Bhlaich ridge can be reached and the first route joined. This route can be used by carless parties from Fort William, using the Camusnagaul ferry.

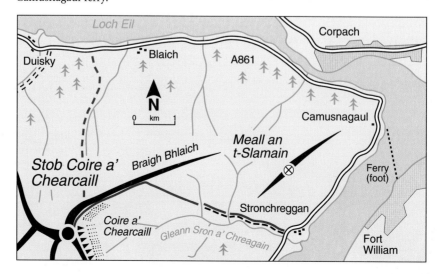

Beinn Odhar Bheag; 882m; (OS Sheet 40; NM846778); *little dun-coloured hill*
Beinn Mhic Cedidh; 783m; (OS Sheet 40; NM828788); *MacCedidh's hill*

Moidart is rough, sparsely populated country bounded on the east by Loch Shiel, on the west by Loch Ailort and on the north by the A830 Fort William to Mallaig road. The highest hills in the district lie near its northern and north-western edge, and are readily accessible from the nearest roads; their southern flanks are remote and impracticable.

Beinn Odhar Bheag, with its slightly lower twin Beinn Odhar Mhor, and Beinn Mhic Cedidh are in the NE corner of Moidart, accessible from Glenfinnan and one or two points on the A830 further west.

These hills are frequently climbed together from the north, starting about 2km east of Loch Eilt. Access used to be possible by stepping stones 200 metres above the mouth of the Allt Lon a' Mhuidhe. However a small dam at the west end of the loch has slightly raised the water level, meaning that the burn is now deep and sluggish and the surrounding ground tends to be water-logged, so the stepping stones are no longer advised. Instead, leave the A830 from a lay-by at 857813. Cross the Allt Lon a' Mhuidhe by a bridge, then over the railway line where it goes through a short tunnel. Climb WSW up fairly easy ground to a skyline notch at 845807 (c400m) on the lower slopes of the NNW ridge of Beinn Odhar Mhor. This ridge is better defined in its upper reaches and gives a straightforward route to the top. Mhor means *large*, yet (not uniquely) is lower than Beinn Odhar Bheag, meaning *small*. Beinn Odhar Bheag lies 1.5km to the south, reached by a pleasant ridge, broad at first, which drops to c750m and becomes narrower and quite rocky, but there are no difficulties and one soon reaches the pointed summit with an inappropriately small cairn – a magnificent viewpoint above the narrow waters of Loch Shiel.

Beinn Odhar Mhor can also be approached from Glenfinnan by the pier road and rounding the Shlatach plantation to follow the Allt na h-Aire to Lochan nan Sleubhaich, passing over spot height 529m to gain the top by Sgurr na Boinaid. The route is rough and requires judgement in assessing the best line.

To reach Beinn Mhic Cedidh, descend the grassy NW ridge to the Bealach a' Choire Bhuidhe (c480m) and grind steadily uphill to the summit, an excellent place from which to admire the east end of the Rois-Bheinn ridge.

The best line back to the road from Beinn Mhic Cedidh is not obvious. Drop down the attractive north ridge to reach a bridge (unmarked on the OS map) over the Allt a' Choire Bhuidhe 500 metres south of the railway line. A rough all-terrain vehicle track goes under the railway at 840813, and after 1km of boggy and tussocky ground one can cross the Allt Lon a' Mhuidhe. Follow the road back to the start. Do not return along the railway line.

An alternative is to return from Beinn Mhic Cedidh to the Bealach a' Choire Bhuidhe, then to drop into Coire Buidhe. Cross the burn at around c320m, and make a gradual rising traverse across grassy slopes to gain a little spur. Continue the traverse to the skyline notch on the NNW ridge of Beinn Odhar Mhor previously mentioned, and return to the starting point.

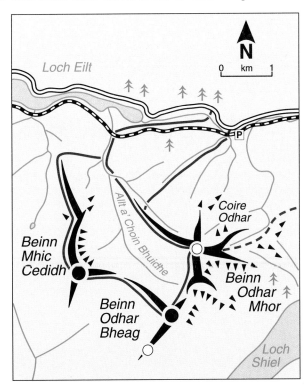

Rois-Bheinn range from Beinn Mhic Cedlidh

Mark Gear

Rois-Bheinn; 882m; (OS Sheet 40; NM756778); *horse hill*
Sgurr na Ba Glaise; 874m; (OS Sheet 40; NM770777); *peak of the grey cow*
An Stac; 814m; (OS Sheet 40; NM763792); *the stack*

ROIS-BHEINN

SGURR NA BA
GLAISE

AN STAC

These mountains in the NW corner of Moidart give very fine ridge walking with views out across the Sea of the Hebrides to the islands of Eigg, Rum and other islands, a view unmatched elsewhere along the west coast. Two possible starting points for the traverse of these peaks and their slightly lower neighbours are Lochailort and Alisary. The traverse from one of these points to the other is a fine expedition, with a pleasant walk along the seaside back to the starting point along the A861 beside Loch Ailort.

Starting at the north end of the group at Lochailort, cars can be parked just off the main road near Inverailort, or on the narrow road beside the River Ailort leading to the Glenshian Lodge Hotel. From either point, tracks lead through a little col immediately south of Tom Odhar and into the lower part of Coire a' Bhuiridh. Continue up the corrie and cross to the east side of the Allt a' Bhuiridh to climb SE up the grassy slopes of Beinn Coire nan Gall. Aim for the lochan at the col between this hill and Druim Fiaclach (869m), and climb the latter by the steep and craggy north ridge.

Druim Fiaclach, although not a Corbett, is possibly the finest peak of this group. The main feature of interest is the SE ridge, which is narrow and has on its crest a number of small tooth-like pinnacles which give the hill its name, *toothed ridge*.

Descend SW from Druim Fiaclach along another fine ridge to a small col and climb south to a tiny lochan perched on the crest of An t-Slat-Bheinn, turning WSW at the lochan along a narrow ridge to reach the summit of this peak (c820m). This undulating ridge culminates 1km further west at Sgurr na Ba Glaise, which has impressive crags on its north face. (7.5km; 1000m; 3h 20min).

Descend steeply NW to the Bealach an Fhiona (701m) where the remains of an old wall are found leading west for 1km to the eastern and higher summit of Rois-Bheinn. (9.5km; 1180m; 4h 10min). The wall continues for 700 metres to the western summit (878m), which although not the highest point is the best viewpoint.

To reach the last peak of this group, return to the Bealach an Fhiona and descend steeply NNW, still following the broken wall, to the col below An Stac, from where a steep rocky ridge leads directly to the isolated summit. (11.5km; 1450m; 5h).

The final descent of the day depends on one's objective. If returning to Lochailort, descend

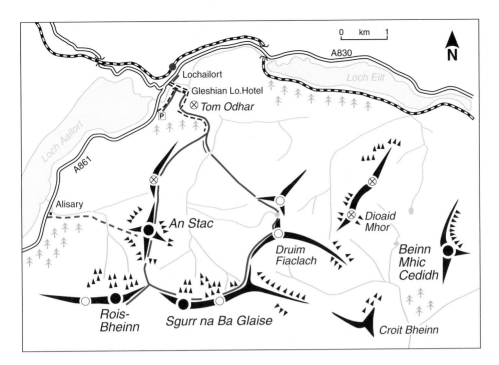

north then NNE over rocky ground to Seann Chruach (521m), and continue NE to rejoin the path near the Tom Odhar col, a short distance from Lochailort.

If making a traverse of the group to Alisary, descend west from An Stac down steep ground with many rocky outcrops to the east corner of the forest on the south side of the Alisary Burn and descend a narrow path on the south side of this burn (keeping close to the forest high above the burn) to reach the A861 beside Loch Ailort 4km from the day's starting point.

Rois-Bheinn from Sgurr na Ba Glaise

Richard Wood

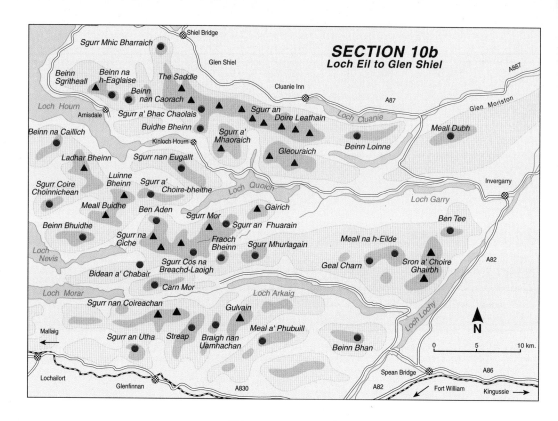

SECTION 10b

Loch Eil to Glen Shiel

Richard Cormack

Sgurr an Utha

Sgurr an Utha; 796m; (OS Sheet 40; NM885839); *peak of the udder*

Sgurr an Utha well justifies its Corbett status and offers a pleasant walk with a good vista from the summit on a clear day. It is the highest point, albeit by only a few metres, of the well-defined group of extremely rocky hills immediately to the NW of Glenfinnan. This massif is bounded on the north by the deep gash of the Chaol-ghlinne, on the east by Glen Finnan, on the west by the Allt Feith a' Chatha and on the south by the A830 from Glenfinnan to Mallaig.

The shortest route to this hill starts where the A830 crosses the Allt Feith a' Chatha (875817). There is space for parking west of the bridge. Follow the forest track which starts from the roadside just east of the bridge through forest plantings not shown on the map. In a few

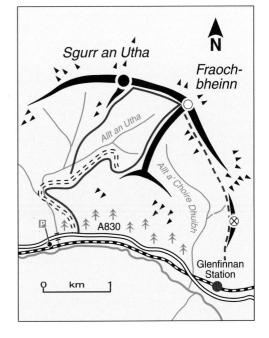

hundred metres the track emerges onto the open hillside and turns NE towards the ridge of Druim na Brein-choille above the Allt an Utha, and this is a convenient route to gain height easily. Follow the track to its conclusion, then gain and follow the ridge to Fraoch-bheinn, traversing across to the col between it and Sgurr an Utha. From here strike up the ridge to the summit which is marked by an obvious cairn perched on the edge of the steep slopes above the Chaol-ghlinne. (4.75km; 690m; 2h 20min). The summit provides an outstanding viewpoint.

The hill can also be climbed by the WSW ridge, reached by crossing the bridge at the foot of the Allt an Utha and climbing north to Sidhean Mor. This is a steep and laborious route, wending a way through crags, and somewhat adventurous in winter.

If one arrives at Glenfinnan by train, the best route to the hill is directly north from the station up the Tom na h-Aire ridge, which is quite steep and rocky, and curves round NW to reach Fraoch-bheinn. The descent to Glenfinnan can most easily be made by dropping south from the col between Sgurr an Utha and Fraoch-bheinn and going down the Allt a' Choire Dhuibh.

Streap from the north

Streap; 909m; (OS Sheet 40; NM946863); *climbing hill*

Streap is the highest summit on the long undulating ridge which separates Glen Finnan from Gleann Dubh Lighe, and can be climbed equally well from either glen. The route from the latter is scenically more attractive and offers the possibility of a traverse over Streap Comhlaidh. For the Gleann Dubh Lighe approach leave the A830 at 931799 and follow the forest track up the west side of the burn to reach the open hillside above the forest plantings. Climb NW below Beinn an Tuim to reach the col between that hill and Stob Coire nan Cearc (887m). Traverse the rocky, undulating ridge over the intermediate knoll (844m) and descend to the col SW of Streap. The final ridge above this col narrows considerably and becomes a steep-sided knife-edge (possibly rather intimidating to the inexperienced) leading directly to the summit of Streap, a magnificent perch. (8km; 1050m; 3h 40min).

Descend SE and climb a short distance to Streap Comhlaidh (898m). The return to the Dubh Lighe goes down the south ridge of this peak to a possibly difficult crossing of the burn if it is in spate. On the east side a path leads south to join an extension of the forest track, which is followed down the glen past the Dubh Lighe bothy (944819) and over the Dubh Lighe to join the uphill route.

For the Glen Finnan approach, follow the private track up the glen to Corryhully bothy. Cross the River Finnan by a footbridge near the bothy and make a steep ascent to the col between Beinn an Tuim and Stob Coire nan Cearc, where the route described above is joined and followed to Streap. (7.5km; 1050m; 3h 30min).

To return to Glen Finnan, descend the SW ridge of Streap and go down a curious diagonal shelf (indicated on the OS map) on the NW flank of the hill to return to Corryhully which could also be used for a quicker ascent.

Braigh nan Uamhachan; 765m; (OS Sheet 40; NM975866); *slope of the caves*

This is the northern and culminating point of the long ridge between Gleann Dubh Lighe and Gleann Fionnlighe. The main part of this ridge is a gently undulating crest which stretches north from Na h-Uamhachan (691m) and gives a pleasant walk.

The Gleann Dubh Lighe approach to Braigh nan Uamhachan goes to the Dubh Lighe bothy (944819) by the route for Streap. From the bothy continue north along the track for about 1km to the fence at the edge of the planting and there head NE uphill to Na h-Uamhachan. The first part of the climb is hard going through tussocky grass, but higher up becomes easier. Once on the ridge, about 3km of effortless walking leads to the summit of Braigh nan Uamhachan. (8km;

850m; 3h 20min). For much of the way along the ridge, as far as the start of the final rise to the top, one follows a well-built dry stone wall.

The approach up Gleann Fionnlighe starts from the A830 just west of the end of Loch Eil and follows the private track to Wauchan and on up the glen for 2km. A cycle can be used to that point. There is tree planting along the SE flank of Na h-Uamhachan not shown on the OS map. Once past this planting, make a rising traverse north across the east face of Sron Liath to reach the ridge at the col 500 metres south of Braigh nan Uamhachan. (8km; 760m; 3h 10min).

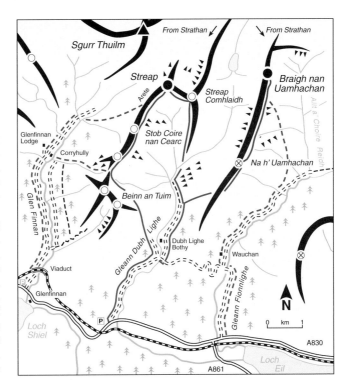

Braigh nan Uamhachan from Sron Liath

Scott Johnstone

Meall a' Phubuill from Gleann Suileag

Meall a' Phubuill; 774m; (OS Sheet 41; NN029854); *hill of the tent*
Beinn Bhan; 796m; (OS Sheets 34 and 41; NN140857); *white hill*

MEALL A'
PHUBUILL

BEINN BHAN

The curving through-valley formed by Glen Loy and Gleann Suileag is bounded on the north and west by a 25km-long ridge of hills of which Beinn Bhan is the eastern termination, with Meall a' Phubuill about two-thirds of the way to the west. The traverse of this ridge is long and tedious, but as neither of the two Corbetts makes a full day's walking on their own, the ascent of both in a day from Glen Loy might be considered.

For the Glen Loy approach to Meall a' Phubuill, park near Achnanellan and follow the right of way track west to the rather struggling wood of Brian Choille. Beyond the trees bear up easily NW to reach the crest of Druim Gleann Laoigh at about 051852 some way west of the lowest point. A dry stone dyke can be followed west along the ridge to Pt.747m, passing a cairn which serves no discernible purpose. Follow the wall down to the deep col east of Meall a' Phubuill where it peters out and a fence turns south towards Gleann Suileag. Breast the slopes ahead to reach the broad summit of Meall a' Phubuill. (7km; 760m; 2h 50min).

Return by descending to the col and following the fence towards Gleann Suileag, passing a long water-slide of fragmental dark rock in the burn. This is the agglomerate of a volcanic vent – a rare phenomenon for the western Highlands. About half way down the burn, cross and bear ESE to regain the track in the glen to Achnanellan.

Meall a' Phubuill can equally well be climbed from Fassfern on the A830. It is possible to cycle up the track on the east side of Gleann Suileag to the north edge of the forest. From there continue along a good path to Glensulaig bothy and climb Meall a' Phubuill by its south flank.

Beinn Bhan is a bulky hill with a 2km long summit ridge which is almost level, forming a crescent round Coire Mhuilinn. This gives a convenient circuit which is best made by starting up the west side of the corrie, as the route thereafter is easier to follow in mist.

Park near the presently derelict house at Inverskillavulin. On either

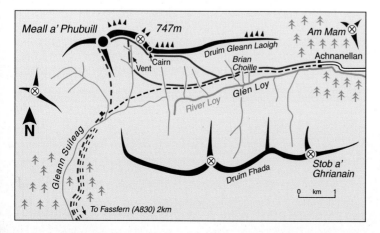

Meall a' Phubuill   747m   Am Mam
Druim Gleann Laoigh   Achnanellan
Cairn   Brian
Vent   Choille
Glen Loy
River Loy
N
Gleann Suileag
Druim Fhada   Stob a'
Ghrianain
0   km   1
To Fassfern (A830) 2km

side of the burn issuing from the corrie above the slopes are fenced off, but there is ample room between fence and burn on each bank for a way to be made easily but steeply to the lip of the corrie and the open hillside above. Starting up the west side of the burn, aim to reach the lip of the corrie well to the SE of the cairn indicated on the Ordnance Survey map.

The route round Coire Mhuilinn is straightforward and in mist a line of fence posts is a useful, if intermittent guide. The summit trig point of Beinn Bhan is not easy to locate in thick mist. In good weather, its position at the northern edge of the summit area is a fine viewpoint. (4.5km; 750m; 2h 20min). To descend, go about 150 metres WSW from the summit, then south, curving

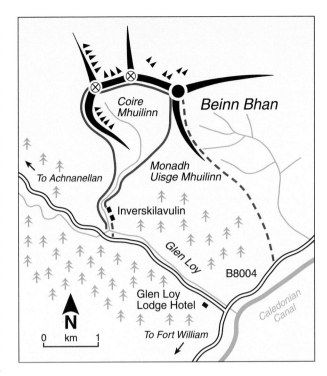

gradually SW to regain the lip of the coire. Then descend a path along the east bank of the stream.

Beinn Bhan can also be climbed from the B8004 1.5km NE of the foot of Glen Roy. Go up beside the forest and over Monadh Uisge Mhuilinn, an easy but dull route relieved by the excellent views up the Great Glen and towards Ben Nevis.

161

Beinn Bhan over Loch Arkaig

Hamish Brown

Ben Tee from the west

Ben Tee; 904m; (OS Sheet 34; NN240971); *fairy hill*

BEN TEE

MEALL NA H-EILDE

GEAL CHARN

Ben Tee is the obvious conical hill rising above the forests in the angle where Glen Garry joins the Great Glen. From points to the west in Glen Garry, and NE up the Great Glen it is the most prominent of the group.

The shortest route is from Kilfinnan, which is reached along the narrow public road from just north of the Laggan Swing Bridge. Park just before a small bridge at the Rights of Way sign. There is a path up the NE side of the Kilfinnan Burn, but this only goes to the Kilfinnan Falls and should not be taken. The better way to Ben Tee is to climb directly NW up the grassy hillside starting a few hundred metres NE of the burn, to reach a stile over a fence (271968). From there, continue WNW across featureless rising moorland which gradually steepens to the NE ridge and becomes rockier as the summit of Ben Tee is approached. (4km; 860m; 2h 20min).

An alternative route from the NW starts at the bridge over Loch Garry at 195020, following the private track to Greenfield and through the forest east to the Allt Ladaidh. A forest track goes south up this burn for 2km to the foot of the Allt Bealach Easain. (It is possible to cycle to that point). Continue up the path on the NE side of the Allt Coire Easain and climb steeply to the summit of Ben Tee. (9km; 810m; 3h 30min).

Meall na h-Eilde; 838m; (OS Sheet 34; NN185946); *hill of the hinds*
Geal Charn; 804m; (OS Sheet 34; NN156942); *white cairn*

These hills, only slightly lower than the neighbouring Loch Lochy Munros to their east, have much the same character. Meall na h-Eilde and its adjacent hills Meall an Tagraidh, Meall Coire nan Saobhaidh and Meall Tarsuinn form a fine undulating ridge which is well seen from Glen Garry to their north. Geal Charn is a more isolated, rounded hill rising above the east end of Loch Arkaig. Good paths lead in from both Loch Arkaig to the south and Loch Garry to the north, but the southern approach is shorter and more often used.

The best starting point from the south is at the Eas Chia-aig, a fine waterfall at the west end of the Dark Mile (*Mile Dorcha*) on the road to Loch Arkaig. From the public car park climb steeply uphill by a fine path through the forest to reach a forest track which is followed north up Gleann Cia-aig, becoming a path before the end of the forest and continuing to a footbridge at 187928. Climb north towards the Bealach an Easain (the col between the Corbett and Meall an Tagraidh) and then NW to the rounded summit of Meall na h-Eilde. (6km; 790m; 2h 40min).

Descend NW to the col (Bealach Choire a' Ghuirein) then west up and along the easy-angled ridge to Meall Coire nan Saobhaidh. From there descend SW down the broad ridge to the little lochan at the Bealach Carn na h-Urchaire and finally climb more steeply to Geal Charn, from where there is a very fine view westwards. (10km; 1040m; 4h). Descend SE to reach the end of the track which goes down the Allt Dubh to Achnasaul, leaving a 2.5km walk along the road back to the Eas Chia-aig.

From the north, Loch Garry, side, several paths head off from Greenfield and these can be worked into a variety of circular routes to take in the Corbetts.

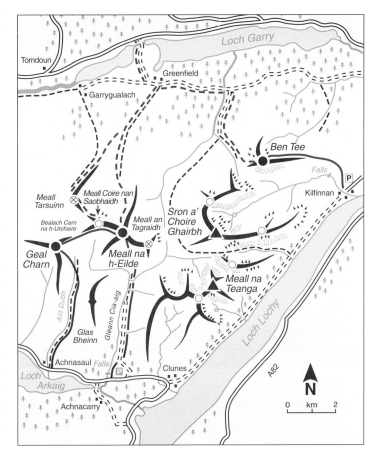

163

Meall na h-Eilde over Loch Garry

Hamish Brown

Fraoch Bheinn and Sgurr Mhurlagain from the south-west

Sgurr Mhurlagain; 880m; (OS Sheet 33; NN012944); *rough-topped peaks*
Fraoch Bheinn; 858m; (OS Sheets 33 or 40; NM986940); *heather hill*
Sgurr Cos na Breachd-laoigh; 835m; (OS Sheets 33 or 40; NM948946); *peak of the hollow of the speckled calf*

164

SGURR
MHURLAGAIN

FRAOCH BHEINN

SGURR COS NA
BREACHD-LAOIGH

These three fine Corbetts lie north of the west end of Loch Arkaig and Glen Dessarry and can be climbed singly or in various combinations. The public road ends at a gate (986915) near the west end of Loch Arkaig. There is no car park and parking can be problematic.

Sgurr Mhurlagain presents a broad grassy flank towards Loch Arkaig above Murlaggan. Higher rocks are unusual, being largely made up of a beautiful pale granite gneiss which marks the junction between the smooth granulite hills to the east and the rugged schist mountains to the west. While the slopes can be climbed from almost any point along the road in less than 2 hours, a better route allows Sgurr Mhurlagain to be combined with Fraoch Bheinn via the long, easy-angled SW ridge. This can easily be reached by taking the path from Strathan up the east side of the Dearg Allt to the col between the two hills. From this col the upper part of the SW ridge leads in less than 2km to the summit. (5.5km; 830m; 2h 30min).

Fraoch Bheinn (despite being slightly lower) is a more interesting hill, particularly on its north side where narrow ridges and steep rocky corries overlook Glen Kingie. Fraoch Bheinn is the most easterly of the craggy schist mountains which stretch westwards into the Rough Bounds of Knoydart and is separated from its neighbours by two passes, each with a stalkers path, which go from Glen Dessarry to Glen Kingie; the Dearg Allt (c460m) to the east and the Feith a' Chicheanais (c360m) to the west.

The ascent of Fraoch Bheinn from Strathan is very straightforward, either directly up the well-defined SSW ridge or by the Dearg Allt path to the point where a ruined fence crosses the path. Cross to the west side of the stream and climb steeply NW through small rocky bluffs to reach the SSW ridge, which is followed to the summit. (4.5km; 810m; 2h 15min).

If time permits, it is worthwhile continuing north for a short distance along the almost level summit ridge to the north top (854m), to look down at a huge rock-slip on the east side of the hill at the head of Coire na Cloiche Moire. This slip is delimited by fissures that seem to cut right through the turf.

Return to Strathan by the SSW ridge, unless one wishes to continue west to include Sgurr Cos na Breachd-laoigh in the traverse. If so, the NW ridge can be descended with care through rocky bands to the top of the Feith a' Chicheanais pass. Alternatively, go down the SSW ridge for about 1km and descend smooth slopes west to reach the Feith a' Chicheanais path at about 300m at the foot of the SE ridge of Druim a' Chuirn.

Sgurr Cos na Breachd-laoigh is the highest point of a horseshoe-shaped ridge to the NW of Glendessarry Lodge, Druim a' Chuirn (822m) being the other high point of this ridge. There is a prominent little pinnacle, called a' Chioch, halfway along the ridge's narrow crest.

For the best circuit take the Feith a' Chicheanais path from Glendessarry Lodge for about 1km and then climb the SE ridge of Druim a' Chuirn. Continue pleasantly along the ridge past a' Chioch to Sgurr Cos na Breachd-laoigh. (From the road-end: 7km; 880m; 2h 55min).

Return directly to the lodge down the easy-angled SE ridge, with a brief steeper section just below the summit.

Carn Mor; 829m; (OS Sheets 33 and 40; NM903909); *big cairn*

The summit of Carn Mor is the highest point of an 11km-long ridge between Glen Pean and Glen Dessarry. The eastern half of this ridge rising above Strathan and over Monadh Gorm (478m) lacks interest and the lower slopes are forested. However, the western half beyond the bealach at the head of Coire an Eich takes on all the rugged and steep-sided character of the Knoydart peaks. The end of the ridge above the head of Loch Morar is as rough and rocky as any of Carn Mor's more famous neighbours.

The approach to this hill is from the Loch Arkaig road end, 1km east of Strathan. Proceed along the well constructed forest track up Glen Dessarry on the south side of the River Dessarry to a point just past a' Chuil bothy. There is a good deal of forestry on the south side of the glen. Beyond the bothy there is a gap in the forest and it is possible to climb SW onto the hill.

Coire an Eich (an approach line itself) is contained by ridges, that to the east joins a crest rising to 616m, and to the west, named Meall nan Spardan, which leads directly to the summit of Carn Mor. (10km; 800m; 3h 25min). A small cairn on one of the several knolls of the summit area marks the top; not easy to find in thick mist.

Carn Mor

Jim Teesdale

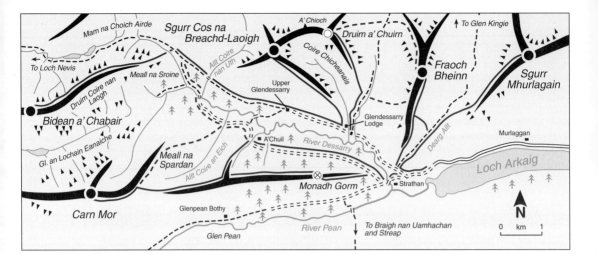

There are stupendous views from the ridge near the summit downwards into Glen Pean over the fissured slopes of a huge land-slip, which has fallen from the summit towards Lochan Leum an t-Sagairt. This is one of the largest landslips in the Highlands, and a descent of that part of the south face of the hill should be avoided, especially in snow conditions. Return by the route to Glen Dessarry or follow the east ridge to Monadh Gorm, and descend roughly through the forestry to regain the track just before Strathan. The rock at the east end of the ridge is reputed to affect the reliability of the compass.

Bidean a' Chabair; 867m; (OS Sheets 33 or 40; NM889931); *pinnacle of the antler*

BIDEAN A' CHABAIR

About 5km west of Glendessarry Lodge, Glen Dessarry divides into two passes, which are amongst the wildest and most spectacular through-routes in Scotland. On the north, the Mam na Cloich' Airde leads to Loch Nevis; on the south, Gleann an Lochan Eanaiche leads to Loch Morar. Between them rises a steep-sided, rocky ridge, whose western end separates the upper reaches of Loch Nevis and Loch Morar. The highest point of this rugged ridge is called Bidean a' Chabair. Seen end on from Loch Arkaig it forms a sharp cone, often mistaken for Sgurr na Ciche. The ascent gives a long and fairly rough climb. (A west top, Sgurr na h-Aide, 859m, was for long shown as the Corbett).

Start from the Loch Arkaig road end. There are two possible ways up Glen Dessarry from Strathan. The right of way to Loch Nevis and Inverie goes along the estate track past Glendessarry Lodge and Upper Glendessarry. A footpath then continues on the north side of the glen to the pass at its head. If one has a cycle, the better way is along the forest track on the south side of the glen. This track goes as far as the junction of the Allt Coire nan Uth and the River Dessarry at 930934, where there is a bridge across the River Dessarry. A path on the north side leads up to join the right of way.

Going to Bidean a' Chabair, continue along the right of way for about 1km past the Allt Coire nan Uth until beyond the forest, and cross the headwaters of the River Dessarry to reach the foot of Meall na Sroine (674m), the east end of the Bidean a' Chabair ridge. Climb steeply up this rocky nose and continue along the undulating ridge of Druim Coire nan Laogh over knolls and past lochans to the final steep rise, which gives some slightly exposed but easy scrambling if climbed direct. (11.5km; 880m; 3h 50min).

The west Top is known as Sgurr na h-Aide (859m), 750 metres away along a fine ridge without too much of an intervening drop and worth a visit for the splendid view west along the extremely rugged ridge that separates Loch Nevis from Loch Morar.

It is possible to climb the north flanks from the Mam na Cloich' Airde. The hillside is steep and slabby, and some scrambling experience is necessary. The south side of the hill above Gleann an Lochain Eanaiche is even steeper and rockier, and is definitely not a hill-walkers' route. Return to Glen Dessarry by the east ridge over Meall na Sroine.

Bidean a' Chabhair with Eigg and Rum in the distance

Bidean a' Chabair from Druim Coire nan Laogh

Sgurr an Fhuarain is very much a lone Corbett among Munros, standing on the long mountain ridge between Gairich and Sgurr na Ciche. Although a shapely pyramid, Sgurr an Fhuarain is more likely to be climbed as part of a traverse of part of this ridge than by itself. Access is not entirely easy as north lies the expanse of Loch Quoich, and to the south the nearest road is the Loch Arkaig one, from which one must cross a pass to Glen Kingie before the foot of the hill is reached.

The quickest route is from the road-end east of Strathan. Go up to Glendessarry Lodge and north from there over the pass of the Feith a' Chicheanais. The path is faint, but the fence line can be followed. Leave the path just north of the pass and descend to cross the River Kingie as directly below the Sgurr Mor-Sgurr an Fhuarain col as possible. In spate conditions the Kingie is difficult to cross and it may be necessary to go far upstream to find a safe crossing place.

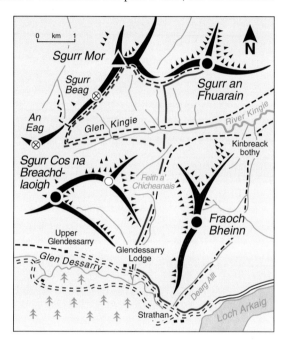

Once on the north side of the river climb easily, if steeply, up the slopes of Doire nan Cluainean to the col and then east to the summit of Sgurr an Fhuarain up the path along the curving ridge which links the hill to Sgurr Mor (1003m). (9km: 1020m; 3h 35min).

Return by the same route, or, with more interest, by climbing Sgurr Mor and continuing by a stalkers path over Sgurr Beag (890m) to the col NE of An Eag, from where one can descend into Glen Kingie and so back to the start.

168

SGURR AN
FHUARAIN

Ben Aden from Druim Leac a' Shith

Mark Gear

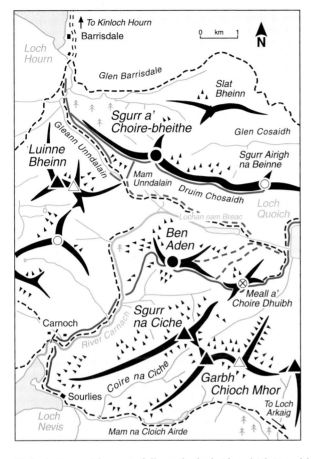

Ben Aden and Sgurr a' Choire-bheithe lie near the west end of Loch Quoich on the eastern boundary of Knoydart. This is one of the most rugged and remote parts of the Highlands, and also one with a very high rainfall, so any trip to these hills must be undertaken with due consideration for the weather. These two mountains lie a long way from the nearest public road, access involves river crossings that may be difficult or even dangerous, and there is little by way of shelter or accommodation, so careful planning is essential.

There is a small bothy at Sourlies, reached by a 13km walk from the Loch Arkaig road-end through Glen Dessarry to the head of Loch Nevis. There is a bothy adjacent to the keeper's house at Barrisdale on Loch Hourn, reached by a 10km walk along the lochside path from Kinloch Hourn, but this too has limited accommodation. The nearest approach to these hills from the public road is along the north shore of Loch Quoich, starting at 986037 on the road to

Kinloch Hourn. The route follows the lochside, which is pathless for the first 5km, but the going is fairly easy. Then the Abhainn Chosaidh has to be crossed. There is no bridge and this is a notoriously difficult crossing, definitely impossible when the river is high. Beyond a good path leads in a further 4km to the west end of Loch Quoich. The 'easy' way to reach the head of Loch Quoich is by canoe or small dingy. There is access to the water's edge at 994034 on the Kinloch Hourn road, but beware of submerged rocks when the water is low.

Ben Aden; 887m; (OS Sheets 33 or 40; NM899986); *hill of the face*

Ben Aden is a superb mountain and a worthy companion to its higher neighbour Sgurr na Ciche, with which it may be combined. Steep and rocky on all sides the tremendous south face dominates the view up the glen from the head of Loch Nevis, and there is a 600m north flank which looms above Lochan nam Breac and the pass from Loch Quoich to Loch Nevis. The ascent of Ben Aden is a test of hillwalking skills, for it needs good route-finding, especially in bad weather when the best way through the many crags and slabs is not easily found.

From Sourlies bothy (868950) the approach goes up the variable path on the west bank of the River Carnach to a junction with the Allt Achadh a' Ghlinne. From there, climb the SW face of the mountain, keeping to the left (N) high up to avoid steep rocks below the summit and gain the NW ridge. Climb this ridge, passing a couple of knolls or false tops before the true summit is reached. (From Sourlies. 7km; 890m; 2h 55min).

From the west end of Loch Quoich one can take the path shown on the map leading up the side of Meall a' Choire Dhuibh (740m). Traverse this peak and continue along the extremely rocky east ridge of Ben Aden, past three lochans and over an intervening knoll. Alternatively, go west from the west end of Loch Quoich along the path to Lochan nam Breac for 1km and from there either climb up the side of the Allt Coire na Cruaiche to reach the east ridge of Ben Aden at the head of this corrie, or follow the sporting ENE ridge to the summit. (From the west end of Loch Quoich: 4km; 690m; 2h).

The summit of Sgurr a' Choire-bheithe is the highest point of the splendid Druim Chosaidh ridge, which extends for 9km from the west end of Loch Quoich eastwards to Barrisdale Bay on Loch Hourn. The north and south flanks of the ridge drop steeply from the narrow crest, which has many knolls and little tops along its length. The summit is near the west end of the ridge, directly above the Mam Unndalain, the pass between Loch Quoich and Barrisdale.

For those starting from Barrisdale, the ascent is very straightforward. Go south along the path to Gleann Unndalain and climb the long easy-angled WNW ridge which rises for 2km at a uniform angle to a prominent knoll beyond which the summit lies 1km due east. (4.5km; 940m; 2h 30min). Return to the col just east of the prominent knoll, then drop down to the top of the Mam Unndalain, and follow the path back to Barrisdale.

Starting from the Kinloch Hourn road, go along the north shore of Loch Quoich as far as the Abhainn Chosaidh. After crossing this river climb up on to the east end of the Druim Chosaidh. Proceed over Meall an Spardain and Sgurr Airigh na Beinne (776m), then follow the undulating ridge for 3km to reach the summit. The rocky crest gives a little mild scrambling on the way. (12.5km; 900m; 4h 10min). If the return along the ridge is too daunting, descend to the Mam Unndalain as already described, and return to Loch Quoich along the path past Lochan nam Breac.

This route should not be attempted during or soon after bad weather as the Abhainn Chosaidh is likely to be impossible to cross, and very dangerous.

For the magnificence of its setting, nearly surrounded by the sea and sea-lochs, and the rugged grandeur of its mountains, Knoydart is justifiably regarded as the epitome of west Highland landscape and character. The area is appropriately known as "the Rough Bounds". No road leads into it, and one must reach Knoydart either on foot by a long walk through the hills, or by boat from Arnisdale or from Mallaig, which is the closest link that the local population has with the outside world.

SGURR A'
CHOIRE-BHEITHE

170

Much of the land is now owned by the community-led Knoydart Foundation, and by the John Muir Trust, meaning that there are few restrictions on access to much of Knoydart, and the area is welcoming to visitors. Knoydart's only village is Inverie, where there is hostel accommodation, B&B's, a shop, a pub, and cottages to let. The Foundation office can be telephoned on 01687 462242, and the web-site is *www.knoydart-foundation.com*. There is a small bothy at Barrisdale adjacent to the keeper's house. Accommodation is limited and a small charge is made. Camping is available at both Inverie and Barrisdale.

Bruce Watt Sea Cruises operates a ferry service from Mallaig to Inverie on Mondays, Wednesdays and Fridays (tel: 01687 462320). It may be possible to arrange boat hire for a crossing

Sgurr a' Choire-bheithe summit from the east

Hugh Munro

Sgurr nan Eugallt

of Loch Hourn from Arnisdale to Barrisdale. Contact Len Morrison, Croftfoot, Arnisdale (tel: 01599 522352). A post-bus service runs between Invergarry, Shiel Bridge and Kinloch Hourn on Mondays, Wednesdays and Fridays.

There are two main walkers' routes to Knoydart : first, from the west end of Loch Arkaig to the head of Loch Nevis (as noted already) and from there over the Mam Meadail to Inverie, second, from Kinloch Hourn to Barrisdale and on over the Mam Barrisdale, then down Gleann an Dubh-Lochain to Inverie. These routes follow rights of way along well-defined paths. Access is also possible along the difficult north shore of Loch Quoich, then by Gleann Cosaidh to Barrisdale, or by Lochan nam Breac and either the Mam Meadail or the Mam Unndalain.

Sgurr nan Eugallt; 898m; (OS Sheet 33; NG927048); *peak of the furrowed rocks* or *precipice*

SGURR NAN EUGALLT

Sgurr nan Eugallt is a fine rocky hill overlooking the head of Loch Hourn at the end of the public road and is the highest point of a 13km ridge parallel to and north of Druim Chosaidh. The last few kilometres of the road to Kinloch Hourn lie below a succession of wild corries on the north side of the mountain and an eastern extension, Sgurr a' Chlaidheimh (841m). The summit is a superb viewpoint towards Ladhar Bheinn, Loch Hourn and the Hebrides.

The climb from the road on the NE side of Sgurr nan Eugallt is simplified by there being a stalkers path up to about 600m, which takes much of the slog out of the ascent. This path starts at the ruined cottage of Coireshubh, and there is space to park cars some 200 metres further north. The path leads almost onto the NE ridge of Sgurr nan Eugallt, and this ridge is followed easily to the trig point (894m). Note that the true summit lies 600 metres or so NW along the undulating ridge. (3.5km; 770m; 2h). The peak of Sgurr Sgiath Airigh (881m) is a little further NW, and possibly makes a better viewpoint.

In good weather a pleasant return can be made by traversing along the main ridge of Sgurr nan Eugallt SE to Sgurr a' Chlaidheimh. Descend to the road through numerous rocky bluffs and slabby slopes. As is the case with so many other hillsides in or near the Rough Bounds, these can be quite confusing in misty conditions, but present no great difficulties when one can see clearly. Down this steep hillside Prince Charles and his small band of men slipped past the Hanoverian troops on a dark night in 1746 to escape northwards to Glen Shiel.

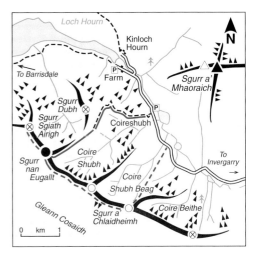

Beinn Bhuidhe with Rum in the distance

Duncan Bryden

Beinn Bhuidhe; 855m; (OS Sheets 33 and 40; NM821967); *yellow hill*

The southern part of Knoydart is occupied by a single massive mountain, Beinn Bhuidhe: a long undulating ridge, about 10km from east to west, with the highest point near the centre. To the south long grassy slopes drop in a single sweep into Loch Nevis; on the north there is a fine series of corries overlooking the right of way in Gleann Meadail. The complete traverse of the Beinn Bhuidhe ridge is a long expedition, but gives unexcelled views of Loch Nevis from its narrow head along to the more open waters of Inverie Bay, and also across to the spire of Sgurr na Ciche.

Start from Inverie, and approach by the Gleann Meadail right of way to the Mam Meadail. From there climb SW to the first peak on the ridge, Meall Bhasiter (718m). An undulating high-level walk leads westwards along the fine ridge to the summit of Beinn Bhuidhe. (13km; 1080m; 4h 30min). A shorter route climbs SE from the Allt Gleann Meadail bridge at 813988 to reach a triple stream junction at c250m. Follow the western burn SSW to the ridge 500 metres west of the summit. (From Inverie: 8km; 910m; 3h 10min).

For the return, continue over Sgurr Coire nan Gobhar (787m) to Sgurr nam Feadan, then drop down complex slopes to Loch Bhraomisaig. Head NE towards the Inverie River and the bridge near the Brocket Memorial on Torr a' Bhalbhain. Some care has to be taken when descending in limited visibility.

Sgurr Coire Choinnichean; 796m; (OS Sheet 33; NG790010); *peak of the mossy corrie*

Sgurr Coire Choinnichean is the shapely cone dominating Inverie Bay, a very prominent landmark as one approaches Inverie from Mallaig. The summit is also a superb viewpoint, looking west over the sea to the Hebrides and east to the mountains of Knoydart's hinterland. For anyone staying in Inverie the ascent of Sgurr Coire Choinnichean is a pleasant short climb though the outing can be extended by traversing its ridge eastwards.

Approach from Inverie along the track to the Mam Uidhe. Once out of the forest, climb east up open slopes to about 450m to the extensive level floor of Coire Choinnichean. Beyond the peak rises much more steeply. Bear SE past the top of the gorge of the Allt Slochd a' Mhogha to gain the lower part of the narrow SW ridge of Sgurr Coire Choinnichean. Climb this pleasantly over a lower top to the main summit. (3.5km; 800m; 2h 5min).

The traverse may be continued along the equally narrow ENE ridge, crossing the peak of Stob an Uillt-fhearna (661m). Descend to the Mam Suidheig, and from there drop south to reach the track in Gleann an Dubh-Lochain. Follow this for 6km back to Inverie.

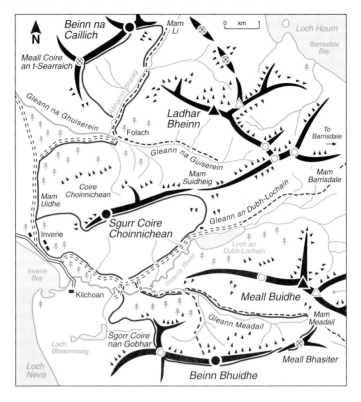

Sgurr Coire Choinnichean

Richard Wood

Beinn na Caillich across Loch Hourn

Beinn na Caillich; 785m; (OS Sheet 33; NG795066); *hill of the old woman*

Beinn na Caillich is a remote and craggy hill which rises 7km north of Inverie and dominates the wild and uninhabited NW corner of the peninsula. The seaward slopes are complex and interesting, whilst the inland ones are grassy and smooth. A long and complicated ridge connects Beinn na Caillich to Ladhar Bheinn 4km to the SE, and the hills may be climbed together.

174

BEINN NA
CAILLICH

    The approach from Inverie is by the Mam Uidhe track and its NE branch through the wood to Gleann na Ghuiserein. Ford the river, or if, necessary, go a short distance east to a bridge near the ruin of Folach. Follow the path up the side of the Abhainn Bheag, cross the river, and continue to just before the Mam Li. Climb west from the 350m contour to scramble up the rough ridge of Carn Dubh to the summit of Beinn na Caillich. (10.5km; 850m; 3h 35min). There are excellent views over the sea to the west, SE towards Ladhar Bheinn and east to Loch Hourn.

    Return by the same route, or descend SW for 2km, passing over Meall Coire an t-Searraich (686m), then down long slopes SE to the Abhainn Bheag. Cross this to pick up the path again, and return to Inverie.

Beinn na Caillich

Derek Sime

Beinn na h-Eaglaise

Beinn na h-Eaglaise; 805m; (OS Sheet 33; NG853119); *hill of the church*
Beinn nan Caorach; 774m; (OS Sheet 33; NG871121); *hill of the rowan berries*

These two shapely hills are the eastern outliers of Beinn Sgritheall and add distinction to the finely sculpted skyline of the Glenelg peninsula. They are easily accessible from Arnisdale on the northern shore of Loch Hourn, and taken together make a fine short round, which may be extended to include Beinn Sgritheall.

BEINN NA H-EAGLAISE

BEINN NAN CAORACH

The traverse of the two Corbetts is best done anti-clockwise, starting with Beinn nan Caorach, thus giving a fairly easy approach along paths and enabling a proper appreciation of the panorama over Loch Hourn and the Knoydart hills on the final steep descent from Beinn na h-Eaglaise. 300 metres before the car park at Corran (848094) a track turns off up Glen Arnisdale, and this is followed for 1.5km to a bridge. Go north past Achadh a' Ghlinne and climb an excellent stalkers path which zig-zags up the east bank of the Allt Utha. At a height of 300m the fine cascade of Eas na Cuingid is passed. Leave the path a short distance further on, cross the burn and climb the rough but straightforward SSW ridge of Beinn nan Caorach which leads direct to the summit. (5km; 770m; 2h 30min).

Follow a line of old fenceposts NW across a broad col of short-cropped grass and onto the Druim nan Bo. This ridge dips SW to a lower col at 550m from where the NE shoulder of Beinn na h-Eaglaise rises impressively as a narrow ridge leading to the summit. This ridge might give good sport in winter, but sadly the crest is disfigured by a line of tall fenceposts. (7.5km; 1040m; 3h 30min).

The linking ridge to Beinn Sgritheall drops very steeply WNW for 200m through outcrops to the Bealach Arnasdail. In wet, misty or snowy conditions this descent is potentially dangerous. From the bealach steep but straightforward slopes of scree and boulders lead up to Beinn Sgritheall's eastern summit.

The best descent from Beinn na h-Eagla-ise to Arnisdale goes SSE over the shoulder of Beinn Bhuidhe which cradles a fine little lochan on the east side, then steeply but without any major obstacles SSW to meet the track in Glen Arnisdale not far from the public road.

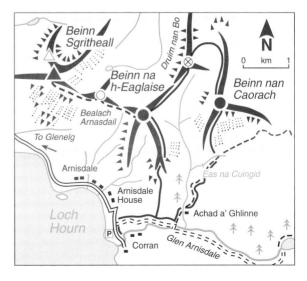

Sgurr Mhic Bharraich

Sgurr Mhic Bharraich; 779m; (OS Sheet 33; NG917173); *peak of the son of Maurice*

SGURR MHIC
BHARRAICH

Viewed from the northern shore of Loch Duich, the range of hills which culminates in The Saddle makes an intriguing prospect. A complex web of spurs and subsidiary tops rings the depths of Gleann Undalain and all but obscures sight of the crowning summit. Sgurr Mhic Bharraich looms large in this beckoning scene, guarding the entrance to the glen on its west side and forming the outpost of The Saddle's long northern ridge. The Corbett however, is sufficiently detatched and buttressed by corries and crags to form a worthy objective in its own right, and offers a satisfying short day from Shiel Bridge.

The best approach is afforded by the excellent path which begins at Shiel Bridge campsite, where there is ample parking. The path climbs over a rock bar into the glen, then crosses a bridge over the Allt Undalain onto the west bank and continues round the SE flank of Sgurr Mhic Bharraich. After 3km the path turns west and climbs out of the glen to Loch Coire nan Crogachan and the pass over to Glen More. The path provides a walking route between Glen Shiel and Glenelg. On the ascent, a left fork in the path should be ignored, and the steeper right branch followed uphill between parallel streams to emerge at the loch at a height of 450m.

From the loch climb the rough upper slopes of Sgurr Mhic Bharraich at their easiest point. Heather-clad slopes lead upwards to reach the mountain's east ridge close to the summit. There are several knolls on the broad summit area, but the highest one is unmistakably marked by a fine cairn. (5km; 770m; 2h 30min).

The long east shoulder of the hill gives a fast and easy return to Gleann Undalain, passing over a craggy eminence and then dropping directly down uniform slopes. The path in the glen is regained a short distance above the bridge.

Two other routes to Sgurr Mhic Bharraich are possible. From Moyle in Glen More on the west side of the hill a path leads to the Loch Coire nan Crogachan col, where the route just described is joined. An approach along the hummocky NW ridge from the highest point of the Bealach Ratagain road is also possible, but the roughness of this route and the many undulations outweigh the advantage of the 340m starting height.

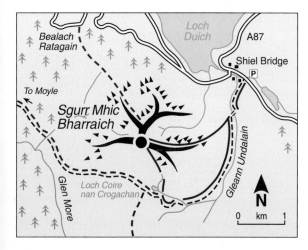

Donald Bennet

Buidhe Bheinn from Loch Coire Shubh

Sgurr a' Bhac Chaolais; 885m; (OS Sheet 33; NG958110); *peak of the hollow of the narrows*
Buidhe Bheinn; 885m; (OS Sheet 33; NG963090); *yellow hill*

These two hills have been given the same height by the Ordnance Survey. As the drop between them is only 122m, they cannot both be Corbetts so have to be regarded as Siamese twins or a part of a double summited Corbett and are given a unique joint status as one Corbett. Both summits should be visited by a prudent hillwalker to claim the Corbett which, while discovering a magnificent linking ridge, also poses logistical problems. Many prefer simply to make two separate expeditions: from Glen Shiel in the north and Kinloch Hourn in the south. The spot height 879m is a SW top and not the summit of Buidhe Bheinn which is shown with a tiny ring contour.

SGURR A' BHAC
CHAOLAIS

BUIDHE BHEINN

If transport can be arranged, a traverse from Glen Sheil to Kinloch Hourn, or vice versa offers the logical option and is a superb outing, a fine as any in the west. Sgurr a' Bhac Chaolais, while on the main South Glen Shiel ridge is somewhat overshadowed by neighbouring hills; Buidhe Bheinn, while simply a southern outlier, because of being such, is a notable viewpoint, looking down on Loch Hourn and to the Rough Bounds of Knoydart. Ascents from Kinloch Hourn (south) and Glen Shiel (north) are outlined. The Kinloch Hourn start avoids the need to traverse the connecting ridge twice.

From Kinloch Hourn start at the car park near the end of the public road (948066), where a small charge may be payable. Cross the bridge 500 metres back along the road and take the track to the lodge. Follow the brutally steep Arnisdale right of way for 1.5km, turn off onto the second of two stalkers paths and follow this steeply north to about 660m on Buidhe Bheinn's SW flank. Gain the NW ridge and

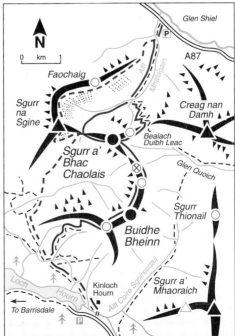

follow this over the 879m top down a narrow rocky ridge and up to the narrow, but flat, summit. (5km; 940m; 2h 35min). Descend by the same route if not going on to add Sgurr a' Bhac Chaolais or take the SE ridge down from the 879m top. From the lochan (958081) either continue down the endless south ridge or work SW to pick up another stalkers path.

The continuation ridge to Sgurr a' Bhac Chaolais is a grand high level route and demanding. (7.5km; 1160m; 3h).

To return to Kinloch Hourn either repeat the crest back to Buidhe Bheinn or, better, head west and descend into Coire Reidh from the col to Sgurr na Sgine., very steep and requiring care. Pick up a stalkers path where it crosses the Allt a' Choire Reidh (940096) and follow it back to Kinloch Hourn. More interesting still, follow the ridge from Sgurr a' Bhac Chaolais to the Bealach Dubh Leac and descend the right of way into Wester Glen Quoich. From there take the path up and over the Bealach Coire Sgoireadail and follow it back to Kinloch Hourn. Despite the reascent, this is no more demanding than the previous descent route.

From Glen Shiel take the right of way path that leads over to Glen Quoich by the Bealach Duibh Leac. This starts near the A87 bridge over the Allt Mhalagain (971139). Layby parking nearby. The path follows the burn, crossing to the west bank after a few hundred metres, then climbs steadily into Coire Toteil. Crossing the burn again, the path zig-zags (sometimes indistinctly) up steep, rough slopes to the 721m Bealach Duibh Leac. A wall, then fence posts, lead WSW over several ups and downs to reach the summit of Sgurr a' Bhac Chaolais. The cairn is perched on a small rock rib. (4.5km; 860m; 2h 30min). The flat summit area is a good viewpoint.

If wanting the second twin, there is no option but to follow the long complex ridge to Buidhe Bheinn (7km; 1120m; 3h 40m) and back again. On the return, the highest points of the ridge can be avoided to the west, but still a big undertaking. Buidhe Bheinn is a finer viewpoint and the 879m SW top best of all.

Descend from Sgurr a' Bhac Chaolais by heading west towards the impressive face of Sgurr na Sgine, skirting one craggy section on the south, then from the bealach head NE to descend Coire Toteil and finish by the path where it crosses the Allt Mhalogain. Another option is to skirt the east face of Sgurr na Sgine to the south to climb the Munro, then follow round to descend via Faochaig's long NE ridge.

178

Beinn Loinne (West Peak), Druim nan Cnamh; 790m; (OS Sheets 33 and 34; NH130076); *elegant hill, bony ridge*

BEINN LOINNE (WEST PEAK), DRUIM NAN CNAMH

Beinn Loinne sprawls to the south of Loch Cluanie, the map giving emphasis to Druim nan Cnamh, *the bony ridge*, which well describes its traverse. From the A87 near Cluanie Inn the old road to Torndoun (locked gate at the start) gives long but easy access. Follow the track to its high point. Traverse wet and boggy moorland which gradually changes into firmer going and, once high, is enjoyable. The summit is not specifically named but has a stark, round trig point. (9km; 570m; 3h). From the A97 in the east one can approach Beinn Loinne via a forest track starting at 214092. From the end of the track, making a rising line to the 775m top of Beinn Loinne, then on to the higher, western peak. Both these routes are assisted by using a cycle while, more unconventionally, a canoe across Loch Cluanie from Lundie gives a pleasant ascent via Coire Beithe.

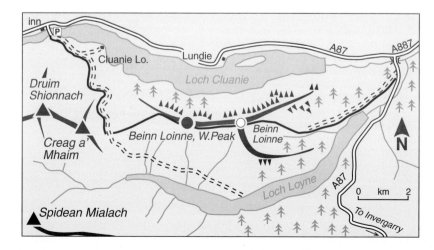

Jim Teesdale

Meall Dubh across Loch Loyne

Meall Dubh; 789m; (OS Sheet 34; NH245078); *black hill*

Meall Dubh stands in an isolated position, the highest point of an extensive area of high moorland between Loch Garry and Glen Moriston. This position makes it an exceptional viewpoint for the mountains of Lochaber and the western Highlands.

The easiest ascent would be from the A87, starting at a gate into the Achlain Beinnen Wood at 208081. However there is no stile. If one is installed, follow the track for just over 1km to a track leading right and upwards. This track emerges from the forest at 221082. Head SE up the very rough hillside. Occasionally faint ridges can be followed, but the going is hard through deep heather. The summit of Meall Dubh is marked by a small cairn with a bigger one not far away. (4.5km; 580m; 2h). Fortunately the summit views are a fine reward for the arduous sections of the ascent.

Forestry plantings have also made access difficult for starting near the bridge over the Allt Garbh-Doire from where one can slog up the heathery slope to the lochans on the crest of Clach Criche and then via Carn Tarsuinn to the summit of Meall Dubh. (5.5km; 520m; 2h 20min).

A route from the north with potentially easier access starts from the A887, 1.6km east of Mackenzie's cairn, where there is a lay-by on the north side of the road and a locked gate on the south side. Beyond the gate, a hill track, with tarmac at first, leads up through pasture to a conifer forest. Follow the main track uphill, disregarding branches. The track ends above the forest at 257097. Rough grass and heather give access to Meall Dubh to the SW and its satellite Beinn an Eoin. (4.8km; 650m; 2h 10min).

A traverse of this extensive area of moorland can be made by continuing from Meall Dubh, first SE then ENE along the rocky crest marked by old fenceposts to the col between Meall Dubh and Mam a' Chroisg. From there descend ESE across easy terrain to reach the Allt Lundie, and go down this stream on its east bank past a series of waterfalls in a fine gorge and reach Loch Lundie. From there one can either follow a track NE down the Invervigar Burn, or south to Invergarry. The ascent of Meall Dubh by either of these routes is long, but enjoyable. (13km; 760m; 4h 20min).

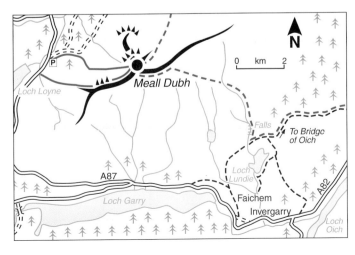

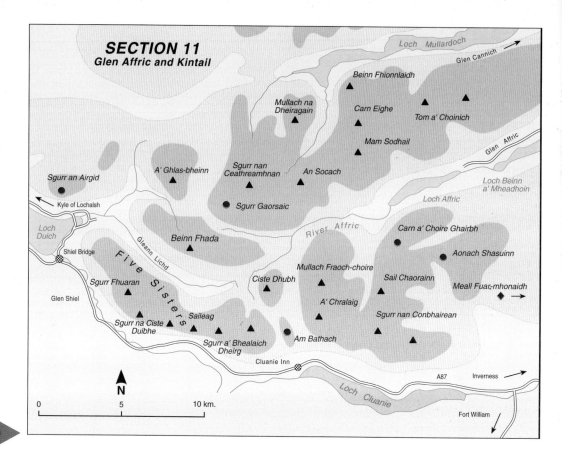

SECTION 11

Glen Affric and Kintail

Meall Fuar-mhonaidh and Loch Ness from Dores

Meall Fuar-mhonaidh*; 696m; (OS Sheets 26 and 34; NH457222); *hill of cold slopes*

Despite its relatively modest height, Meall Fuar-mhonaidh (Mealfuarvonie) is a prominent feature of views up and down Loch Ness, for it is much higher than its neighbouring hills and rises almost directly above the loch on the NW side of the Great Glen. It has the distinction of being the highest hill in the country made from rocks of the Old Red Sandstone system, although its summit rocks consist, not of sandstone proper, but of a very coarse conglomerate whose resistance to weathering has resulted in the hill's prominent outline. It is a long whale-backed ridge, flanked by cliffs on its NW and SE sides, and is a favourite tourist ascent, notable for its views of Loch Ness and the Great Glen. It is normally approached from the NW, turning off the main A82 immediately south of the bridge at Lewiston, near Drumnadrochit, and driving up a minor road to Balbeg (signposted to Bunloit). This road climbs very steeply, with awkward hairpin bends, to high moorland about 250m above Loch Ness. From there on the road is very narrow, with blind summits, and with a cycle track (part of the Great Glen Way) on one side.

Just before Grotaig there is a car park at 493240 with a sign indicating "hill footpath". The first part of the path follows a stream through a delightful birch wood, and is way-marked. Emerging onto the open hillside, the path continues and climbs to the shoulder of the hill, where a deer fence is crossed by a tall stile. The long NE shoulder of the hill is then climbed to the summit.

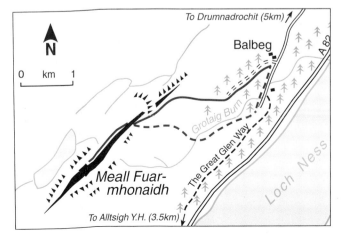

There are several cairns, the true summit being the furthest one. (4km; 500m; 1h 40min). Descend by the same route.

The Great Glen Way from Alltsaigh (Loch Ness Youth Hostel; OS Sheet 34) on the A82, 4km NE of Invermoriston can also be followed to reach Meall Fuar-mhonaidh; after traversing the forest above Loch Ness it rises to join the standard route at Grotaig.

These two hills lie to the south of Glen Affric, one of Scotland's longest and most beautiful glens, and with one of the best preserved remains of the old Caledonian pine forest to set off the backdrop of mountain and loch.

To climb these two mountains from Glen Affric, start from the Forestry Commission car park at the end of the public road 1.5km east of Affric Lodge. Cross the bridge just west of the car park and follow the forestry track west through the Pollan Buidhe forest, where large sections of the native pinewood have been fenced off and the regeneration of young trees has been very successful. A white cottage is passed just before reaching the Allt Garbh. Follow a footpath up the west bank of this burn, at first muddy, then through lanky heather, and climb the steep slopes and crags of Na Cnapain. This is a superb viewpoint to Glen Affric with its woodlands and lochs. Continue WSW to Carn Glas Iochdarach (771m) and slightly down along a broad ridge to a col at 707m. Then climb gradually to Carn a' Choire Ghairbh, where there are two tops about 200 metres apart, the north one being the 863m summit. (8.5km; 690m; 3h).

Descend SW down a broad slope, keeping clear of the steep hillside to the west overlooking Gleann na Ciche, to reach the col called the Cadha Riabhach (664m). From the col climb SE up the broad ridge of Carn a' Choire Ghuirm to reach flatter ground near Loch a' Choinich. From the loch bear NE across a little plateau, crossing a bump (863m) and descending the narrowing ridge of An Elric to the Bealach an Amais (652m). (The bealach can be reached more quickly from Carn a' Choire Ghairbh by taking a direct line beneath Carn a' Choire Ghuirm, but this misses the views from the latter.) From the bealach climb due east for 1km to the 875m west top of Aonach Shasuinn, and finally go ESE for 750 metres to the summit. (15km; 1140m; 5h 20min).

To avoid the steep headwall of Coire Gorm, it is best to return to the west top and descend north then NE from there down the broad ridge of Ceann Aonach Shasuinn to reach the Allt Garbh near Loch an Sguid. Cross the burn and continue down its NW side to rejoin the ascent route near the tree line. It is also possible to continue the horseshoe from Aonach Shasuinn by traversing Carn nan Coireachan Cruadh and Cnap na Stri (724m), then descend NW to cross the Allt Garbh further down and join the lower part of the return route just described. This extension gives excellent views over the Guisachan Forest to the NE, but it should be avoided when the Allt Garbh is in spate.

Aonach Shasuinn can also be climbed from Ceannacroc in Glen Moriston by a long, but easy and scenically attractive route along the private track up the River Doe. This track is very rough and would be hard going for cycles. From the end of the road in Coire Dho climb steeply north up to the broad ridge of Carn a' Choire Bhuidhe and continue NW to Aonach Shasuinn.

CARN A' CHOIRE
GHAIRBH

AONACH
SHASUINN

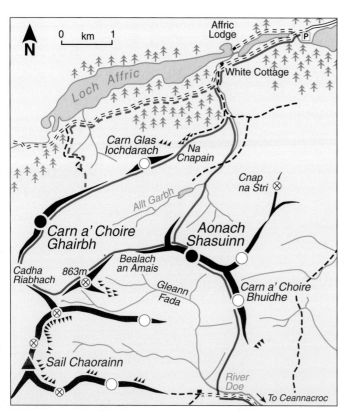

Richard Wood

Sgurr an Airgid above Loch Duich

Sgurr an Airgid; 841m; (OS Sheet 33; NG940227); *peak of silver*

This hill rises very prominently and steeply at the head of Loch Duich, directly above the north end of the causeway which takes the A87 across the head of the loch. The ascent is very short, suitable for an afternoon's exercise, but the reward on a good day is a fine view of the higher peaks of Kintail in one direction, and the western lochs and Skye in the other.

Park on the A87 lay-by below the churchyard (945211) and walk along the minor road on the north side of Strath Croe. There is a stalkers path marked on the map, but its lower part is hard to find. Higher up its line upwards across the steep hillside is clear. Follow the path, passing through a gate in the deer fence, almost to the col east of Sgurr an Airgid, and then climb west up the rocky double crest to the summit. (3.5km; 830m; 2h 10min). Return by the same route. A path from the col skirts the north side of the crest to the summit, providing an easier ascent or descent route.

Sgurr Gaorsaic; 839m; (OS Sheet 33; NH036219); *peak of horror*

This hill is in a remote situation at the watershed between the eastward flowing streams along Glen Affric and northward flowing waters which plunge down the Falls of Glomach to Glen Elchaig. The hill is surrounded by higher mountains, in particular its near neighbour, the mighty Sgurr nan Ceathreamhnan, and hillwalkers approaching this mountain from the west are advised to traverse Sgurr Gaorsaic on the way.

There are two popular ways to Sgurr Gaorsaic. The shortest route is from Strath Croe at the head of Loch Duich. One can either start at the car park at the end of the public road near Dorusduain, or at Morvich on the opposite side of the strath. Both routes converge at the foot of Gleann Choinneachain and follow the fine path up that glen under the impressively steep northern spurs of Beinn Fhada (Ben Attow). The path leads to the Bealach an Sgairne, a splendid pass to the head of Glen Affric. Descend from the pass along the path which goes round the south end of Loch a' Bhealaich, and once past the loch climb NE directly up the steep slopes of Sgurr Gaorsaic to the flat summit, with a lochan at its west edge. (7.5km; 950m; 3h 20min. 1.5km further from Morvich).

Another possible route is from the east up Glen Affric and Gleann Gniomhaidh as its upper reaches are called, a route most likely to be followed if staying at Alltbeithe (Glen Affric) Youth Hostel.

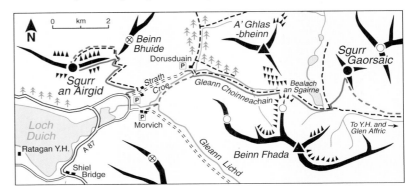

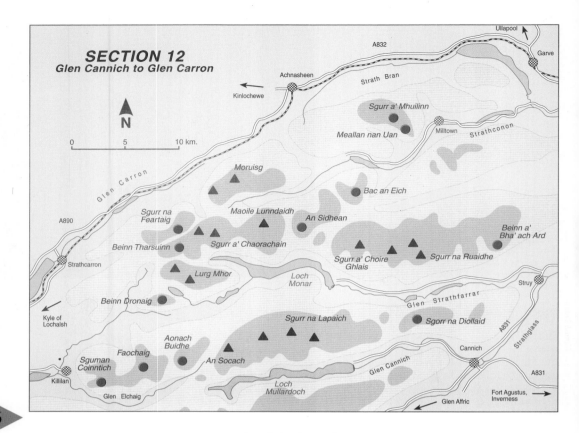

SECTION 12
Glen Cannich to Glen Carron

SECTION 12

Glen Cannich to Glen Carron

Hamish Brown

Aonach Buidhe from Maol-bhuidhe

Aonach Buidhe; 899m; (OS Sheet 25; NH057324); *yellow ridge*

Aonach Buidhe occupies an isolated position at the head of Glen Elchaig, in the centre of the great wilderness that extends from Glen Cannich to Glen Carron. Despite a lack of stature relative to the encircling Munros, the hill is finely shaped, with distinctive spurs on all sides, and is separated from its neighbours by deep passes to the west and SE. These passes carry the stalkers path from Glen Elchaig to Maol-bhuidhe bothy, and the right of way to Pait Lodge on the shore of Loch Monar.

Unless the ascent is included in a camping or bothying expedition, only Glen Elchaig offers a feasible approach to Aonach Buidhe for the day walker. The private track up the glen is a right of way, but cars are not allowed beyond Killilan. As a result, a 13km walk up the glen is necessary just to reach the foot of the hill near Iron Lodge, and this of course must be reversed at the end of the day. The use of cycles is therefore strongly recommended, and will shorten the expedition by some 3 hours. The cycle run up Glen Elchaig is very pleasant, and the return run down the glen even more so.

From the road end at Iron Lodge a track continues up the north side of the Allt na Doire Ghairbhe for 300 metres, and then splits into two paths which go through the hill's bounding passes, as described above. Follow the right path to cross the An Crom-allt for the south ridge of Aonach Buidhe. After a steep start, this ridge gives an easy and undistinguished climb direct to the summit. (From Iron Lodge: 3.5km; 770m; 2h 10min). Descend via Loch Mhoicean and the path down to Iron Lodge.

The best feature of the hill is its NE ridge, which narrows pleasingly below the subsidiary top of An Creachal Beag (870m). This ridge is the obvious route if one is climbing the hill from Maol-bhuidhe bothy to the north, but it may also be reached from Iron Lodge by continuing across the pass at Loch Mhoicean. Although very circuitous, this route enables the hill to be traversed and the remote northern side to be explored.

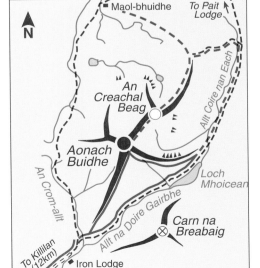

Ben Killilan and Sguman Coinntich from Loch Long

Sguman Coinntich; 879m; (OS Sheet 25; NG977303); *mossy peak*
Faochaig; 868m; (OS Sheet 25; NH021317); *the whelk*

SGUMAN
COINNTICH

FAOCHAIG

These two summits are the culminating points of the broad tract of hill country which bounds Glen Elchaig to the north, and forms the heart of the Killilan Forest. Sguman Coinntich makes a picturesque back-cloth on the drive up Loch Long from Dornie, and is readily accessible from the public road near Killilan. By contrast, Faochaig lies in the remote interior 5km NE of its neighbour, and hides its virtues (the chief of which is a finely scalloped eastern corrie) from all except dedicated hillwalkers. The two Corbetts are linked by a long undulating ridge, and can advantageously be combined in a grand day's tramp of some 22km from Killilan.

There is a parking layby at the public road end (941303) 1km before Killilan. A path ascends the immediate north bank of the Allt a' Choire Mhoir from Killilan, joining an estate track above plantations. At a height of 450m the angle eases and the stream valley broadens into the Coire Mor which divides Sguman Coinntich from its lower northern outlier, Ben Killilan. By crossing the stream and striking up rough but uncomplicated slopes to the SE, the summit ridge of Sguman Coinntich is gained and the summit reached in a further 100 metres. (4.5km; 870m; 2h 30min).

If time or energies do not permit the onward traverse to Faochaig, then in clear weather Ben Killilan should be traversed on the return journey in order to enjoy the superb westward vista to Skye. However, this traverse involves a steep scramble down through the crags guarding the Bealach Mhic Bheathain.

Alternatively, the southern flanks of Sguman Coinntich can be descended to reach a stalkers path in the Ghlas-choire which leads down to the right of way in Glen Elchaig.

The crossing from Sguman Coinntich to Faochaig is an enjoyable high-level walk of 6km, with 360m of ascent over many little knolls, mainly on short-cropped grass save for a rougher patch over the intermediate top of Sron na Gaoithe, which may be tricky in mist. There are fine rocky exposures over Coire Shlat, and throughout the walk excellent views towards Sgurr nan Ceathreamhnan. (10.5km; 1250m; 4h 30min).

The summit of Faochaig stands on a boulder outcrop at the SW end of a broad plateau. Descending, long easy slopes southwards leads to the catchment valley of the Allt Domhain, a favourite haunt of deer. As the valley deepens, a stalkers path can be picked up on the east side of the stream, and this leads steeply down to Carnach in upper Glen Elchaig.

There remains an 11km hike along the right of way down the attractive glen to Killilan. Faochaig can also be ascended from Maol-bhuidhe bothy to its NE, following the path up the Allt na Sean-luibe almost to the pass and then the stalkers path which climbs steeply west to a height of 750m on the hill's NE spur.

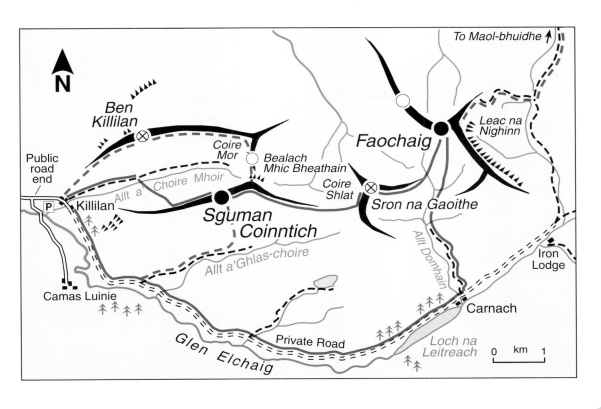

Faochaig from Aonach Buidhe

Jim Teesdale

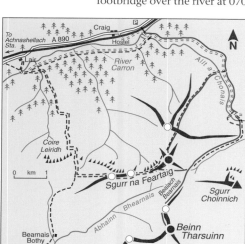

Beinn Tharsuinn with Bidean a' Choire Sheasgaich beyond

Ronald Turnbull

Beinn Tharsuinn; 863m; (OS Sheet 25; NH055433); *transverse hill*
Sgurr na Feartaig; 862m; (OS Sheet 25; NH055453); *peak of the sea-pink (thrift)*

BEINN
THARSUINN

SGURR NA
FEARTAIG

These two hills lie SE of Achnashellach in Glen Carron, and suffer from the proximity of higher and more popular mountains round the head of Loch Monar and above Achnashellach. Beinn Tharsuinn has little interest in itself, but as it lies on the most direct route to Bidein a' Choire Sheasgaich and Lurg Mhor, so is commonly traversed en route to those mountains. Sgurr na Feartaig, however, is an attractive hill, forming a long level ridge with steep corries on the northern side overlooking Glen Carron which provides a grand circuit, with fine views of the mountains round Coire Lair and the Torridonian giants beyond.

Both hills are easily climbed from Craig in Glen Carron, 3.5km east of Achnashellach station. There is a public parking area off the A890, beside the railway level crossing. The private track along the Allt a' Chonais is suitable for cycling.

To reach Beinn Tharsuinn follow this track for 5km from Craig to a footbridge at 074466, and climb up a stalkers path SW to the triple Bealach Bhearnais. From the bealach climb steeply SW towards Beinn Tharsuinn. Once above this steep section, continue along the broad grassy ridge, knobbly in character, to the summit. (10km; 810m; 3h 30min).

Sgurr na Feartaig can also be approached by the track up the Allt a' Chonais as far as a footbridge over the river at 070482. From there a stalkers path continues up the hill and along the summit ridge, passing a short distance NW of the large summit cairn. (7km; 810m; 2h 50min).

The two hills can easily be combined in a single traverse. After climbing Beinn Tharsuinn return to the Bealach Bhearnais and climb NW for 270m up a steep slope of grass and boulders to the summit of Sgurr na Feartaig.

Alternatively, an easier but less direct ascent can be made by following broad grassy slopes from the bealach on a rising traverse west to reach the ridge of Sgurr na Feartaig a few hundred metres WSW of the summit. (13.5km; 1080m; 4h 5min). Descend NE to the Allt a' Chonais by the stalkers path already mentioned.

To make an alternative descent from Sgurr na Feartaig, follow the path WSW from the summit along the ridge for almost 3km to the flat col west of the hill. Descend north by the path down Coire Leiridh to the River Carron which must be waded as there is no longer a bridge over the river near Lair. The crossing is not possible if the river is in spate when the forestry track south of the river can be followed to the start.

Hamish Brown

Ben Dronaig from Lurg Mhor, Sguman Coinntich beyond

Beinn Dronaig; 797m; (OS Sheet 25; NH037381); *hill of the knoll* or *ragged hill*

Beinn Dronaig sits squat and remote in the outback of the Attadale Forest to the east of Loch Carron. From either Attadale by Loch Carron or Achintee in Strathcarron, the ascent necessitates a round trip of at least 25km, and involves a long walk just to reach Bendronaig Lodge at its foot. This lodge lies in the valley of the Black Water which flows south into Glen Ling and thence to Loch Long.

The route from Attadale to Bendronaig Lodge follows an estate track and may be made easier by the use of a cycle. The Achintee approach takes a fine stalkers path over loch-strewn moorland, crossing the Bealach Alltan Ruairidh to join the Attadale track west of the lodge, which lies directly beneath the hill at a height of 270m.

Beinn Dronaig is climbed by the steep slopes to the SE of the lodge to reach the undulating summit ridge, which is followed ENE to the top. (From Attadale: 14km; 880m; 4h 40min). An attractive alternative is to cross the Coire na Sorna pass and Loch Calavie and ascent the ESE ridge, using paths shown, then descend the route above.

The crowning trig point is well sited and affords a magnificent survey of the encircling wilderness. Save for a glimpse of Lochcarron, no public road or settlement disturbs the solitude.

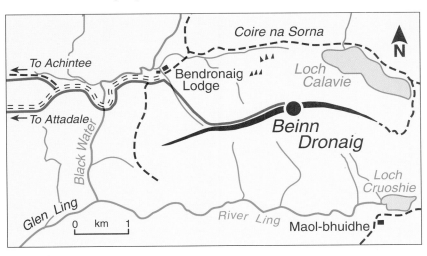

Sgorr na Diollaid

Sgorr na Diollaid; 818m; (OS Sheet 25; NH281362); *peak of the saddle*

This fine little rocky peak lies between the lower reaches of Glen Cannich and Strathfarrar and provides an excellent short day with particularly good views of the Strathfarrar, Mullardoch and Glen Affric hills, worth saving for a fine day.

SGORR NA
DIOLLAID

The hill is inclined to be wet, rough and heathery, but on the higher southern slopes the terrain is more slabby. Two prominent rocky knolls mark the summit, from which the northern slopes drop steeply into Strathfarrar.

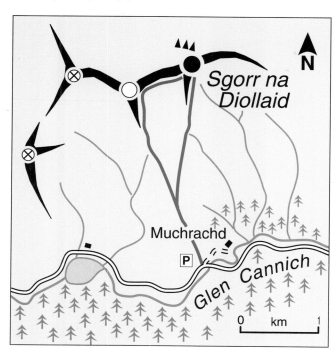

The best approach to Sgorr na Diollaid is from the south. Park at the bridge in Glen Cannich where the road crosses to the north side of the river near Muchrachd. Ascend by a line slightly east of north, seeking the easiest going up the quite steep hillside. Bearing to the right of a prominent knoll, easier ground is soon reached and slabs provide pleasant walking. Finally, the rocky comb approaching the summit gives interesting scrambling over a series of knolls. (3km; 660m; 1h 50min).

The lower 777m top lying 1km SW of Sgorr na Diollaid may be traversed by descending east over rough ground at first. Easy walking then leads SSE to Muchrachd.

Alec Keith

Beinn a' Ba'ach Ard

Beinn a' Bha'ach Ard; 862m; (OS Sheet 26; NH360434); *hill of the high byre*

This triple-topped hill stands on the north side of Glen Strathfarrar near the junction with Strath Glass at Struy and is the highest point of a large area of rolling heathery upland between Glen Orrin and Strathfarrar, a very prominent hill, well seen from points to the east such as the Kessock Bridge over the mouth of the Beauly Firth. Being so isolated, the hill commands splendid views all round.

Beinn a' Bha'ach Ard is best approached from Glen Strathfarrar, starting from Inchmore where there is a locked gate across the road. Walk up the glen for 2km to the power station at Culligran, and from there follow a track WSW then west for 2km through pleasant birch woods to the point where the track emerges from the wood (366401). From there strike NNW up the hillside which is initially craggy, but not difficult. Higher up, climb a broad ridge over exposed slabs but little heather, which gives easy going. Pass a prominent surveyor's marker at 400m and continue north to the summit of Beinn a' Bha'ach Ard. (7km; 810m; 3h).

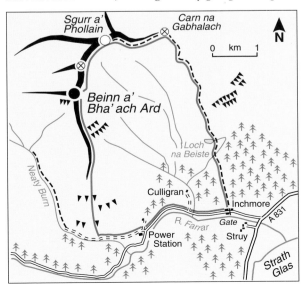

Continue NNE along the broad ridge over Pt.834m, then NE to the flat summit of Sgurr a' Phollain. Descend steeply SE to reach the end of a stalkers path which is followed down to a col and up a slight rise for 500 metres to Carn na Cabhalach. From there descend SSE over rough moorland, the path shown on the map being almost non-existent for much of the way, and reach Loch na Beiste. A good path, becoming a track in due course, leads downhill through attractive birch woods to Inchmore.

An Sidhean is a rounded heathy hill with few marked features and has a feeling of remoteness, standing as it does in the tract of wilderness north of Loch Monar and at the very head of Strathconon. Above 650m the hill has an extensive undulating plateau which provides good summer grazing for deer and pleasant going for hillwalkers. There is a choice of approaches to this hill, north or south, but the southern approach, starting from the Loch Monar dam, is recommended as being the more scenic and following better paths. The road up Glen Strathfarrar above Inchmore near its foot is private, but access by car is permitted during the summer except on Tuesdays and Sunday mornings before 1.30p.m. Application to drive past the locked gate should be made at the cottage beside the gate. (For access during the winter months it is advisable to telephone 01463 761 260 to make enquiries).

One can drive as far as the Loch Monar dam and park near there. Continue on foot along the road for 1km to Monar Lodge, and thereafter follow the well-maintained stalkers path crossing several attractive deep-cut ravines along the north shore of Loch Monar. After 4km take the well-graded path up the hillside west of the Allt na Cois. Leave it at about 500m and continue north up the shoulder of Mullach a' Gharbh-leathaid. This broad ridge is steep at first, but opens out onto a wide plateau and the prominent summit cairn is reached 2.5km after leaving the path. (7.5km; 600m; 2h 40min).

To vary the return route, descend 2km SE to the col (c590m) at the head of the Allt na Cois and contour east round the north side of Meall Dubh na Caoidhe into the steep-sided glen of the Allt a' Choire Dhomhain. Follow the stalkers path down this glen to Loch Monar and so back to Monar Lodge and the dam.

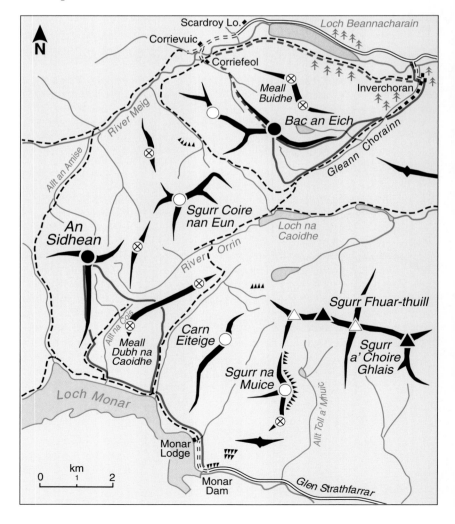

Hamish Brown

Bac an Eich from the north ridge of Maoile Lunndaidh

Bac an Eich; 849m; (OS Sheet 25; NH222489); *bank of the horse*

This is a bold hill with steep slopes to the NE, and is very prominent in views up Strathconon from Milltown. The hill rises above the deer farm at Inverchoran, and is in the heart of stalking country, with stalkers paths right round it.

The shortest route to Bac an Eich starts at Inverchoran. Follow the track which climbs quite steeply south from the farm and goes SW up Gleann Chorainn for 1.5km. Then take a path going down to the burn, which is crossed most easily just beyond the outcrop of Scots pines on the NW bank (252492).

Make a rising traverse WSW to cross the stream which flows from Loch Toll Lochain high up above a lower rocky ravine. Continue up the shoulder which forms the south wall of Coire an Lochain, climbing steeply between rocks to reach the more level ridge above the corrie. Finally go along this ridge over peat hags, bearing WNW up the final gentle slope to the summit. (5km; 700m; 2h 20min).

Descend southward from the summit and then SE to join the stalkers path at an obvious col at the 450m contour (Torran Ceann Liath). Gleann Chorainn provides a pleasant return to Inverchoran.

Alternatively, descend the NW ridge of Bac an Eich for about 1.5km, then bear north to cross a stream above its lower ravine and descend north bounding ridge to Corriefeol. Follow the path down the River Meig and along the south side of Loch Beannacharain, with some rough going where it is necessary to climb a bit to avoid crags which drop steeply into the loch. Finally, the path continues through the forest back to Inverchoran.

These two hills, Bach an Eich and An Sidhean, can be traversed in one day from either Scardroy or Inverchoran but the return is long and demanding.

Meall nan Uan and Sgurr a' Mhuilinn from Creag Ruadh

Meallan nan Uan; 838m; (OS Sheet 25; NH263544); *little hill of the lambs*
Sgurr a' Mhuilinn; 879m; (OS Sheet 25; NH264557); *peak of the mill*

MEALLAN NAN
UAN

SGURR A'
MHUILINN

This small group of attractive hills lies west of Milton in Strathconon. They look particularly interesting when viewed from the Black Isle or across Strath Bran.

There are six well-defined summits in the group. Sgurr a' Mhuilinn and Meallan nan Uan lie in the centre, 2km apart and separated by a col at 675m with the small Loch Coire a' Mhuilinn nestling in a stony corrie at 600m between them. About 2.5km to the NW of Sgurr a' Mhuilinn, and very prominent in views from Strath Bran, lie the attractive twin tops of Sgurr a' Ghlas Leathaid (844m) and Sgurr a' Choire Rainich (847m) (spelt incorrectly and given a height of 248m on the map). Creag Ruadh (734m) is the termination of the fine undulating SE ridge of Meallan nan Uan. The sixth top, Creag Ghlas (686m) overlooks Gleann Meanich, but being a rather low outlier separated from the other tops by some very rough ground, is seldom climbed. Gleann Meinich to its south is a fine example of a U-shaped valley.

A clockwise circuit of the tops is suggested. Park just south of Strathanmore where there is information on deer stalking and climb west, steeply at first, up grass and bracken covered slopes, then turning SW to the prominent summit of Creag Ruadh. From there a very pleasant walk leads NW for 1.5km along a narrow ridge with aerial views down into Gleann Meinich, over an intermediate knoll to the final steeper 120m climb to Meallan nan Uan. (3.5km; 800m; 2h 10min).

Descend NW along a broad ridge for 1km over another knoll (Carnan Fuar) to reach the col at 675m which is at the centre of the group. The summit of Sgurr a' Mhuilinn is only 1km NE, (5.5km; 1005m; 3h), but the addition of the two western summits is recommended first. Contour across the slopes of Sgurr a' Mhuilinn NW to another col at 700m, (249565) then ascend in turn the cones of Sgurr a' Ghlas Leathaid and Sgurr a' Choire Rainich. Return ESE for 2km to Sgurr a' Mhuilinn along a broad ridge of pleasant springy grass passing a lochan on the way. (9.5km; 1230m; 4h 10min).

To return to Strathanmore follow the ridge which drops steeply ESE from the summit of Sgurr a' Mhuilinn. Lower down, where the ridge merges into more level peaty slopes, bear SE and cross the Allt an t-Srathain Mhoir to make the final descent to the road in the glen.

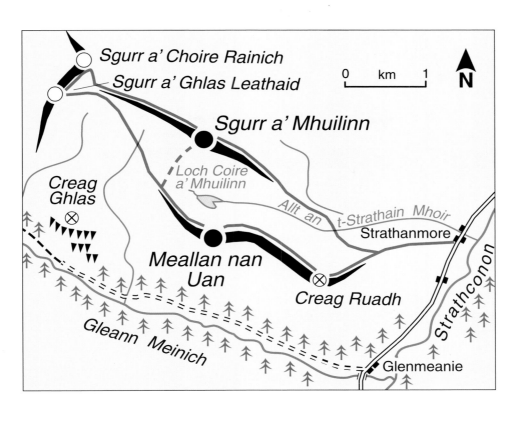

Sgurr a' Choire Rainich
Sgurr a' Ghlas Leathaid
0 km 1
N
Sgurr a' Mhuilinn
Creag Ghlas
Loch Coire a' Mhuilinn
Allt an t-Strathain Mhoir
Strathanmore
Meallan nan Uan
Creag Ruadh
Strathconon
Gleann Meinich
Glenmeanie

Sgurr a' Mhuilinn from Meallan nan Uan

Richard Wood

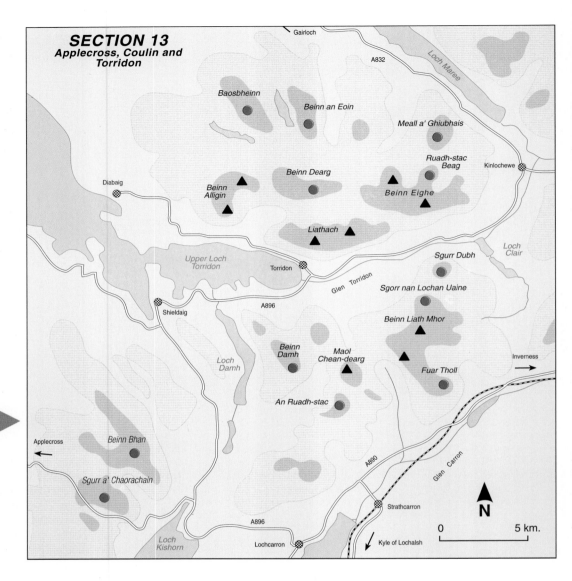

SECTION 13
Applecross, Coulin and Torridon

SECTION 13

Applecross, Coulin and Torridon

Clarrie Pashley

Sgurr a' Chaorachain and the Cioch Nose above Loch Kishorn

Sgurr a' Chaorachain; 792m; (OS Sheet 24; NG796417); *peak of the little sheep*

Sgurr a' Chaorachain may not be the highest of the Applecross summits, but certainly appears the most impressive in the view across Loch Kishorn from Achintraid. From there one looks directly into Coire nan Arr (*the giants' corrie*), and the great cliffs and buttresses are a spectacular example of Torridonian mountain architecture, with terraces and walls of sandstone rising directly from the floor of the corrie. The most impressive feature is A' Chioch, a steep tower rising above the inner recess of the corrie and connected to the main mass of mountain by a narrow serrated ridge.

SGURR A'
CHAORACHAIN

The upper part of Sgurr a' Chaorachain forms a horseshoe ridge facing east above Coire nan Arr, the highest point being at the SE end. Near the middle of the horseshoe is the lower top (776m) which has a radio mast on its summit and a rough track leading from the nearest point of the Bealach na Ba road 1km to the west. This narrow twisting road climbs steeply round the south side of Sgurr a' Chaorachain on its way from Kishorn to Applecross and reaches a height of 630m at the bealach, making this hill one of the most easily accessible of Corbetts.

Three routes to the summit are possible, the easiest one being from the Bealach na Ba. From the car park near the top of the pass follow the access track towards the radio mast for about 500 metres and bear SE, gaining height gradually across the bouldery hillside to reach the col between the two tops of the mountain. Continue east along the broad ridge, climbing over (or round) a sandstone tower and up the final grassy slope leading to the summit. (3km; 300m; 1h 30min).

This short route is hardly worthy of such a fine mountain and better lines are available for those prepared for some easy scrambling. A fine, long traverse which reveals the grandeur of Coire nan Arr starts near the bridge which takes the Applecross road over the Russel Burn (814413). From the bend in the road 300 metres NW of the bridge, where there is limited space for parking, follow the track to the dam on Loch Coire nan Arr, then go along the west side of the loch over rough ground and make a rising traverse towards the great tower of A' Chioch. Continue WSW up the burn flowing from the inner corrie which is enclosed by Sgurr a' Chaorachain's towering sandstone cliffs to reach a little lochan. From there climb SW up a steep slope of grass and boulders to reach the col on the summit ridge where the previous route is joined and followed to the summit. (4.5km; 700m; 2h 30min).

To return to the starting point by the most direct route, descend ESE along the broad ridge, which becomes steeper and is crossed by small cliffs and terraces. Provided one stays on the crest of the ridge on a bearing SE as it steepens there are no serious obstacles. Scramble down a succession of short easy walls with grassy ledges between them until the angle eases and a walk east down the rough lower slopes leads back to the road near the Russel Burn.

John Cleare

Coire na Feola and Beinn Bhan from the south

Beinn Bhan; 896m; (OS Sheet 24; NG803450); *white hill*

BEINN BHAN

The highest and most imposing summit in Applecross is Beinn Bhan, a great 8km ridge whose eastern face forms a series of six corries, typically Torridonian in their architecture of terraced cliffs and dark gullies.

The best view of the mountain and its corries is from the A896 a few kilometres north of Loch Kishorn on the way to Shieldaig. The western side of the mountain is a long slope of grass, scree and low terraced cliffs. The summit is near the south end of the long narrow plateau formed between these east and west facing slopes.

The most convenient point of approach to Beinn Bhan is the bridge over the River Kishorn at the head of Loch Kishorn, 500 metres along the road to Applecross from Tornapress on the A896. From that point the slopes dropping from the south end of the mountain look dull and featureless, and the ascent of these slopes is similar in character, although giving the shortest route to the summit.

The most interesting route, and one that everyone seeking to discover the true character of Beinn Bhan should follow, is to visit Coire na Poite, the grandest of the corries, and make the ascent to the summit from there. Take the path from the River Kishorn bridge northwards for 2.5km to the crossing of the streams flowing from Coire na Poite, and then climb up to Lochan Coire na Poite, set in a superb position at the mouth of the corrie between the high spurs of A' Chioch and A' Poite.

For those with a good head for heights and competent scrambling ability, the best route of ascent from the corrie is up the ridge over A' Chioch. Start 500 metres south of Lochan Coire na Poite and climb easily up to A' Chioch. Scramble down a short rocky ridge to a col and traverse another little top to reach the foot of the steep climb to the plateau. This is quite exposed, up several short rock steps and walls, but there are traces which show the best route to follow. The plateau is reached 500 metres SE of the summit. (6.5km; 950m; 3h 20min).

The A' Chioch ridge is a proper scramble in summer, best avoided when wet and slippery, and, in winter, becomes a Grade II climb. If this route seems too intimidating, an ascent can be made from the next corrie north (Coire an Fhamhair), via the NW slopes. Minimal easy scrambling leads to the plateau near the tiny Loch na Beinne Baine, from where a walk south along the edge of the corries leads to the summit. (7.5km; 900m; 3h 10min).

The descent goes SE down the narrowing plateau, past Coire na Feola and Coire Each, and on down the wide slopes above the tidal flats of Loch Kishorn to reach the River Kishorn bridge.

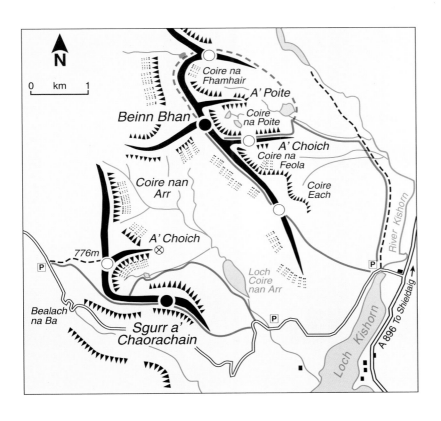

The eastern corries of Beinn Bhan

Dave Broadhead

An Ruadh-stac

Clarrie Pashley

An Ruadh-stac; 892m; (OS Sheet 25; NG921480); *the red conical hill*

The quartzite cone of An Ruadh-stac crowns the tangled moorland to the north of Strathcarron. With its northern precipice in profile, the mountain is also well seen from Loch Coultrie on the Kishorn to Shieldaig road to the west. Although the summit lies in the midst of some of the roughest country imaginable and is 4km distant from the nearest road, the ascent is helped by a stalkers path leading up to the Bealach a' Choire Ghairbh at a height of 580m on its NE side. Using this approach, the ascent of An Ruadh-stac can be conveniently combined with the Munro Maol Chean-dearg, 2km to the north.

The starting point is at Coulags bridge (958451) on the A890 7km NW of Lochcarron village where there are parking spaces by the road. The right of way to Torridon starts just east of the bridge and passes left of a new shooting lodge to follow the east bank of the Fionn-abhainn, climbing gradually towards Coire Fionnaraich.

After 2.5km the stream is crossed by a bridge, and shortly beyond one passes Coire Fionnarach bothy and Clach nan Con-fionn (*the stone of Fingal's dogs*), to which the legendary Fingal is said to have tied his hunting dogs. In 500 metres the path divides; taking the left fork, the boggy floor of the corrie is soon left and the path climbs under the craggy nose of Meall nam Ceapairean to the triple bealach.

The great north face of An Ruadh-stac is a magnificent sight with cliffs harbouring four lochans, each one at a different level. Leave the bealach and go south, then SW along a knobbled rocky ridge above two of these lochans to gain the steep final ramparts of the peak. These give a rough 340m climb with some bits of scrambling to the summit. There are two eminences on the top, the southerly being the higher. (7.5km; 900m; 3h 10min).

A challenging return to Strathcarron can be made by descending due south over the moors, although clear weather is recommended to appreciate the beauty as well as to navigate over this bewildering trackless terrain. Quartzite ridges and outcrops hide a series of jewel-like lochans, which are revealed in a glorious succession as far as the final eminence of Torr na h-Iolaire, from which easy slopes lead down to the Strathcarron road.

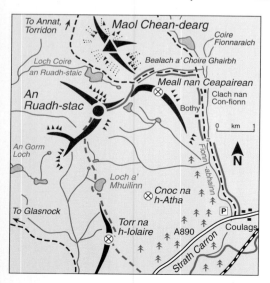

Alan O'Brien

Fuar Tholl

Fuar Tholl; 907m; (OS Sheet 25; NG975489); *cold hole*

Rising at the head of Strathcarron is Fuar Tholl, the triple-topped profile as seen from Loch Carron giving rise to the local name 'Wellington's Nose', a reference to the tip of the Mainreachan Buttress which can just be seen over the skyline of the mountain. The easiest way up Fuar Tholl is from Coulags or Balnacra on the A890 on the south side, but the finest approach starts at Achnashellach, several kilometres further up Glen Carron where the great sweeps of red Torridonian sandstone tower over tiny Auchnaschellach railway station.

There is a car parking area at the side of the A890 opposite the station access track. Take this track to the station, cross the line directly and 100 metres further turn left where there is a junction of forest tracks. Follow the track for 600 metres until a small path leads down left just beyond a small stream (cairn). In 50 metres this path joins the original path up Coire Lair which here goes close alongside the River Lair. The path climbs steadily out of the forest and through magnificent scenery, the river cascading down a deep and narrow gorge on the left with pine tress clinging to inaccessible ledges.

At an elevation of 370m, with Coire Lair opening out, the gradient eases and the path divides. Take the left (west) fork and cross the River Lair. In spate this can be difficult, and a lengthy detour round Loch Coire Lair is necessary.

Continue west along the path to a height of 630m, then bear off south into Coire Mainnrichean and climb towards the foot of the stupendous Mainreachan Buttress. Whatever one's experience, it will be agreed that this is as impressive a mountain setting as can be found in Scotland. Keeping the buttress on one's right, climb steeply up grass, then stones and scree to a col on the summit ridge, the crowning trig pint and shelter being 50m higher and 200 metres to the NE. (6km; 870m; 2h 50min).

Descend by traversing west to the top of the Mainreachan Buttress (895m), continuing NW over the third top and dropping steeply north to rejoin the Coire Lair path, which is also another ascent option. The obvious SE ridge to the railway 400 metres from Achnashellach station is very rough and not recommended. In bad weather a descent can be made down the SW spur over Carn Eididh, then south to Balnacra on the A890.

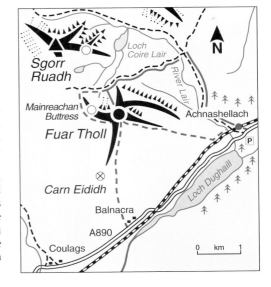

Beinn Damh

Beinn Damh; 903m; (OS Sheets 24 and 25; NG892502); *hill of the stag*

BEINN DAMH

Beinn Damh is the most prominent of the hills situated on the south side of Loch Torridon. The hill stands in splendid isolation, rising steeply from the southern shore of the loch to the craggy top of Sgurr na Bana Mhoraire (687m), then sweeping gracefully SE over two subsidiary tops to the highest peak, Spidean Coir'an Laoigh, which is dramatically buttressed on the east side.

The classic ascent starts from the Loch Torridon Hotel on the A896 (889542) where cars can be parked. A stalkers path leaves the road 100 metres to the west of the bridge over the Allt Coire Roill and cuts through rhododendron thickets and climbs uphill through a forest of native Caledonian pines and planted firs with the Allt Coire Roill roaring down on the left in a gorge. At the head of this gorge the river makes a spectacular 30m plunge over a sandstone cliff which may be glimpsed from the path.

Just beyond the waterfall, where the forest thins, the path divides. Take the right fork and climb SW into the corrie of Toll Ban. The path becomes less distinct on the steep upper slopes but gains the broad col which separates Sgurr na Bana Mhoraire from the main mass of Beinn Damh. A detour NW to this outlier is recommended as giving superb views of Loch Torridon.

From the col easy slopes lead up SE to the first of the subsidiary tops, which may be bypassed on the west side. Traverse quartzite boulders across a slight dip to the next top, from which a narrow ridge leads up to the main summit. (6km; 900m; 2h 50min). The crowning cairn is perched on the brink of the very steep east facing corrie, and commands a fine panorama, SE to the Achnashellach hills, and north to the Torridonian giants.

The NE ridge of Beinn Damh called Stuc Toll nam Biast is an alternative route of ascent which gives a good scramble from the Drochaid Coire Roill. The left fork of the normal approach path is taken and followed for a further 2.5km to this pass, giving grand views of the gullied NE cliffs of the mountain. From the pass climb a rocky ridge SW then more steeply west up a buttress to reach the short NE ridge of Beinn Damh. Any difficulties on the buttress can be avoided on the left.

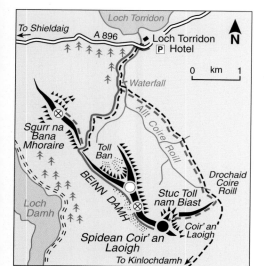

Hamish Brown

Beinn Dearg from Mullach an Rathain

Beinn Dearg; 914m; (OS Sheets 19, 24 and 25; NG895608); *red hill*

This hill is left by many for their last Torridonian peak as surrounding kin are better known and more accessible; but its very centrality makes Beinn Dearg ideal to climb first for the excellent and unusual views of its prominent neighbours. Beinn Dearg is a gem of a hill and, if the narrowest of the towers along the crest are taken direct, a steady hand and a good head for heights are required. There are, however, no difficulties that cannot be avoided. The height of 914m (2999ft) has it as joint highest Corbett.

Start at the Coire Mhic Nobuil car park (869576). Follow the path up the corrie and shortly after crossing the Abhainn Coire Mhic Nobuil take the left branch which goes close under the imposing Horns of Alligin towards the Bealach a' Chomhla. Go almost as far as the wide, flat bealach and then climb the west spur of Stuc Loch na Cabhaig (888m). The ascent is steep, with some small crags to avoid and needs some route finding ability in mist. An airy ridge with some easy scrambling on the narrowing rocky crest leads to the flat top of Beinn Dearg. (7km; 960m; 3h 10min).

Continue the traverse SE at first down an easy ridge. In 200 metres the main ridge turns east and a short steep descent leads to a col. Beyond, the ridge rises again for a short distance and becomes narrow and rocky, giving a pleasant easy scramble along the crest which is quite exposed on the north side above Loch a' Choire Mhoir. Descend two or three short rock steps to reach the broad and easy continuation of the ridge eastwards. (The scramble along the crest can be avoided by traversing ledges on the south side of the ridge).

The traverse along the east ridge to its end at Carn na Feola (761m) is straight forward. The descent from there is best made by going south, aiming to reach the path beside the Abhainn Coire Mhic Nobuil about 500 metres west of Loch Grobaig. The south side of the east ridge of Beinn Dearg is steep and rocky for much of its length, with typically Torridonian terraced cliffs, and care is needed descending. If one does not go as far as Carn na Feola, but wishes to descend further west, a possible route lies beside a little stream which flows down the steep hillside, at 906604.

The south side of Beinn Dearg is in National Trust for Scotland territory, and there is no restriction on climbing the mountain by the route described during the stalking season.

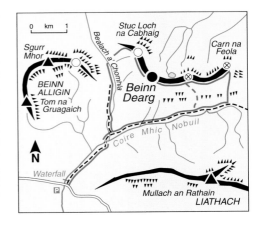

Ruadh-stac Beag

Chris Townsend

Ruadh-stac Beag; 896m; (OS Sheet 19; NG973614); *small red peak*
Meall a' Ghiubhais; 887m; (OS Sheet 19; NG976634); M22; *hill of the fir tree*

RUADH-STAC BEAG

MEALL A'
GHIUBHAIS

The drive west into Glen Docherty is always a moment to be savoured: Loch Maree, the surrounding mountains and the Outer Isles conspire to appear at the same breath-catching moment. The descent to Kinlochewe unfolds these two Corbetts which can be combined in a pleasant walk.

The hills are climbed using the Mountain Trail (shown on the map), starting from the Glas Leitir car park beside Loch Maree. This nature trail climbs up through the ancient Caledonian forest with many points of interest along the way. A satisfying circuit can be made by ascending the rocky SE trail to a large cairn, which is an excellent viewpoint. Then head SW to the Allt Toll a' Ghiubhais and follow this stream up between Ruadh-stac Beag and the main ridge of Beinn Eighe. Ruadh-stac Beag is well defended by cliffs and scree, and the only easy ascent is from the south. The unstable flanking screes are best avoided by following the burn upwards until it is possible to bear west to gain the SSW spur of the hill above a lochan nestling in the col. From there the way is clear to the top, although the large boulder scree requires care. (6.5km; 926m; 3h).

In descent tackle the screes more directly if wished. Return down the burn, then head north and finally up NW to the small summit plateau of Meall a' Ghiubhais. There are two tops, the higher one being at the SW end of the plateau. (11.5km; 1386m; 5h). In descent take an ESE line to avoid the unstable SE boulder field and return to Loch Maree by the more straightforward NW Mountain Trail. (15km; 6h).

The Pony Track which starts 1km NW of Kinlochewe, also gives access to these hills. The ascent of this path slowly reveals more of the inner Torridonian grandeur, with Creag Dubh, the NE peak of Beinn Eighe, dominating the view southwards.

At the highest point of the path head for the Allt Toll a' Ghiubhais to climb Ruadh-stac Beag, then Meall a' Ghiubhais as described above.

Meall a' Ghiubhais and Ruadh-stac Beag are in the Beinn Eighe National Nature Reserve, where access is restricted during the stalking season, but access via these routes is usually acceptable all year.

Jim Teesdale

Sgurr Dubh

Sgorr nan Lochan Uaine; 871m; (OS Sheet 25; NG969531); *peak of the little green loch*
Sgurr Dubh; 782m; (OS Sheet 25; NG979558); *black peak*

These two hills occupy a large part of the Coulin Forest, the wild and open country lying between Lochs Clair and Coulin to the NE and the Coire Lair peaks to the south. They are well seen, but rarely identified by travellers on the Achnasheen to Kinlochewe road, who naturally look for the more famous Torridonian peaks on the western skyline. Whilst they lack the height and grandeur of their neighbours on the opposite side of Glen Torridon, their ascent is recommended as giving a fine appreciation of Torridonian scenery.

The round trip taking in both summits may conveniently be started from the carpark (957568) at the foot of Coire Dubh on the A896 in Glen Torridon. A path leaves the road 100 metres east of the carpark, and goes south past Lochan an Iasgair and the Ling Hut. The path continues SW close to the Allt Frianach, passing a fine waterfall and entering Coire a' Cheud-chnoic (*corrie of a hundred hillocks*) filled with innumerable moraine mounds of regular proportions.

The path steers a course through this maze of hillocks, and is followed for about 3km until Sgorr nan Lochan Uaine is passed and one is below the col on its SW side. Continue SE for about 1km up heathery slopes towards this col in which the Lochan Uaine is cradled. At about 550m bear north of east across a little stream and climb grassy slopes to the broad crest of the NW shoulder of Sgorr nan Lochan Uaine. Continue along this to the final cone of quartzite scree and boulders to the grassy summit. (6km; 800m; 2h 50min).

SGURR NAN
LOCHAN UAINE

SGURR DUBH

A broad and contorted ridge 2.5km long and dropping as low as 510m links this peak to Sgurr Dubh. Miniature lochans abound on the Sgurr Dubh flanks, a navigational challenge in mist, and the slopes are barren and rough. The summit views across Glen Torridon are magnificent. (9km; 1070m; 4h 10min).

From the quartzite summit boulderfields of Sgurr Dubh a rough descent can be made to the Ling Hut, moving SW initially to outflank sandstone cliffs then weaving through quartzite outcrops to easier lower slopes.

An easier but much longer descent can be made by returning SW along the ridge for 800 metres and then dropping SE to reach a path in Coire an Leth-uillt which leads down to Coulin Lodge. From there a path leads along the west shore of Loch Clair and the A896 is reached 3km east of the Coire Dubh car park.

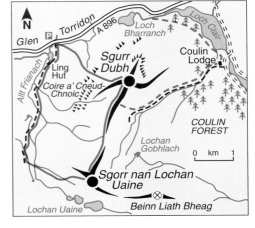

Baosbheinn

Baosbheinn; 875m; (OS Sheets 19 and 24; NG870654); *hill of the forehead*
Beinn an Eoin; 855m; (OS Sheet 19; NG905646); *hill of the bird*

The two ridges on opposite sides of Loch na h-Oidhche radiate like spokes NW from the central Torridon group. These are wild and lonely hills set amongst grand scenery, where paths are few and visitors rare. They have an air of seriousness due to their length and remoteness when compared with the more frequented Torridon peaks to their south. The route described traverses both mountains in a long circuit from the A832 to their north.

BAOSBHEINN

BEINN AN EOIN

Start from a small car park by a green shed (current colour, but known locally as the Red Barn) at 856721 on the A832 west of Loch Maree. The track has a signpost indicating the Bad an Sgalaig Native Pinewood, the planting of a million trees grown from locally collected seed as part of the Millennium Forest project to recreate the Caledonian forest which once grew there. Cross the footbridge over the outflow of Am Feur-loch and follow the track SE for 5km (ignoring a branch off to the right after about 3km) to the stepping stones across the Abhainn Loch na h-Oidhche (886676). The odd divergence of streams was made to prevent flooding in Kerrysdale.

Follow the path for 400 metres until near two huge glacial erratics (boulders dumped by the retreating glacier), then turn SSE off the path towards the NW buttress of Beinn an Eoin. A gully to the north, or easier ground further north, allows this barrier to be passed and the main ridge reached. Traverse over three minor tops to a stiff ascent which leads to the much narrower final ridge. This can be climbed direct with minor scrambling, or follow the path just below the west side to gain the summit. (9km; 820m; 3h 30min).

To continue the traverse descend steeply south for about 400m, then west to the bothy of Poca Buidhe which nestles against the hillside at the head of Loch na h-Oidhche. This has one end open for travellers and can be used for shelter, with space for two. There is also a good howff 10 metres south of the bothy. If only climbing Beinn an Eoin walk back along Loch na h-Oidhche (*the loch of night*).

To continue to Baosbheinn, from the bothy go SW then west between small lochans to gain the low SE ridge (Drochaid a' Ghorm-locha) which leads up to Baosbheinn. Follow the switchback ridge over two minor tops of 707m and 806m before making the steep ascent to the summit, Sgorr Dubh. (15km; 1480m; 5h 50min). The main ridge drops steeply NW to a col from where it is possible to descend the NE spur, moving left lower down into An Reidh-choire to reach a footbridge just below the outflow of Loch na h-Oidhche. From there regain the path and the long haul back to the Red Barn. This return route from the summit misses out much of the mountain's interest so to complete the traverse, continue along the main ridge NW from the col over three minor tops to its end at Creag an Fhithich. The very steep NW face of this peak which overlooks Gairloch was caused by a massive landslide in post-glacial times. Descend the NE flank, and continue NNE to cross the Abhainn a' Gharbh Choire by a bridge at 866694. Head east across flat boggy ground to gain a bull-dozed track which leads to the main track about 3km from the road.

An alternative descent can be made to Loch Bad an Sgalaig. The strange shapes of water worn and long dead pine trees line the shore and provide interest as you follow the extremely rough lochside back to the Red Barn at the end of a long and memorable day.

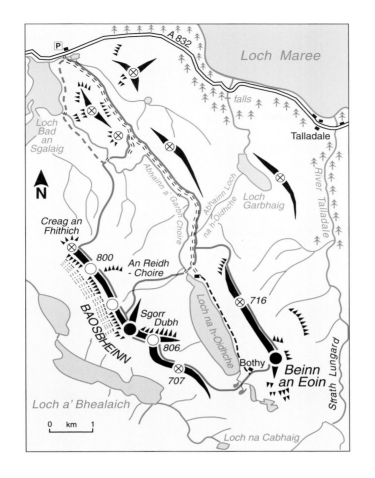

Beinn an Eoin

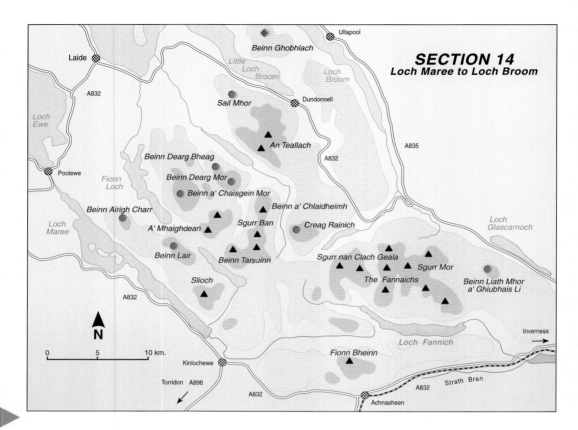

Beinn Ghobhlach

Ullapool

Laide

Little
Loch
Broom

Loch
Broom

A832

Loch
Ewe

Sail Mhor

Dundonnell

A835

An Teallach

A832

Beinn Dearg Bheag

Poolewe

Beinn Dearg Mor

Fionn
Loch

Beinn a' Chaisgein Mor

Beinn Airigh Charr

Beinn a' Chlaidheimh

Loch
Glascarnoch

A' Mhaighdean

Sgurr Ban

Creag Rainich

Loch
Maree

Beinn Lair

Beinn Tarsuinn

Sgurr nan Clach Geala

Sgurr Mor

Slioch

The Fannaichs

Beinn Liath Mhor
a' Ghiubhais Li

A832

Inverness

N

Loch Fannich

0   5   10 km.

Kinlochewe

Fionn Bheinn

Torridon A896

A832

Strath Bran

Achnasheen

A832

SECTION 14

Loch Maree to Loch Broom

Alec Keith

Beinn Airigh Charr

Five of the hills described in this and the following pages are in the Letterewe and Fisherfield forests to the north of Loch Maree. This is one of the finest wilderness areas in the Highlands, combining some magnificent mountains in a very remote and inaccessible setting. Distances from the perimeter into the heart of this area are long, and accommodation within it is limited to the bothy at Shenavall and the barn at Carnmore which has been repaired and provides spartan shelter.

Access to the three southerly Corbetts is best made from Poolewe. It is no longer possible to obtain permission to drive to Inveran, but if mountain bikes are used it is possible to cycle past Kernsary to the edge of the plantation.

These two deer forests are prime stalking country and should be avoided for six weeks following 1st September. After that date enquiries should be made from the keeper at Kernsary.

BEINN AIRIGH
CHARR

Beinn Airigh Charr; 791m; (OS Sheet 19; NG930761); *hill of the rough shieling*

This is a prominent hill at the western edge of the Letterewe Forest well seen across Loch Maree and from the low-lying coastal area round Loch Ewe. A characteristic feature is the steep tower on the north face named Martha's Peak after a legendary shepherdess who fell to her death on the cliffs while tending her flock.

Being at the west end of the Letterewe Forest, Beinn Airigh Charr has the easiest access of all the chain of hills along the north side of Loch Maree. The approach is along the track from Poolewe past Inveran to Kernsary. Shortly after passing Loch an Doire Ghairbh take a path (look for small cairn at the side of the track), which goes SW and in 1km joins the track from Kernsary to Ardlair. (Alternatively cycle along this track via Kernsary). Continue along this track south towards Loch Maree until an old stone sheep fold can be seen about 100 metres left of the path at 894768. From there an excellent path goes east, contouring round the valley to a stream and continuing uphill beside it east, then SE.

The path continues uphill for about 3km and eventually reaches the col between Spidean nan Clach and Meall Chnaimhean. To the south the whole range of Torridon mountains is suddenly and superbly revealed, while the objective of Beinn Airigh Charr is easily gained by flanking the large bowl between the Corbett and Spidean nan Clach. (From Poolewe: 10.5km; 800m; 3h 50min).

The summit of Spidean nan Clach is the conical top that has beckoned all the way up the lower path, so it is fitting to complete the traverse by going NW to its sharp rocky summit. From there descend south and then SW to reach the col and the end of the ascent path and the miles back to Poolewe. Another worthwhile diversion is to the other top, Meall Chnaimhean, for excellent views westwards over Loch Maree.

Beinn Lair from A' Mhaighdean

BEINN LAIR

Beinn Lair; 859m; (OS Sheet 19; NG982732); *hill of the mare*

Beinn Lair is a hill of two contrasting aspects: on the SW side long slopes of grass and heather at a fairly gentle angle from the wooded shore of Loch Maree, on the NE side a continuous line of cliffs 5km long dropping precipitously from the summit to Gleann Tulacha and Lochan Fada. The latter is one of the finest, and probably the longest, mountain walls in the Highlands, and is given added character by being in such a remote setting. Between these two sides the broad summit ridge extends for 5km, with the highest point near the middle, and the slightly lower top of Sgurr Dubh 1km to its SE.

Beinn Lair is almost equidistant from Poolewe and Kinlochewe, a long way from both villages. The Poolewe approach is shorter if one starts by cycling to Kernsary and along the tracks beyond. Letterewe Estate are happy for cycles to be used on vehicle tracks but not on footpaths. Go past Kernsary and along the track leading east to a fork by a plantation. Go through the plantation for just over 1km then off, right (cairn), to follow a path out of the plantation and across moorland above the Allt na Creige. This is a new path, at a higher level than that shown on the current map and provides easy walking on a good hard surface. Continue along the path SE to the foot of Srathan Buidhe and cross the stream in this narrow glen to follow the path as it drops below the NE face of Meall Mheinnidh towards Fionn Loch. Not far from the loch turn right up another path heading for the Bealach Mheinnidh and Letterewe. Climb to this bealach, between Beinn Lair and Meall Mheinnidh. From there climb the ridge of Beinn Lair, NE at first for 1.5km then SE, all the way along the edge of the stupendous cliffs overlooking Fionn Loch and Gleann Tulacha. At about 800m there is a very fine promontory which juts out over the north face and gives dramatic views of the cliffs and lochs below. The summit itself is a wide dome which requires accurate navigation in mist, but the huge summit cairn is unmistakable. (From Poolewe: 18km; 920m; 5h 40min).

On the return to Poolewe a good alternative route from the Bealach Mheinnidh is to climb Meall Mheinnidh, (720m, a Graham), via a 230m ascent up the SE ridge past a little lochan just above mid-height. Descend by the NW ridge, which has some short slabby cliffs low down which are easily avoided. Towards the foot of the ridge drop into Srathan Buidhe and cross the stream to regain the outward paths back to Kernsary and Poolewe.

This is a very long day's hillwalking, the total distance being about 36km, and a time of 11 hours, excluding stops.

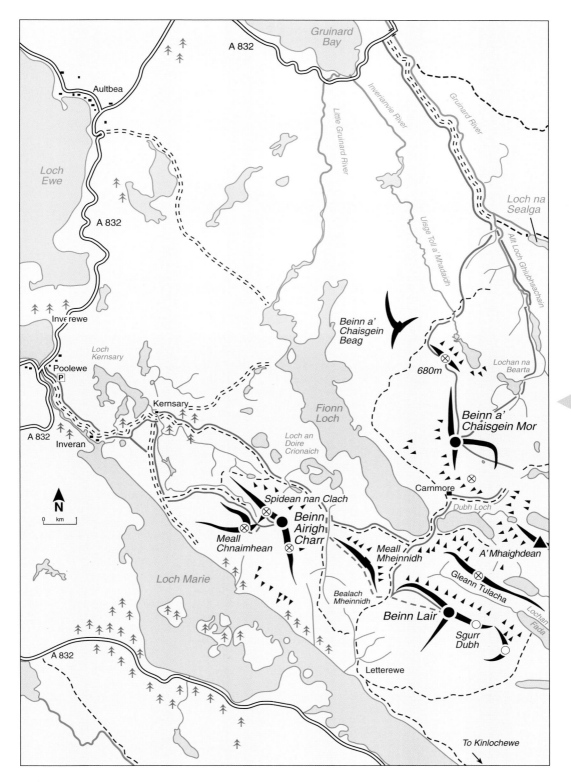

Alec Keith

Beinn a' Chaisgein Mhor from Beinn Lair

Beinn a' Chaisgein Mor; 856m; (OS Sheet 19; NG982785); *big forbidding hill*

This great flat-topped hill stands on the border between the Letterewe and Fisherfield forests on the east side of Fionn Loch, one of the most inaccessible hills in the area between Loch Maree and Little Loch Broom. On the south side of the hill, overlooking the lodge at Carnmore, are two huge crags – Carn Mor and Sgurr na Laocainn.

The route to Beinn a' Chaisgein Mor from Poolewe is the same as that for Beinn Lair as far as the junction of paths near Fionn Loch. At that point continue NE along the path which goes round the head of the loch and across the causeway between Fionn Loch and Dubh Loch. Follow the excellent path which makes a rising traverse east below the cliffs of Sgurr na Laocainn, then NE up the Allt Bruthach an Easain to Lochan Feith Mhic'illean. From there climb WNW for just over 2km up an open hillside with no features except for a tiny lochan halfway up to the Corbett summit. (From Poolewe: 22km; 920; 6h 40min). The most practical return to Poolewe is by the same route.

Climbing Beinn a' Chaisgein Mor in a day from Poolewe is very long and not to everyone's taste. A night in the barn at Carnmore is an option and could allow a combination with Beinn Lair. Assuming the use of a cycle, the following is a more enjoyable route and takes one through wild country. Start where the A832 crosses the Gruinard River (962912). "Mountain bikes are welcome", says the sign. Cycle up the track on the SE side of the river, somewhat rough in places, to where it crosses the Allt Loch Ghiubhsachain (993856). Dry conditions are recommended for the circuit, both for crossing the stream and because the valley is very boggy. Follow the west bank of the Allt for about 600 metres to where it steepens, then cross and follow the east bank. A gorge section is best avoided higher up the hillside. Just short of Loch Ghiubhsachan, cross again to the west side and continue along the west shore of the loch to flat ground at its far end. Pass under the sweep of slabs known as Na Bearta Buttress, where the keen rock climbers can do a route, observe a log cabin which looks very incongruous and head up the stream to the lovely Lochan na Bearta. Skirt the south side and go up to follow the east ridge of Beinn a' Chaisgein Mor to the summit. The summit is a cluster of angular gneiss rocks set in a great moss plateau reminiscent of the Cairngorms. The central position in the Fisherfield Forest rewards with a panorama from An Teallach to Mullach Coire Mhic Fhearchair and round to Beinn Lair. For a wonderful descent, choose a fine day and head north to Pt.680, walking over the rounded tops into the afternoon sun with the light reflected from the myriad of lochans in a vast tract of low-lying land stretching to the sea at Loch Ewe and Gruinard Bay. Head down to the col to Beinn a' Chaisgein Beag and pick up a stalkers path down to the Uisge Toll a' Mhadaidh and up the other side. Near the high point, leave the path and head for a stream which leads down to the Allt Loch Ghiubhsachain only about 300 metres from the cycle. The run back is remarkably easy, but bone shaking.

Beinn Dearg Bheag can also be climbed in a sensible day using this cycle approach and the very determined might combine both. Beinn a' Chaisgein Beag (680m) is worth the small diversion.

Mark Gear

Beinn Dearg Mor and Beinn Dearg Bheag from Shevanall

Beinn Dearg Mor; 910m; (OS Sheet 19; NH032799); *big red hill*
Beinn Dearg Bheag; 820m; (OS Sheet 19; NH019811); *little red hill*

These two hills, rising grandly on the SW side of Strath na Sealga, are just as remote as the Corbetts in the Letterewe Forest, but unlike them they are best approached from the north, leaving the A832 at Corrie Hallie 4km up Strath Beag from the head of Little Loch Broom. Beinn Dearg Mor, in particular, is a magnificent mountain, comparable with An Teallach on the opposite side of Loch na Sealga, with the same narrow ridges, deep corries and steep sandstone cliffs, a peak to be treated with respect.

Leaving the A832 at Corrie Hallie, follow a track south for 3km until near its highest point on bare moorland to the west of Loch Coire Chaorachain. There a path leads off to the right (cairn) level for 1.5km across the end of the An Teallach range and then dropping to Shenavall bothy in Strath na Sealga. This bothy is often used by walkers and liable to be crowded.

From the bothy cross the Abhainn Strath na Sealga, then a kilometre of very wet bog and finally the Abhainn Gleann na Muice to reach Larachantivore. This will usually be possible in reasonably dry weather, but difficult and even dangerous in or after wet weather, when this expedition may be impossible. From Larachantivore go south along the path for a short distance and then make a rising traverse SW up a rather steep slope to reach a little hanging corrie SE of Beinn Dearg Mor. Climb NW up the centre of this corrie, trending north at its head

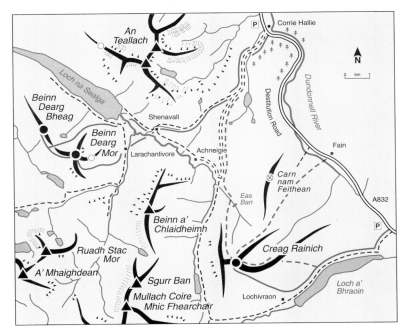

to reach the summit of Beinn Dearg Mor. A more interesting route can be made by climbing the narrow rocky ridge which bounds the corrie on its SW side. (11.5km; 1180m; 4h 40min).

Descend SW from the summit of Beinn Dearg Mor, soon turning NW down the ridge to Beinn Dearg Bheag. This goes along the rim of the Toll an Lochain, a classic example of a circular corrie with its little loch lying in a hollow scooped out by ancient glaciers. Finally the ridge rises to the airy summit of Beinn Dearg Bheag. (14km; 1400m; 5h 30min).

The very long return to Corrie Hallie can be shortened slightly by descending, with due care, the steep slope on the NE side of the col at the head of the Toll an Lochain. This descent leads down to the path on the south side of Loch na Sealga and one has to cross the combined streams flowing into the loch, which may be more difficult than the crossing of the streams separately on the outward route. Both in the interest of aesthetics and safety these hills are best kept for a clear day.

Creag Rainich; 807m; (OS Sheets 19 or 20; NH096751); *bracken crag*

'The Destitution Road' is the name given to the A832 as it sweeps over the bare moorland from Braemore Junction to Dundonnell. The derelict half way house, Fain, was a staging post in the days of the famine relief scheme that built the road. The huge moors to the SW swell upwards to the unobtrusive Corbett Creag Rainich, a fine viewpoint, but a long slow ascent over the bogs and braes if tackled from Fain.

A better route to this hill starts 4km SE of Fain at the point on the A832 where a private road branches off to Loch a' Bhraoin. While no shorter, one can follow first a track and then a fairly good path. Walk down the private road to the NE end of the loch and continue along the path on the north shore to Lochivraon. From there climb NW up open grassy slopes over a knoll at 748m to the summit of Creag Rainich. (8.5km; 600m; 3h). A shorter variant is to traverse uphill to the east ridge from part way down the loch. The two variants can be combined for a pleasant circuit.

The longer approach to Creag Rainich, starting from Corrie Hallie and following the track to Strath na Sealga, is also recommended and would be the natural choice if based at Shenavall.

Creag Rainich from Beinn Bheag

Jim Teesdale

Jim Teesdale

Beinn Liath Mhor a' Ghiubhais Li

Beinn Liath Mhor a' Ghiubhais Li; 766m; (OS Sheet 20; NH280713); *big grey hill of the coloured pines*

This hill is an outlier of the Fannichs and stands above Loch Glascarnoch: a featureless dome of rough grass and heather. Forest plantings NW of the hill have made it less accessible than formerly.

The best start is the car park beside the A835 near the NW end of Loch Glascarnoch at 287737. Walk 100 metres SE along the road to the east end of the forest and then climb south along the forest edge up to the shoulder of Meall Daimh. Continue across a shallow col and more steeply up 260m to the summit of Beinn Liath Mhor a' Ghiubhais Li. (3km; 510m; 1h 40min).

The view from there is remarkably fine, for on one side is the whole length of the Fannaich chain, while, north, rises the Beinn Dearg group.

Nowadays, none of the old pines that gave the hill its name survive, but upper parts show some of the finest examples of solifluction boulder ramparts to be found in Scotland. They may be the relicts of a time when the summit of the hill protruded from glacier ice.

An alternative route is to park at the west end of the Loch Glascarnoch. This parking is often used to access the eastern end of the Fannichs range. Nearby is an automated Metrological Office weather station, complete with automatic web camera.

Walk a short distance east along the road and the follow a forest track south. Leave the track at a suitable point and ascend the west ridge to the summit.

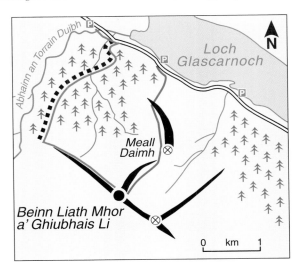

Sail Mhor; 767m; (OS Sheet 19; NH033887); *big heel*

Sail Mhor lives up to its name, being a big lump of a hill rising from the elevated moorland several kilometres NW of An Teallach. The north side drops steeply to Little Loch Broom, and it is from that side that the ascent is made, starting at the foot of the Allt Airdeasaidh, the Ardessie Burn.

The path up the burn is on the east side, but if there is a spate, a possibly difficult crossing higher up can be avoided by climbing up the west side. The splendid falls and cascades of the Ardessie Falls are the first point of interest on the climb. Once in the flatter upper valley, cross to the west side of the burn and follow a smaller stream up into the corrie between Sail Mhor and Ruigh Mheallain for 1km before bearing north and climbing steeply to the SE end of Sail Mhor's curving crest. The walk round the rim to the cairn gives superb views of the sea and far islands. (4.5km; 750m; 2h 20min).

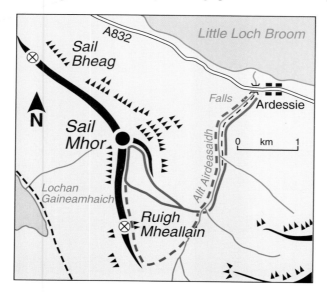

SAIL MHOR

218

Descend south along the edge of the steep west face to reach the col to Ruigh Mheallain, and either traverse that top or else go more directly down the corrie east to return to the Alt Airdeagaidh and the uphill route.

Sail Mhor

Gill Nisbet

Gill Nisbet

Beinn Ghobhlach

Beinn Ghobhlach*; 635m; (OS Sheet 19; NH055943); *forked hill*

Beinn Ghobhlach is a prominent little hill which occupies a strategic position at the tip of the peninsula between Little Loch Broom and Loch Broom. The hill commands a superb view in all directions, the high mountains of An Teallach, Beinn Dearg and the Coigach in an eastward arc, and the sea-lochs, The Minch and their islands to the west.

The approach to the south side of the hill is along the narrow road to the tiny village of Badrallach. From the parking area at the end of the road, walk along the fine footpath which leads to Scoraig and after about 1km make a rising traverse NW up the hillside to the little col near Pt.338m. Descend a little and bear NNE between Loch na h-Uidhe and Loch na Coireig and continue up the SW flank of Beinn Ghobhlach to reach the west ridge a short distance from the summit. The final walk up this bare sandstone ridge leads to a fine cairn and the spectacular summit panorama. (3.5km; 640m; 2h 10min).

On a clear day it is worth walking round the broad stony ridge to the small cairn at the NW prow which gives fine views out to sea and the distant islands.

From there drop south into Coire Dearg to return along the Scoraig coast path back to Badrallach.

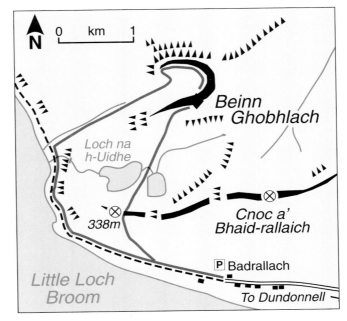

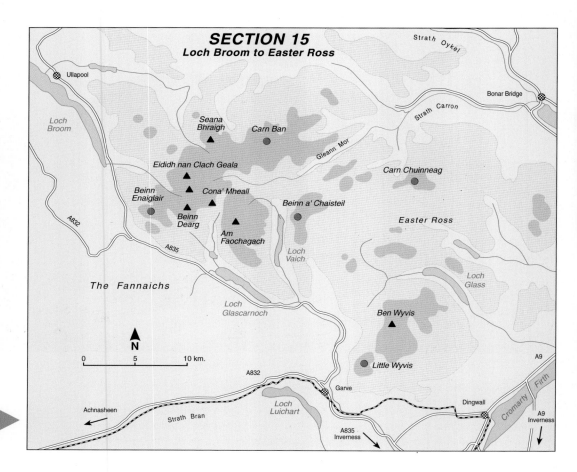

SECTION 15
Loch Broom to Easter Ross

SECTION 15

Loch Broom to Easter Ross

Beinn Enaiglair is an outlier of the Beinn Dearg group of hills, and is situated about 4km north of Braemore Junction on the A835 from Dingwall to Ullapool. Although not as high as the principal Beinn Dearg group or the nearby Fannaichs, Beinn Enaiglair is an obvious feature to travellers approaching Braemore Junction from Garve, Ullapool or Gairloch, and the summit gives extensive views of the Ross-shire hills. The south and west slopes are generally grassy, but the north flanks are steeper and quite rocky.

The ascent of Beinn Enaiglair can conveniently be combined with that of Beinn Dearg across the intervening summit of Iorguill (872m), and this is a good route to Beinn Dearg. Start from the A835 about 150 metres east of Braemore Junction. From the convenient stile cross the open hillside NNW aiming to cross the Home Loch outflow at a useful ford (204789). From the ford follow the route markers (white posts) to join a track to the north end of the Home Loch. Head NW up the stream to a junction of paths at 208797, paths which encircle Beinn Enaiglair. The shortest route is to take the right path east to the bealach between Beinn Enaiglair and Meall Doire Faid (730m) and from there climb north to the broad and mainly grassy summit plateau. (5.5km; 710m; 2h 30min).

For a more interesting and varied ascent, take the left branch of the path which skirts round the NW end of Beinn Enaiglair and steadily ascends beside the Allt na h-Ighine towards the bealach between Beinn Enaiglair and Iorguill. Follow a path (not on the map) which climbs above this bealach by zig-zags and traverses into the small grassy corrie from which springs the west source of the Allt Mhucarnaich. Follow the path west up the floor of this little corrie, then SW up a steep slope onto the summit of Beinn Enaiglair. (9km; 610m; 3h 10min).

The descent can be made by either of the two routes described, and the combination of them makes a good walk.

If appropriate transport arrangements can be made, a longer descent can be made to Loch Droma some 7km east of Braemore Junction. Descend the SE ridge of Beinn Enaiglair to the junction of stalkers paths above Loch Feith nan Cleireach. The continuation SE of this path goes for a further 3km along an undulating ridge, with good views of the SW side of Beinn Dearg, to reach a col north of Lochdrum. From there either descend the path south to the A835 at the west end of Loch Droma, or continue over a few more undulations of the ridge to reach a path (not on the map) which descends to the east end of Loch Droma.

221

BEINN ENAIGLAIR

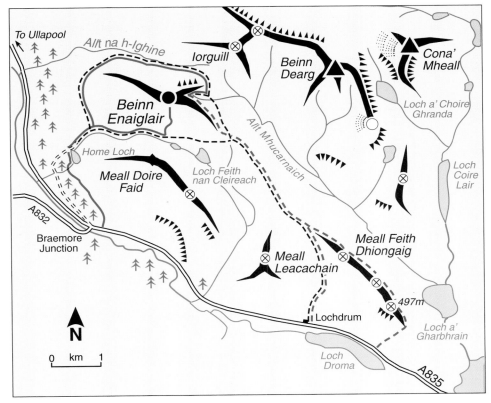

Beinn a' Chaisteil and Meall a' Ghrianain from the SW

Jim Teesdale

BEINN A' CHAISTEIL

Beinn a' Chaisteil; 787m; (OS Sheet 20; NH370801); *castle hill*

This mountain lies 9km north of the A835 from Dingwall to Ullapool, and forms the highest point of a ridge on the east side of Loch Vaich. The summit is separated from Meall a' Ghrianain (772m) at the south end by 2.5km and a col at 650m. Both hills have uniform steep heathery slopes on all sides, but a stony plateau above 650m gives easy walking.

Beinn a' Chaisteil is best approached from the south along the private estate road up Strath Vaich from the A835 (as for Carn Ban). Park at Black Bridge 2.5km east of Aultguish Inn and follow the estate road for 4km. Just before the road crosses the Abhainn Srath a' Bhathaich near Lubriach a rough track takes off through a locked gate, keeping to the east of the river. Continue up this track for a further 5km to semi-derelict Lubachlaggan with its rusty red-roofed bothies, now only inhabited by sheep. It is possible to cycle to this point.

The burn flowing down from Beinn a' Chaisteil is followed on its north bank, remnants of an old stalkers path making the ascent a little easier. Its ends at a small cairn at 500m, and from there another 2km of fairly easy climbing NE brings one to the summit. (11km; 630m; 3h 40min).

There are fine views of Seana Bhraigh to the NW, and, through one of its cols, an unusual view of Suilven.

To include Meall a' Ghrianain go south along the undulating ridge for less than 1km, then descend SSW for 1km to the 650m col, from where there is a climb of just over 1km to the top. Descend the broad south ridge, joining a path which zigzags down the steeper part and follow a fence which turns an intervening hill, Meallan Donn, on the west side to reach a track. From there a path leads SW down to Lubriach and the road back to Black Bridge.

To Carn Ban

Beinn a' Chaisteil

N

Lubach-laggan

Loch Vaich

Meall a' Ghrianain

Allt Coire a' Chundrain

Meallan Donn

Strathvaich Lodge

0   km   1

Lubriach

To Black Bridge and A835

Little Wyvis

Little Wyvis; 764m; (OS Sheet 20; NH429645); *little awesome hill*

Little Wyvis forms a fairly insignificant outlier to the SW of the dominant massif of Ben Wyvis and only just makes Corbett status. The hill is extensively planted with conifers on all lower slopes except due west where deer and exotic species are raised and walkers not welcome. (This accounts for the scarring hill tracks). The only practical ascent is via the Allt a' Bhealaich Mhoir, the normal route for Wyvis with which the Corbett could be combined. Park by the A835 near Garbat.

Follow the Ben Wyvis path up the north bank of the Allt a' Bhealaich Mhoir to above forest level and angle up to Tom na Caillich (or the dip just to its west) and continue along the ridge to the summit. (5km; 620m; 2h 10min).

If the Allt a' Bhealaich Mhoir is in spate keep on until safe to cross and ascend Litte Wyvis from the Bealach Mor.

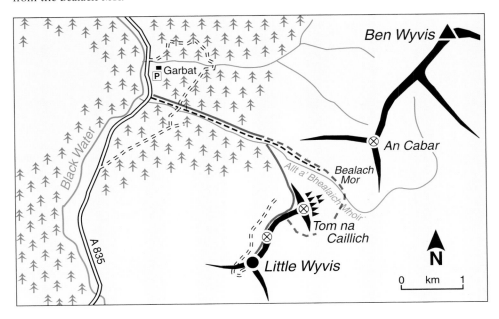

Carn Ban and the Toll Lochain

Jim Teesdale

Carn Ban; 845m; (OS Sheet 20; NH338875); *white cairn*

This great dome-shaped hill is situated in the heart of some of the most remote hill country in Scotland. In the Freevater Forest at the centre of Ross-shire, Carn Ban forms a continuation eastwards of the Seana Bhraigh plateau, from which it is separated by Coire Mor. Being so remote, there is a very long walk from any starting point and a cycle is a considerable advantage along the roads and tracks that lead far into the glens surrounding it.

CARN BAN

Four approaches are possible, all more or less equally long: from the head of Loch Broom in the west: from Corriemulzie Lodge in the north: from Strathcarron in the east: and from Strath Vaich in the south. The Strath Vaich route is probably easiest and is described, the start being as for Beinn a' Chaisteil (see page 222).

Continue along the track on the east side of Loch Vaich and on round Meall a' Chaorainn, then follow the NW branch of the track into Gleann Beag. Cross the river by a bridge and go up the glen for a further 1.5km to a second bridge.

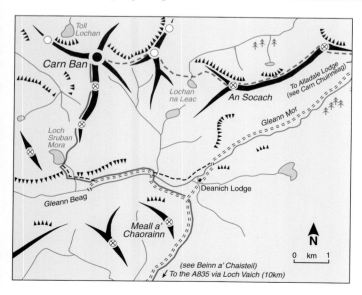

A stalkers path, starting at a small quarried area, goes up the hillside below the crags of Cail Mhor, making a rising traverse towards (and crossing) the burn coming down from Loch Sruban Mora. In wet weather it may be difficult to cross this burn, in which case climb steeply up the east bank of the burn to the loch. From there follow a faint path then head NNE over peat hags and bogs and past occasional cairns onto the shoulder of Carn Ban. Once on the long south ridge continue over three undulating tops of moss and fine scree, and reach the summit. (21.5km; 650m; 5h 50min).

The logical return is by the same route unless one is equipped for a major traverse, in which case the descent east either down the Alladale River or Gleann Mor might be considered.

Jim Teesdale

Carn Chuinneag from the north-east

Carn Chuinneag; 838m; (OS Sheet 20; NH484833); *hill of the churn (bucket)*

Carn Chuinneag, with its distinctive twin tops, enjoys an isolated position amongst the rolling hills and deer forests of Easter Ross. The hill is best approached from Ardgay at the head of the Dornoch Firth, taking the public road up Strathcarron to The Craigs, then turning south to Glencalvie Lodge. Cars should be left just before the bridge near the lodge as the track up Glen Calvie is private.

Go through the gates and keep left of the lodge along the road past the keeper's house towards the river. Continue up Glen Calvie through birch woods which end just before Diebidale Lodge. There take the stalkers path up the north shoulder of the west top of Carn Chuinneag to a cairn at the junction of paths. Either continue south along the path for a short distance, climb the SW ridge to the west top and then along to the central top, the true summit (trig point), or follow the path NE from the cairn almost 1km until past boulders (and onto less steep ground) where an ascent ESE leads to the summit of Carn Chuinneag. (9km; 750m; 3h 20min).

Various initial lines of descent are indicated on the map (left), then follow the track down Glen Calvie.

Croik
The Craigs
Strathcarron
N
0   km   1
To Alladale Lodge (1km)
Glencalvie Lodge
Glen Calvie
Diebidale
Loch Chuinneag
Carn Maire
Carn Chuinneag

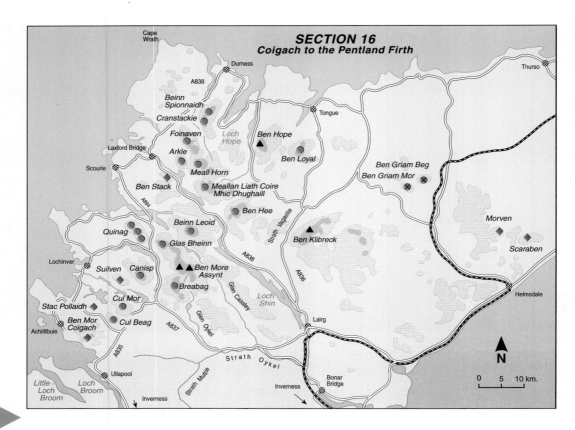

SECTION 16
Coigach to the Pentland Firth

SECTION 16

Coigach to the Pentland Firth

Ben Mor Coigach

Ben Mor Coigach*; 743m; (OS Sheet 15; NC094042); *big hill of Coigach* (Coigach is place of the fifths, a celtic land division)

Seen from the A835 Ullapool to Inchnadamph road, Ben Mor Coigach appears as a rather massive wall-sided mountain, whose western end plunges down in sea-cliffs (almost unique on the Scottish mainland). This appearance conceals the fact that the top of the wall is a fine narrow ridge behind which is a grand complex of shapely peaks and deep cliff-backed corries. This array of peaks is best seen from the minor road which branches off to Achiltibuie along the north side of the range. These fine peaks and corries, and the prospect over sea and islands from them, make the traverse of Ben Mor Coigach one of the most attractive in the NW Highlands. Although not high enough to achieve Corbett status this fine hill contains 2 Grahams, Ben Mor Coigach and Sgurr an Fhidhleir, and also the adjacent Graham of Beinn an Eoin, across Lochan Tuath.

Ben Mor is easily climbed from the end of the public road beyond Achiltibuie near Culnacraig. From there climb up the steep west end of the high ridge which has the unlikely name Garbh Choireachan and continue for almost 2km along this splendid narrow, but fairly level ridge to the summit of Ben Mor Coigach. If the crest is adhered to this gives enjoyable easy scrambling, but a traversing path on the north side avoids any difficulties. (3.25km; 610m; 1h 45min).

To complete a fine traverse, continue ENE from the summit for about 1km to the edge of the east facing corrie then turn NW along the edge with spectacular views as one drops down to the col before Sgurr an Fhidhleir. Climb this very fine peak, which although not the highest, is perhaps the most spectacular of Ben Mor Coigach's array.

Head west and traverse Beinn nan Caorach to Conmheall, but do not attempt to descend from this last summit due south as the ground is steep and rocky. Return east for a few hundred metres before descending south towards Culnacraig.

The ascent of Ben Mor Coigach from the NE is possibly the finest route as one can penetrate into the very heart of the range at Lochan Tuath below Sgurr an Fhidhleir. Near the east end of Loch Lurgainn there are stepping stones where a fence crosses the burn by a bridge. The bridge is blocked by the fence but could be used if the burn is in spate. Car parking is limited. A small path leads across boggy ground to the Allt Claonaidh, where there is a faint path on the south side of the burn. Any other crossing of this ground starting further SE is not recommended due to extensive tree planting and fencing. The path beside the Allt Claonaidh leads up to Lochan Tuath, splendidly situated at the foot of the huge prow of Sgurr an Fhidhleir. For the fit there is a possible diversion 1km north to the Graham of Beinn an Eoin.

To continue the ascent from Lochan Tuath, climb west into the little corrie on the south side of Sgurr an Fhidhleir where an intermittent path on the north bank of the stream leads steeply up rough ground to the broad summit ridge. After climbing Sgurr an Fhidhleir, continue to Ben Mor

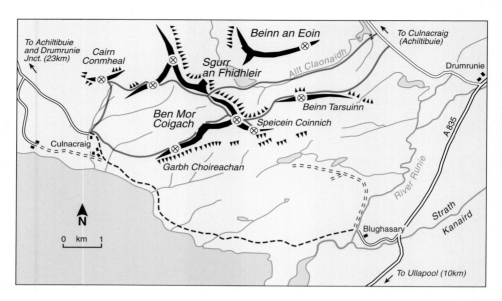

Coigach.   (6.5km; 785m; 3h). Given sufficient time adding the fine narrow ridge of Garbh Choireachan is well worthwhile. Continue along the ridge east to Speicin Coinnich, which is a fine pointed peak. Return about 400 metres west to a small col and descend NE down a steep grassy slope to reach the ridge to Beinn Tarsuinn. The north side of this hill is rockier than the map indicates, so continue at least 1km east from the top to find easy slopes leading down to more level ground and the return to the day's starting point. Alternatively, from Speicein Coinnich, continue down the narrow rocky, but easy east ridge to its foot then head ENE to cross the ridge of Beinn Tarsuinn and back across moorland to the road.

Cul Mor from Stac Pollaidh

Alan O'Brien

Cul Beag; 769m; (OS Sheet 15; NC140088); *small back*
Cul Mor; 849m; (OS Sheet 15; NC162119); *big back*

Cul Beag rises immediately above the narrow single track road on the north side of Loch Lurgainn, so the approaches are short and steep. As with neighbour Cul Mor, care should be taken to avoid the bands of sandstone cliffs on the upper part of the hill facing west and north.

Rather than ascend and descend by the same route, a traverse is suggested which, though short, is a very attractive. Start from the single track road 500 metres east of Linneraineach where a good stalkers path ascends north by a small group of Scots pines. Follow the path to just beyond Lochan Fhionnlaidh, then climb steep slopes ESE to reach a shallow col on the north ridge of Cul Beag. Continue steeply south up this ridge, taking care to avoid the sandstone crags of the west face, to reach the summit. (2.5km; 700m; 1h 50min). To complete the traverse descend SSE for 1km, then SSW for a further 1km to reach the road at the head of Loch Lurgainn 2km from the start.

Cul Mor is the highest of the Assynt Corbetts, and has very steep flanks: south, west and north. Only the east side is easy-angled, and offers a straightforward ascent. When combined with Cul Beag the traverse provides a magnificent day's walk.

Start at a gate in the fence on the west side of the A835 500 metres north of Knockanrock. A good footpath crosses boggy ground and continues north diagonally up the hillside to reach the rather ill-defined east ridge of the mountain. Continue WNW up the broad ridge to reach Meallan Diomhain. Head to a tiny lochan. then on SW up the steep ridge, bounded on the NW by the precipitous Coire Gorm, to end abruptly at the summit. (6km; 620m; 2h 30min). If a traverse is not intended, return by the same route.

The traverse of both mountains is better than climbing each on its own, but the terrain between is rough, and the time required may be more than the distance suggests.

From the summit of Cul Mor descend SW to the saddle to Creag nan Calman. Skirt well to the east before turning SW to angle down to Lochan a' Chuil Mhoir. Swing round under the prow of An Laogh to Lochan Dearg and from there head up west to reach the shallow col on the north ridge of Cul Beag and climb that ridge to the summit. (11km; 1230m; 4h 45min).

From the summit of Cul Beag descend east to the lochan and over Meall Dearg. Continue east and follow the crest of Creag Dhubh to pick up a stalkers path just south of Loch nan Ealachan which leads to the A835 500 metres south of Knockanrock.

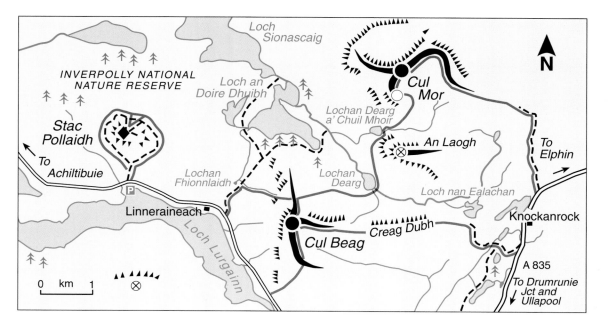

Stac Pollaidh

STAC POLLAIDH*

SUILVEN
(CAISTEAL LIATH)*

Stac Pollaidh*; 613m; (OS Sheet 15; NC107106); *peak of the peat moss*

Stac Pollaidh (Polly) is a unique little hill (a Graham), which shows to an extreme extent the results of the weathering action of rain, frost and wind on a softer version of Torridonian sandstone. Horizontal strata of varying resistance to these effects have been etched out into ridges and pinnacles of bizarre shape along the flanks of the narrow crest which is about 500 metres long and terminates at both ends in steep rounded buttresses. Geologically and scenically outstanding, the hill well justifies a place in the Inverpolly National Nature Reserve.

The popularity of Stac Pollaidh led to severe erosion problems so a new path has been built to circle the hill with a branch to the summit ridge. The new path leaves the car park (108095) and climbs up to the eastern flank of the hill before contouring the north side on a traversing line. Soon there is a fork with the right traversing branch continuing round the mountain and the left leading to the summit ridge. The summit ridge provides some scrambling, some of which is avoidable but none is as difficult as the unavoidable final "formidable" obstacle (Stac Pollaidh scale). Tackle this tower on the right on good holds with one awkward move. On the descent, the other side (right looking down) is easier until a one metre jump lands you on the col. An alternative line of ascent, slightly harder but not at all exposed, is a chimney reached by descending the gully to the south for a few metres. This leads back behind the pinnacle from where it is an easy 100 metres to the summit cairn. (1.5km; 550m; 1h 20min).

For the descent, return to where the path reaches the ridge. Once back at the path there is a descending leg westwards to rejoin the circuit without backtracking. Follow the path round the western flank of the hill and so back to the car park.

Suilven (Caisteal Liath)*; 731m; (OS Sheet 15; NC153183); *the pillar* (Norse), *the grey castle*

Surprisingly Suilven fails by a fair margin to reach Corbett height, though it is a Graham. Nevertheless, by any mountain standard Suilven yields nothing to any of the higher Scottish hills. An `Inselberg', or `Island Mountain' of Torridonian sandstone, surrounded by a sea of Lewisian gneiss from which the softer rocks have been stripped, the Grey Castle when viewed from the west stands as a rather forbidding bastion defying the ravages of wind and weather. In fact this appearance, and also its pinnacle form when seen from the east, is rather misleading, as the mountain is really a narrow serrated ridge with three main summits, presenting no great difficulty to the ascent of the highest (western) top by way of the Bealach Mor.

The two commonly used approach routes are very similar as regards length and quality. Both are long, but until near the base of the hill follow good paths.

The route from Inverkirkaig leaves the road at 085193 and follows the pleasant wooded glen of the River Kirkaig, whose 20m falls are an attraction in themselves. The mountain is hidden from view for several kilometres, but comes as a dramatic sight when first seen close-to. Beyond the Falls, at a small cairn, make sure to take the path which shortcuts the peninsula at the NW end of Fionn Loch. This path is boggy, but the route round the loch-side is longer and rougher. Although various cairns may suggest diversions from the path marked on the map, it is best to continue along the NE shore of the Fionn Loch until the stream from the Bealach Mor is reached at 143168. A boggy stretch up the burn leads to a heather-clad debris fan leading very steeply up to the Bealach Mor. The path is eroding and the steepness may seem intimidating to some. The bealach is reached near a remarkable wall, and through a gap the route continues WNW along the ridge, with some easy scrambling to the rounded summit of Caisteal Liath. (10.5km; 730m; 3h 40min).

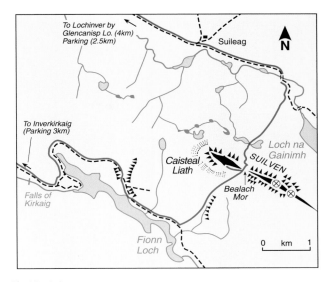

From Lochinver one can drive to the west end of Loch Druim Suardalain, about 1km west of Glencanisp Lodge, where there is a small parking area. From the lodge a good path leads up Glen Canisp following the meandering river with numerous lochans. At first the scenery is gentle with scattered primroses and violets in springtime, but gradually becomes more rugged and desolate as the wilderness is penetrated. The brooding bulk of Suilven increasingly dominates the scene. After crossing the bridge to the south of the river, continue up the path for about 600 metres to the point 167198 where a cairn marks the start of a rough path leading SSW over boggy ground. This leads between two lochans at the foot of the mountain, then climbs steeply up a shallow gully to the Bealach Mor where the route to the summit described above is joined. (9.5km; 730m; 3h 20min).

231

The middle peak of Suilven, Meall Mheadhonach, can be reached from the Bealach Mor by some easy but exposed scrambling, however, the continuation of the traverse to the SE peak, Meall Bheag, involves some more serious scrambling and is for experienced climbers only.

Suilven

Andrew Dempster

Duncan Bryden

Canisp and Loch Assynt

Canisp; 847m; (OS Sheet 15; NC203187); *white hill*

Canisp, like near neighbour Suilven, rises abruptly from a tableland of Lewisian gneiss, but although higher by 115m, Canisp lacks the steepness and sharply serrated spine of Suilven that makes the latter such an outstanding peak. Nevertheless, because of its isolation, Canisp is well worth climbing for the excellent views of the other Assynt hills.

The hill is a steep-sided ridge running from SE to NW, and may be approached from either end. The walk from the NW, starting at Lochinver or Little Assynt, is much longer than the south-eastern approach, so the latter is recommended.

Four kilometres north of Ledmore the River Loanan flows out of the north end of Loch Awe where there is a footbridge to simplify an otherwise difficult crossing. Follow the path from the footbridge to Loch na Gruagaich, then along the Allt Mhic Mhurchaidh Gheir to a lochan under the north flank of Meall Diamhain.

The hillside becomes progressively more stony, and several cairns should be ignored as they have no significance. From the lochan climb SW to the col immediately west of Meall Diamhain, and from there continue up the rounded ridge of Canisp or, if the not infrequent strong SW wind is blowing, up the shallow corrie on its north side. These two routes join at 750m and a further 100m of climbing brings one to the summit. (6km; 690m; 2h 30 min).

CANISP

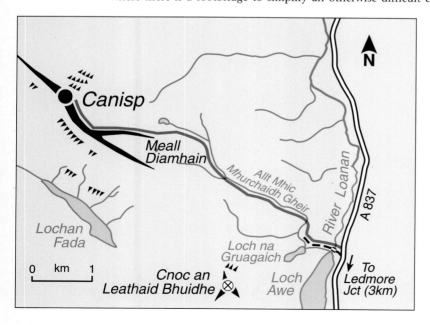

Jim Teesdale

Breabag from the south-west

Breabag; 815m; (OS Sheet 15; NC286157); *little height*

Breabag forms a high tableland between the upper reaches of the River Oykell to the east and the A837 from Ledmore to Inchnadamph to the west. The highest point of this plateau is at the south end, and is not named apart from the name Creag Liath which applies to the crags to the SW. Although the mountain is composed of quartzite which forms the broken cliffs of its eastern corries the approach from the west traverses glens where Durness limestone predominates.

BREABAG

The most interesting approach starts from the A837 5km north of Ledmore at a salmon hatchery where there is a car park. The route follows the glen of the Allt nan Uamh along a path which has been much improved. One kilometre from the road, the river wells up from a spring in the floor of the glen while, above, the river bed is dry. Further up the glen, the path forks, the right climbing to prominent caves at the foot of a cliff on the south side (Bones of long-extinct mammals have been found in these caves, providing evidence of the presence of early man). Take the left fork which passes the entrance to a deep cave on the left just before a rock step. At that point climb the slopes to the east which are initially steep. One kilometre on there is a break in the escarpment, just north of a prominent quartzite slab. Climb through this break onto the upper part of the mountain. The summit lies 1km to the south with 200m of ascent. (5km; 680m; 2h 20min).

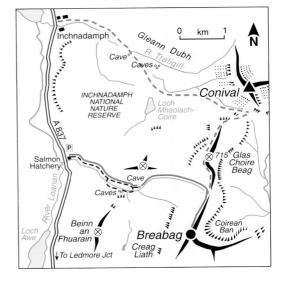

Rather than return to the A837 by the same route, traverse Breabag northwards and descend Gleann Dubh. From the summit head NNE initially down gently sloping ground to a col at 630m (293170). From there the terrain changes to quartzite slabs (slippery if wet) which are followed to the north top (718m). Continue to the deep and narrow pass between Breabag and Conival, and then descend the Allt a' Bhealaich (which soon disappears down a limestone pot). Thereafter follow the dry bed of the stream to meet the path from Loch Mhaolach-coire. Soon after it is worth making a short detour to the right to view the caves through which the stream may be seen rushing. Continue down Gleann Dubh to the A837 at Inchnadamph, 4km north of the salmon hatchery.

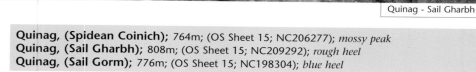

Gill Nisbet

Quinag - Sail Gharbh

Quinag, (Spidean Coinich); 764m; (OS Sheet 15; NC206277); *mossy peak*
Quinag, (Sail Gharbh); 808m; (OS Sheet 15; NC209292); *rough heel*
Quinag, (Sail Gorm); 776m; (OS Sheet 15; NC198304); *blue heel*

234

QUINAG,
(SPIDEAN
COINICH)

QUINAG,
(SAIL GHARBH)

QUINAG,
(SAIL GORM)

Quinag is an eye-catching mountain from any direction, being one of the great peaks of the
North West, and it presents a formidable array of rocky features. Quinag is probably derived
from Cuinneag, meaning *milk bucket* or *water stoup*. The walker may be relieved to know that
the three main summits can be gained relatively easily.

The most dramatic view of Quinag is from the north; the rock prows of Sail Gharbh and
Sail Gorm tower above the sea at Kylesku. From the west the hill appears as a long wall of
cliffs. Only to the SE does it relent, and it is from that side that walkers will almost invariably
approach. Other routes on the mountain are best left for those with exploratory or climbing
experience.

The start is from the A894 between Loch Assynt and Kylesku at 233274, where there is a
large parking area and the beginning of a stalkers path. From there the broad ridge of Spidean
Coinich faces one, with its northern edge clearly marked by crags. The ascent goes up this
ridge, whose angle is determined by the tilt of the quartzite strata, and much of the way is up
bare rock, in places littered with boulders. A rocky bump is crossed before the cone of Spidean
Coinich is reached. From afar it appears to be cliff-girt, but the crags all face NE and there are
no problems for the walker. (3.5km; 550m; 1h 50min).

The biggest surprise when on Quinag is that it is such a green mountain. The areas of rock
are less extensive than expected, and are well demarcated, offering the walker ground that is
either easy (though steep) or obviously impossible. The long traverse north takes one over the
airy crest of Pt.713m and along the twisting path down to the Bealach a' Chornaidh (c 555m),
where one should study the line of the path descending the eastern corrie, the route off the
mountain.

The path zig-zags up to Pt.745m and then drops to a more knobbly col (c 555m) and the
ridge out to the spectacular prow of Sail Gorm, the northernmost spur of the mountain.
(5.75km; 870m; 3h 20min). This route is reversed to return to the knobbly col, but the ascent
to Pt. 745m can be avoided by a traverse across its north side to reach the ridge leading to
Sail Gharbh. This peak is the highest point of Quinag; at it the grey quartzite just overlaps
the sandstone, and the summit is the high point on a ridge which extends nearly 1km further

NNE to end above the great cliffs which are the finest feature of the mountain. (8km; 1030m; 4h 45min).

Return along the west ridge to its lowest point and again avoid an ascent of Pt.745m by a descending traverse SE to the Bealach a' Chornaidh, below which one reaches the start of a path which leads down to the north of Lochan Bealach Cornaidh. This path joins the stalkers path back to the starting point on the A894.

It is also possible to drop down SW from the Bealach a' Chornaidh. A narrow path makes a descending traverse south of barring cliffs to easier, but still steep, ground above the Bealach Leireag. From the top of this pass descend 2km SW along the path to Tumore on the A837 by Loch Assynt.

An even longer end to the day can be made by walking NW from the Bealach Leireag down Gleann Leireag to the B869 near Nedd. Using two cars or some such arrangement is necessary for these alternatives.

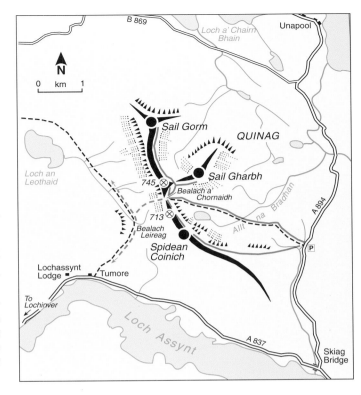

Quinag - Spidean Coinich

Hamish Brown

Alan O'Brien

Glas Bheinn

Glas Bheinn; 776m; (OS Sheet 15; NC254264); *grey hill*

This is rather a neglected hill, being surrounded by such grand peaks as Quinag, Suilven and Ben More Assynt, but the discerning will quickly realise what fine views such a summit must have. Glas Bheinn is also the start of one of the finest high-level walks in the northern Highlands, southwards to Conival and Breabag. There is plenty of rough rocky ground on the hill, but it is easily avoided.

GLAS BHEINN

The start, which is not too obvious, is just north of the highest point of the A894 between Loch Assynt and Kylesku at 238284. Start east on the path which goes round the south end of Loch na Gainmhich, but soon leave it to climb up the grassy edge of the crags on the NW ridge of the hill. This ridge is followed, and after several steps and more level sections leads onto the broad, mossy summit plateau. (3km; 550m; 1h 40min).

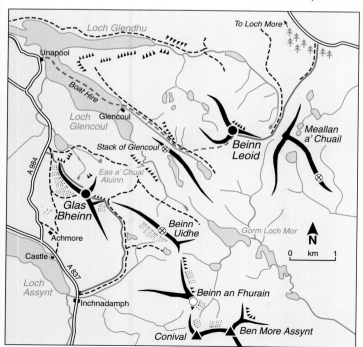

The route can be reversed on the descent, or a steep way taken SW to return to the start by the path which goes from Achmore round the foot of the hill. The best continuation goes SE then east down a narrow ridge to the col between Glas Bheinn and Beinn Uidhe. A stalkers path crosses this col and is followed for 6km past Loch Fleodach Coire down to Inchnadamph. This leads back to the road several kilometres from the day's starting point, but offers a very fine traverse in grand surroundings.

Beinn Leoid; 792m; (OS Sheet 15; NC320294); *McLeod's hill*

Beinn Leoid is not a tame mountain being remote and if one approaches from the west there is some wild country to be crossed. From the east, however, the ascent can be made quite easily starting from the A838 between Lairg and Laxford Bridge and following stalkers paths to reach the hill. The landscape between Beinn Leoid and Glas Bheinn is an amazing chaos of bare rock, deep glens, and a proliferation of lochs and bogs, a magnificent wilderness enhanced by the starkly prominent peak of the Stack of Glencoul and the cascade of Britain's highest waterfall, the Eas a' Chual Aluinn. For the strong walker these are the approaches to explore, but the easy route is described first.

The best starting point on the A838 is 2km SE of Loch More at 357333, limited parking. From there a stalkers path climbs steeply south between forest plantings to end after 2km on a broad saddle on the north ridge of Meallan a' Chuail. From there make a descending traverse SW to join another much longer stalkers path from Lochmore Side which leads to the col between Meallan a' Chuail and Beinn Leoid, whose east ridge leads directly to the summit. (7km; 760m; 2h 50min). As a variant on the return, it is possible to take in Meallan a' Chuail with little more extra climbing than is involved by following the outward route.

The easiest approach from the west is by sea. In recent years it has been possible to hire a boat at Unapool to be taken to Glencoul. Local enquiries should be made to ascertain the present situation. From Glencoul a good path goes up the glen below the dramatic Stack of Glencoul to end just beyond Loch an Eircill. From there Beinn Leoid is 2km NNE. (7km; 800m; 3h).

The return can be made down the NNW ridge for 1km then north to join a path leading down to Glen Dubh, and out along the north shore of Loch Glendhu to Kylestrome. As an approach route, this is the easiest one entirely on foot from the west.

Beinn Leoid

Gill Nisbet

Ben Stack from Loch Laxford

Ben Stack*; 721m; (OS Sheet 9; NC269423); *steep hill*

Standing to the west of and close to Loch Stack on the A838 from Lairg to Laxford Bridge, this elegant little mountain is worthy of attention in spite of its modest height and the short distances involved in an ascent. Moreover, Ben Stack is a superb viewpoint. Seen from the SE approaching along Loch More, the mountain dominates the view.

The SE approach to Ben Stack starts from the A838 at the entrance to the private road to Lone, 1km north of Achfary. Follow a rock rib up the broad SE ridge of Ben Stack, named Leathad na Stioma on the map. The rocky crest makes a pleasant staircase, interspersed with heather and grass. Alternatively an ATV track can be followed on the SW side of the rib to about 300m. A minor eminence at 540m followed by a short level stretch leads to the summit cone of steeper grass. The summit is split by a landslip into two nearly level ribs, the trig point and stone shelter at 719m being on the lower southern one, and the summit cairn about 100 metres further on at the western end of the northern one, at 721m, past an incongruous solar-powered aerial. (3.5km; 680m; 2h).

Looking westwards from the summit, the eye is drawn down to the low ground that extends to the distant and much-indented coastline; is a landscape in which water seems to predominate over rock in intricate mixture.

An alternative route starts from a building on the roadside at 265437 near Lochstack Lodge. Follow the stalkers path that climbs west until a small burn is reached at about 230m then strike SE up steeper broken slopes direct to the top. With conveniently placed cars, or a willingness to walk 5km along the road beside Loch Stack, a pleasant traverse of the hill can be made by the two routes described. The northbound afternoon postbus may be a help.

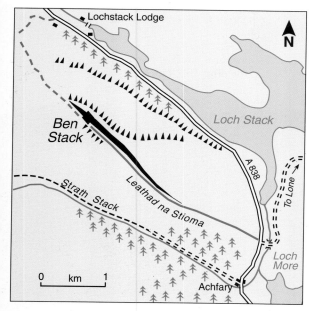

Chris Townsend

Fionaven from Arkle

Foinaven (Ganu Mor); 914m; (OS Sheet 9; NC315507); *white hill (big wedge* or *head)*
Arkle; 787m; (OS Sheet 9; NC302461); *peak of the chest*
Meall Horn; 777m; (OS Sheet 9; NC352449); *hill of the eagle*

239

This group of hills lies at the heart of the Reay Forest in the angle of the A838 east of Laxford Bridge, and holds some of the greatest climbing interest to be found in NW Sutherland.

Foinaven is just short of Munro height (2,998 ft), and can be considered an outstanding mountain in any context, its long narrow crest bearing many summits, the sweep of quartzite screes on the SW flank, and the grandeur of its corries and spurs on the NE flank all contribute to the superb mountain architecture. Arkle is composed of the same sharp angular quartzite as Foinaven, and is of a similar character, although a smaller hill. The walking on both these mountains is generally rough, and care is required on their summit ridges, particularly when the rocks are wet. Neither mountain is recommended for inexperienced hillwalkers in adverse weather or winter conditions.

FOINAVEN
(GANU MOR)

ARKLE

MEALL HORN

Meall Horn, together with its adjacent hills, is much less impressive. There are some very rocky faces on its NE side, but seen from the SW is rounded and lacking in any special character. Meall Horn can be climbed as an extension to a day on either of the other two, but is only a short day's climb by itself.

The easiest approach to this group is from the A838 1km north of the village of Achfary. There is a parking area about 100 metres down the private road to Lone just before a bridge. Walk or cycle past the keeper's cottage at Airdachuilinn to the buildings at Lone (permission to drive along this road is no longer obtainable). Follow the left track a short distance after the last building. This leads in 500 metres through a gate between two remarkable boulders to a small pine plantation, and above the trees zig-zags up the steep hillside and continues as an excellent stalkers path at an easy gradient beside the Allt Horn. The three mountains can be climbed from different points on this path.

For Foinaven take the path to the Bealach Horn, its highest point at 510m (339460), then strike due north to Creag Dionard (778m, but height/name not on the map) over grass, boulders and bare rock. The upper part tends to be featureless, in contrast to the rest of the mountain, and careful navigation is required in mist. The pink flowers of thrift and moss campion abound in June.

From Creag Dionard the broad stony ridge leads to Pt.808m, which is the start of the summit ridge proper. From there descend steeply to the next col, Cadha na Beucaich, over loose rocks and unstable scree, keeping close to the crest. Continue up the ridge, which is steep and narrow, or along its west flank to Pt.869m. The route continues NW over a minor top and along a much broader, but still rough, ridge to reach the highest point, Ganu Mor. There are two cairns about 100 metres apart. (14.5km; 1130m; 5h 10min). One more top on the main ridge can be added if desired; Ceann Garbh (902m), which is about 1km north along a mainly grassy ridge.

An alternative starting point for the ascent of Foinaven is the track which leaves the A838 at Gualin House (306564). Follow this track up Strath Dionard for about 7km, then aim for Cnoc a' Mhadaidh (589m). From there continue up steep broken ground to reach Ceann Garbh and the start of the main ridge. Given suitable transport arrangements, the two routes just described can be combined to give a splendid traverse of the mountain.

For the ascent of Arkle, leave the stalkers path 1.5km beyond Lone at 321432 and strike north up mixed heather and stony slopes between two small burns until the flat top of Meall Aonghais is reached. An apparent bull-dozed track up the slope, well seen from a distance, changes on closer inspection to a quartzite steam bed scoured of vegetation, in dry weather an easy and interesting route. Open stony slopes lead on to the start of the summit ridge at Pt.758m. The true summit is 1km further on at the end of a magnificent curving ridge, which is narrow and rough going for one short stretch along a natural pavement of quartzite. An alternative to the route on the crest at the narrow section is on the west side. (8.5km; 840m; 3h 20min).

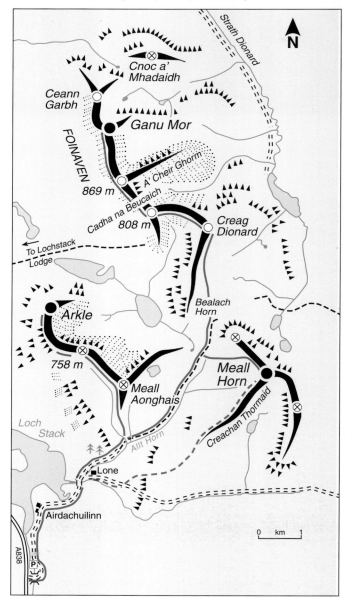

Derek Sime

Arkle from Loch Stack

The route to Meall Horn goes up the stalkers path to about 400m at 336452. Bear east through a gap in a line of incipient crags, then NE up steep grass, ablaze with thrift in June, to the col on the broad summit ridge. From there the summit is about 500 metres SE up easy ground. (9km; 760m; 3h 20min). The return route may be varied by descending the SW spur over Creachan Thormaid.

There is another good stalkers path from Loch Stack Lodge (off the A838 at 268435) which circles Arkle and ends on the slopes of Foinaven and this can be used to give further variations and combinations of routes.

Meall Horn from Arkle

Scott Johnstone

Meallan Liath Coire Mhic Dhughaill

Meallan Liath Coire Mhic Dhughaill; 801m; (OS Sheets 9, 15 and 16; NC357391);
grey hill of MacDougall's corrie

**MEALLAN LIATH
COIRE MHIC
DHUGHAILL**

This hill, with several radiating spurs and ridges, lies to the NW of Loch More, from where the summit appears as a broad dome. The hill is in the centre of the Reay Forest and hence a good vantage point. Although its northern corries are crag-lined, the southern slopes are easier angled and the walking pleasant, particularly on the summit ridge.

The best starting point is near Kinloch at the SE end of Loch More. Follow a private road to Aultanrynie, but just before reaching the house take a stalkers path up the hillside to the east and continue uphill by a series of easy zig-zags. The path bears SE to reach the south end of the broad undulating ridge of Meallan Liath Beag. This is followed to the Corbett's long east ridge. Carn Dearg (796m) can be climbed before heading west, then NW and finally SW up the final slope where slabby stones make a pleasant staircase to the summit of Meallan Liath Coire Mhic Dhughaill. (9.5km; 850m; 3h 40min).

Leave the summit south, bearing slightly left to avoid incipient crags and rough scree, and descend east of Meall Reinidh. Cross the Allt an Reinidh at a convenient point to rejoin the stalkers path above the zig-zags. Continue down the path to Kinloch.

A longer but more interesting approach to this hill can be made from Lone at the east end of Loch Stack. Follow the stalkers path east up the Abhainn an Loin and either climb the Sail Rac ridge or continue up to the Bealach na Feithe and climb south to Meall Garbh (754m). A pleasant traverse can be made by combining any of these routes.

The inconvenience of needing three maps can be avoided by making ones own composite.

(Map labels:)
To Lone (Foinaven)
Sabhal Beag
Bealach na Feithe
Abhainn an Loin
Sail Rac
Meall Garbh
Carn an Tionail
Meallan Liath Coire Mhic Dhughaill
Carn Dearg
Meall Reinidh
Meallan Liath Beag
A' Ghlaise
Loch More
Allt an Reinidh
Aultanrynie
Kinloch
A838
N
km

Derek Sime

Ben Hee

Ben Hee; 873m; (OS Sheet 16; NC426339); *fairy hill*

Ben Hee lies on the eastern edge of the Reay Forest, and when seen from the road in Glen Mudale to the west of Altnaharra rises prominently above a moorland wilderness. From most viewpoints Ben Hee appears as a rounded hill, and except for steeper ground in east facing corries, gives easy walking.

The most convenient approach is from the SW, leaving the A838 at West Merkland. Follow the private track for 1.5km to a stalkers path, which leads off east about 50 metres before the bridge. The path leads up the Allt Coir' a' Chruiteir into the corrie enclosed by the west slopes of Ben Hee. Continue up the head of the corrie to the summit. There is a small cairn with a trig point 20 metres SE of it. (5.5km; 830m; 2h 40min).

There is a fine all-round view including Beinn Mor Assynt, Quinag, Ben Stack, Foinaven, Ben Hope, Ben Loyal and the boggy moor to the SE. There are abundant cushion-forming alpines of moss campion, cyphel and thrift on the higher stony slopes which give splashes of colour in June.

The simplest return is by the route of ascent or continue SW down the rock strewn ridge over Meallan Liath Mor and directly down to West Merkland. Alternatively go west along the broad ridge leading to Sail Garbh and descend SW to rejoin the outward route, but the going is rather rough.

A traverse of the hill over its unnamed NE top can be made by continuing along the private track to the historic Bealach nam Meirleach (*robbers' pass*). A path branches off SE between Loch an t-Seilg and Loch an Aslaird. Follow this and climb the NW flank of Ben Hee, passing north of a small hidden lochan, to reach the 851m NE top. From there traverse SW along a well-defined ridge, passing an obvious area of old landslips on the east flank, to reach the summit. (9km; 850m; 3h 30min).

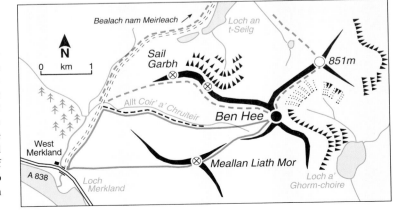

Beinn Spionnaidh and Cranstackie

Cranstackie; 801m; (OS Sheet 9; NC350555); *rugged hill*
Beinn Spionnaidh; 773m; (OS Sheet 9; NC362573); *hill of strength*

CRANSTACKIE

BEINN
SPIONNAIDH

These twins, rising east of the A838 from Rhiconich to Durness, and west of Loch Eriboll, lie in the northern reaches of the Reay Forest. Not only is Beinn Spionnaidh the most northerly Corbett, but the two hills together form the most northerly high ground of any consequence in Britain.

From the shores of Loch Eriboll they rise in interminably long and featureless slopes, which are afforested at lower levels. The southerly extension of Cranstackie falls in very steep, rocky slopes into Strath Dionard, thus leaving the western flank as the best approach.

The walking is pleasant and undemanding, while in common with all the isolated mountains of Sutherland the views are extensive. In favourable conditions Orkney can be seen across the Pentland Firth.

Start the ascent from Carbreck on the A838 (333593), and proceed for 2km along the private track to the shepherd's house at Rhigolter. From there bear SE up steep grassy slopes into the high corrie between the two hills and reach the col between them at 550m.

Cranstackie can be climbed directly up the well-defined NE ridge (5.5km; 750m; 2h 30min). Return to the col and continue up the broader SW slopes of Beinn Spionnaidh. The trig point stands at the north end of the short summit ridge. (7.5km; 970m; 3h 20min).

Descend by the NW ridge and leave it at a convenient point before incipient crags are reached to drop down steep slopes back to Rhigolter.

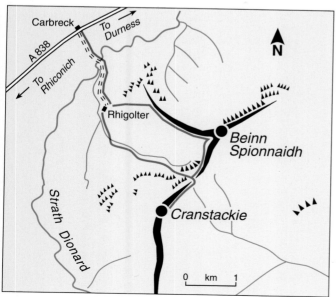

James Lamb

Ben Loyal

Ben Loyal (An Caisteal); 764m; (OS Sheet 10; NC578488); *law hill (the castle)*

Ben Loyal lies about 7km south of the village of Tongue and 4km west of Loch Loyal and is regarded as one of the finest hills in Scotland. The isolated position and striking appearance more than compensate for lack of height, only just sufficient for Corbett status. The striking outline of its four granite peaks is best seen across the Kyle of Tongue, but the formidable appearance of these peaks belies their difficulty, and the traverse of the mountain is a delightfully easy walk.

Ben Loyal is almost invariably climbed from the north, for that route shows the best of the mountain. The alternative approach from the east (Loch Loyal) is dull by comparison and the ground on that side is often boggy and wet.

BEN LOYAL (AN CAISTEAL)

Leave Tongue by the minor road which goes south to the farm of Ribigill (583538), where a car can be left. A track, wide at first then narrowing to a footpath, continues due south to the deserted shepherd's cottage of Cunside. Head towards Sgor Chaonasaid and bear leftwards to climb steep grass and heather slopes to the east of the rocky prow of this peak. From the bold summit rocks of Sgor Chaonasaid (708m) the broad ridge continues due south 1km to the main summit, An Caisteal. The rocks of the intervening Sgor a' Bhatain (700m) are easily bypassed on their east side, and the granite tor of An Caisteal should be tackled on the west. (6km; 710m; 2h 40min).

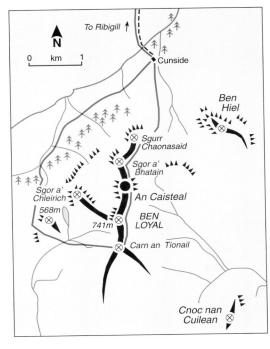

To complete the traverse continue south from An Caisteal over Pt.741m by a well-defined but easy grass ridge. The spur which juts out NW from this point to Sgor a' Chleirich (642m) is not a suitable route of descent, for the west prow of that peak is very steep and rocky. Continue south to Carn an Tionail (714m) and from there descend grassy slopes west towards the prominent conical Pt.568m which is the right most summit of Ben Loyal as seen from the Kyle of Tongue. Descend the Allt Fhionnaich to about 400m and round the flank of Pt.568m, along deer tracks to about 350m until a stream can be followed down to the Coille na Cuile. Once clear of the trees, at a height of about 100m, walk back to Cunside. (Retracing the outward route is as easy and as quick an option.)

Roger Wild

Ben Griam Beg from the south-east

Ben Griam Mor*; 592m; (OS Sheets 10 and 17; NC806389); *big dark hill or peak stack hill*
Ben Griam Beg*; 580m; (OS Sheets 10 and 17; NC832412); *little dark hill or peat stack hill*

BEN GRIAM MOR*

BEN GRIAM BEG*

These rounded sandstone hills stand 3.5km apart among the headwaters of the River Helmsdale and the Halladale River, some 10km NW of Kinbrace. Ben Griam Beg's summit has the remains of the highest hill fort in Scotland, consisting of a thick stone wall enclosing an area of about 150 metres by 60 metres. On the south flank there are other walls and enclosures which suggest a larger occupied area.

Although an approach to these hills can be made by leaving the A897 near Ballach Cottage and following the private track to Greamachary and onwards NW over boggy ground to Ben Griam Beg, a better route starts from the B871 at a small quarry (787378) about 5km north of Badanloch Lodge.

Start along an anglers path heading north towards Loch Coire nam Mang across the moorland below the west flank of Ben Griam Mor. After 1km leave the path and choose the best line east to reach the crest of the NW shoulder of Ben Griam Mor. Continue up the crest where the sandstone outcrop presents no difficulty and onwards over stony ground to the summit. (3km; 430m; 1h 30min).

Descend the NE ridge of Ben Griam Mor, keeping to the crest to avoid sandstone outcrops on the NW flank. Cross flat boggy ground near the south end of Loch Druim a' Chliabhain and climb NE up the broad grassy slopes of Ben Griam Beg, keeping above the sandstone outcrops overlooking the loch. Steeper rocky heath-clad slopes lead to the summit past the hill fort and other remains. (6.5km; 780m; 2h 50min).

Descend to the south end of Loch Druim a' Chliabhain and head west below the north side of Ben Griam Mor to reach Loch Coire nam Mang and the anglers path back to the B871.

Jim Teesdale

Morven from Scaraben

Morven*; 706m; (OS Sheet 17; ND004285); *big hill*
Scaraben*; 626m; (OS Sheet 17; N066268); *divided hill*

Morven is the highest hill in Caithness, and is well seen from as far away as the south side of the Moray Firth, the isolated position and steep conical shape being very distinctive.

The best route to Morven starts at Braemore, reached by road from the A9 at Dunbeath. Park at the bridge (073304) and continue past Braeval and west along a track below Maiden Pap (484m) to reach Corrichoich. Continue up the river for 500 metres to a grassy knoll, on which is sited the remains of an ancient wheelhouse. From there head SW over rough moorland to the saddle east of Morven. A steep and rough ascent of 400m over heather and scree, passing south of a rocky bluff, leads to the summit. (7km; 560m; 2h 30min). On a clear day the views extend as far as Orkney, where the Old Man of Hoy can just be seen. The best return is by the same route, although the very fit might elect to traverse the rough intervening hills and moorland to Scaraben. The ascent of this hill is, however, better done as a separate walk from Braemore.

Scaraben is a long quartzite ridge with three very distinctive whitish stony summits. Cross the bridge from Braemore and follow a track SE. After 1km head south on rough moorland towards East Scaraben (590m), which is reached in 3km over gradually steepening ground. Continue WSW along the ridge to the main summit. (5km; 630m; 2h 10min). Finally, West Scaraben (600m) can be reached in a further 1.5km. From there descend NE over the moors to return to Braemore, or head north over rough boggy ground to climb Maiden Pap and drop down to the track on its north side.

MORVEN*

SCARABEN*

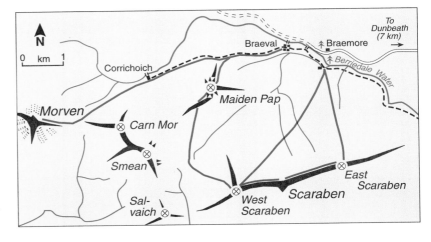

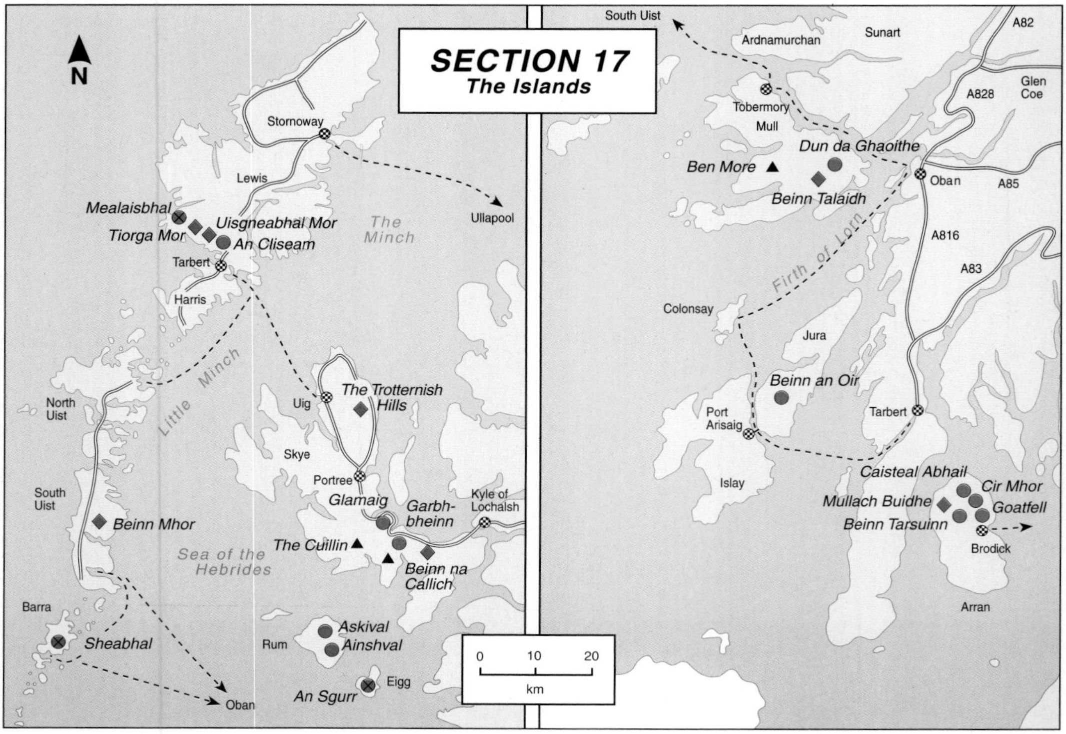

N
SECTION 17
The Islands
Stornoway
Lewis
Mealaisbhal
Uisgneabhal Mor
Tiorga Mor
An Cliseam
The Minch
Ullapool
Tarbert
Harris
Little Minch
North Uist
Uig
The Trotternish Hills
Skye
Portree
South Uist
Glamaig
Garbh-bheinn
Kyle of Lochalsh
Beinn Mhor
The Cuillin
Sea of the Hebrides
Beinn na Callich
Barra
Sheabhal
Askival
Ainshval
Rum
Eigg
An Sgurr
Oban
0
10
20
km
South Uist
Ardnamurchan
Sunart
A82
Glen Coe
A828
Tobermory
Mull
Dun da Ghaoithe
Ben More
Oban
A85
Beinn Talaidh
A816
Firth of Lorn
A83
Colonsay
Jura
Beinn an Oir
Port Arisaig
Tarbert
Islay
Caisteal Abhail
Cir Mhor
Mullach Buidhe
Goatfell
Beinn Tarsuinn
Brodick
Arran

SECTION 17

The Islands

Goatfell, Arran — *Graham Little* 249

Beinn Tarsuinn, Cir Mhor and Caisteal Abhail, Arran — *Graham Little* 250

Mullach Buidhe*, Arran — *Graham Little* 252

Beinn an Oir, Jura — *Derek Fabian* 253

Beinn Talaidh*, Mull — *Rob Milne* 254

Dun da Ghaoithe, Mull — *Rob Milne* 255

An Sgurr*, Eigg — *Graham Little* 256

Askival and Ainshval, Rum — *Donald Bennet* 257

The Eastern Red Hills*, Skye — *Hamish Brown* 260

Garbh-bheinn and Belig*, Skye — *Donald Bennet* 262

Glamaig, Skye — *Hamish Brown* 263

The Trotternish Hills*, Skye — *Hamish Brown* 264

Sheabhal*, Barra — *Derek Fabian* 266

Beinn Mhor* and Hecla*, South Uist — *Derek Fabian* 267

Tiorga Mor*, Oireabhal*, and Ulabhal* North Harris — *Derek Fabian* 269

Uisgneabhal Mor*, Teileasbhal* and Stuabhal*, North Harris — *Derek Fabian* 271

An Cliseam (Clisham), North Harris — *Derek Fabian* 272

Mealaisbhal* and Cracabhal*, Lewis — *Derek Fabian* 274

Scott Johnshtone

Goatfell and Brodick Peir

Arran

Goatfell; 874m; (OS Sheet 69; NS991415); *goat hill*

This famous mountain, the highest on Arran, receives perhaps more ascents than any other **GOATFELL** island peak, its commanding situation and accessibility proving an irresistible attraction. Three main ridges radiate from its lofty summit: to the north the pinnacled Stacach ridge (linking it to its lower brother North Goatfell), to the east (the upper part of which is the tourist route) and to the south.

The tourist route, the most popular approach, starts at Cladach, about 3km from Brodick Pier. The route is well signposted and passes through the castle grounds, initially as a rough track and then after about 1km as a well maintained path. Following the east side of the Cnocan Burn the path breaks out of the woodland and takes a well defined cairned line up into Coire nam Meann and thence onto the east ridge of the mountain at a height of 630m. This is also the junction with an alternative ascent that starts below the charming settlement of High Corrie and initially follows the north bank of the Corrie Burn. The path crosses the burn then follows the east ridge over Meall Breac, to join the tourist route. About half a kilometre of quite narrow and rocky ridge leads upward to the summit of Goatfell which is adorned with a triangulation pillar, a viewpoint indicator and several perched boulders. (5km; 870m; 2h 40min).

The views are truly spectacular, the drop into Glen Rosa to the west is quite breathtaking. Although the ascent and descent of Goatfell makes a fine outing, the day can be extended by traversing north (skirting the pinnacles of the Stacach ridge) to North Goatfell (810m), then over Mullach Buidhe (819m) and down over the delightful little peak of Cioch na h-Oighe (*the maiden's breast*) (661m) and into Glen Sannox. Although the path avoids all technical climbing, the traverse and descent of Cioch na h-Oighe requires care (not a walking route in winter). A limited public bus service or taxi hire allows a return to the starting point.

Cir Mhor from the south

Arran

Beinn Tarsuinn; 826m; (OS Sheet 69; NR959412); *traverse hill*
Cir Mhor; 799m; (OS Sheet 69; NR972431); *great comb*
Caisteal Abhail; 859m; (OS Sheet 69; NR969443); *forked keep* (popularly, *The Castles*)

BEINN TARSUINN

CIR MHOR

CAISTEAL ABHAIL

These three splendid hills form part of the great granite ridge that lies west of Glen Rosa and Glen Sannox. They can be ascended individually by a variety of routes (see below) but in combination they form an outstanding ridge walk extending from Beinn Nuis in the south to Suidhe Fhearghas in the north (the usual traverse direction). Including the initial ascent from Glen Rosa and the descent of lower Glen Sannox, the traverse comprises about 16km of challenging walking. Following the true ridge-line for its full length involves rock climbing skills on the A' Chir Ridge and the Witch's Step but both can be easily avoided.

Start at the Glen Rosa road end (001375) about 3km from Brodick Pier (campsite by the river). Follow the track to the footbridge over the Garbh Allt. Cross, then follow the rather muddy path on the north side of the burn. Alternatively take the obvious diagonal path some way before the Garb Allt to follow the south side of the burn. On reaching a confluence, ford the burn and follow a rather vague path over moorland heading directly for the SE shoulder of Beinn Nuis. As the path gains height it skirts the edge of the great eastern precipice to gain the summit cairn (792m). A wide ridge runs north passing several rock towers flanking the wild Coire a' Bhradain then over several false tops to the summit of Beinn Tarsuinn. (7km; 790m; 3h). A splendid viewpoint with the A' Chir ridge below and the great grey comb of Cir Mhor beyond. The steep descent down the NE ridge to Bealach an Fhir-bhogha (*pass of the bowmen*) requires care as the path twists and turns avoiding a number of rocky sections – if in doubt keep to the west. The path bifurcates at the col, the right branch leading onto the famous A' Chir ridge (745m), where rock climbing skills are required for a safe passage, the left skirting the base of the slabby west face of the mountain. Taking the left hand path, with only a slight loss of height, the ridge is regained a short distance before the A' Chir/Cir Mhor col. Magnificent views of the massive architecture of the Rosa Pinnacle, on the south flank of Cir Mhor, can be enjoyed during the steady ascent to the airy summit. The feeling of being at the very centre of the Arran hills and the great sense of void to the north add to the magic that is Cir Mhor – one of Scotland's finest peaks. (9.5km; 1050m; 4h).

Descend to the NW and look back at the awesome dark, dank northern precipice, almost Alpine in proportions.

A curving ridge, known as the Hunters' Ridge leads on to Caisteal Abhail, passing the famous, well cairned springs and overlooking the wilds of Coire na h-Uaimh to the east. The summit area, in keeping with the mountains alternative name of The Castles, features several rocky castellations. (11km; 1280m; 4h 40min). Although the third Corbett of the day has been climbed, much interest lies ahead as the ridge is followed eastwards to the striking gap of the Witch's Step. This great rift, resulting from the erosion of a basalt dyke, can look very intimidating, especially in misty weather. However, the descent to the gap involves easy scrambling and the rock climbing on the east side can be avoided by descending the gully to the north for about 15m to gain an obvious path outflanking the steep rocks of the summit tower of Ceum na Caillich (Witch's Step) (727m).

The path now leads easily on to Suidhe Fhearghas (Fergus's Seat) (660m), a fine viewpoint, and down into North Glen Sannox to gain the A841 at North Sannox Bridge. Alternatively, from the foot of Suidhe Fhearghas, strike east to join Glen Sannox at the old barytes mines and thence to the road at Sannox Bay. A limited public bus service or taxi hire allows a return to Brodick.

Individual ascents of the three Corbetts can be made as follows:

Beinn Tarsuinn – follow the first part of the traverse described above to the summit. (7km; 790m; 3h). The day can be enhanced by continuing to the SE over Beinn a' Chliabhain (675m) back into Glen Rosa.

Cir Mhor – gain The Saddle between North Goatfell and Cir Mhor by walking up either Glen Rosa or Glen Sannox then follow the path up the east ridge of the mountain, through rock outcrops, to end abruptly on the summit. (5.3km; 800m; 2h 30min).

Caisteal Abhail – either reverse one of the alternative endings of the traverse described above or walk up Glen Sannox and on into Coire na h-Uaimh to gain the south ridge of the mountain from the Cir Mhor / Caisteal Abhail col Alternatively, either of the ridges flanking Garbh Coire to the north give enjoyable and less frequented routes. Both can be approached by following the path up North Glen Sannox. (6.5km; 860m; 3h).

BEINN TARSUINN

CIR MHOR

CAISTEAL ABHAIL

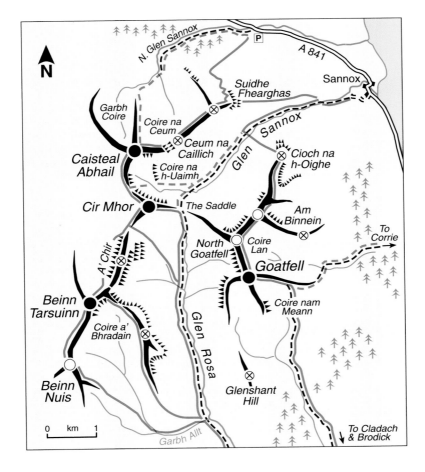

Arran: Mullach Buidhe and Beinn Bharrain

Arran

Mullach Buidhe*; 721m; (OS Sheet 69; NR901427); *yellow hill*

MULLACH
BUIDHE*

Glen Catacol and Glen Iorsa cut off the 12km hill range of western Arran. The grouping of Beinn Bhreac (711m), Mullach Buidhe (721m) and Beinn Bharrain (715m) offers good routes from Pirnmill. The hills are blessed with splendid views over the Kilbrannan Sound to west Kintyre, Islay and Jura, whilst, to the east, the main ridges of Arran are viewed over Glen Iorsa.

The most convenient starting point is at the Post Office in Pirnmill. Immediately to the north a rough farm track runs up between houses, bends left then sharply right and after about 100 metres bends left again. Leave the track at this point and follow a rather muddy path that ascends the sparsely wooded hillside on the north side of the Allt Gobhlach. Waterfalls and a narrow gorge add interest. Cross the burn well above the gorge and follow an indistinct path running SSE across rather boggy ground to the foot of the ridge defining the west flank of Coire Roinn. The path improves and leads at a regular gradient to Beinn Bharrain. Passing the striking tor of Casteal na h-Iolaire (*stronghold of the eagle*), a curving ridge leads to the col and then on to the triangulation pillar on the summit of Mullach Buidhe. (4.5km; 790m; 2h 20min). A more sporting and direct ascent of Mullach Buidhe can be made by following the ridge defining the east flank of Coire Roinn. This is narrower and rockier and involves some unavoidable scrambling – care required, especially in winter.

A good alternative to descending either of the ascent routes is to descend the NE ridge to Bealach an Fharaidh then ascend the whaleback ridge to Beinn Bhreac (711m). A descent of the steepish western slopes can then be made towards Pirnmill.

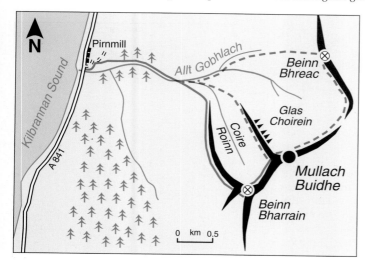

Alan O'Brien

Beinn an Oir and Beinn a' Chaolais from Beinn Shiantaidh

Paps of Jura

Beinn an Oir; 785m; (OS Sheet 61; NR498749); *hill of gold*
Beinn Shiantaidh*; 757m; (OS Sheet 61; NR513747); *holy hill*
Beinn a' Chaolais*; 733m; (OS Sheet 61; NR488734); *hill of the narrows*

Beinn an Oir is the central, highest and finest of the renowned Paps of Jura. These three hills in the southern third of the island of Jura are all characterised by high dome-shaped summits, separated by deep bealachs, and by rough quartzite scree and boulder slopes. Their island location makes the shapely paps a prominent feature of the western seaboard of Argyll.

Access to Jura is by ferry from Kennacraig on the mainland (the Kintyre peninsula) to Port Askaig on Islay; from Port Askaig a small car ferry crosses the narrow Sound of Islay, where the tidal stream can be fierce, to Feolin Ferry on Jura's west coast. Cycles can be useful as transport on Jura. The best starting point for an ascent of Beinn an Oir, as well as a round of two or all three paps, is on the A846 near the bridge over the Corran River (543720). Climb NW past a small forest plantation over a low shoulder to reach the Corran River about 1km east of, and below, Loch an t-Siob. Continue west to pass south of this small lochan, to reach the steeper SE slopes of Beinn an Oir. The ascent is easiest by a long grassy rake rising from south to north up the east face of the hill, avoiding the worst of the rough boulders and scree. This rake gains the NE ridge and the final climb leads past two prominent dry-stone enclosures and along a stone pathway, constructed during early triangulation work. (6km; 770m; 2h 40min).

BEINN AN OIR

BEINN SHIANTAIDH*

BEINN A' CHAOLAIS*

A traverse of the three paps is a classic but a much longer day's expedition. Make the same approach to Loch an t-Siob, but pass to the east of the loch and climb the SE steep shoulder of Beinn Shiantaidh, descending then by the west ridge to the col from where the NE ridge of Beinn an Oir, as described above, leads to its summit. Descend by the fairly steep bouldery south ridge, which requires care, and climb Beinn a' Chaolais by the NE shoulder on unstable scree which gives way higher up to pleasant mossy ground. The easiest descent is east by south, largely down scree, to the col to Beinn Mhearsamail and then NE by gentler slopes to reach Gleann an t-Siob, returning from there to the start. (13.5km; 1380m; 7h).

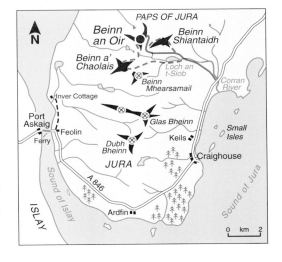

Beinn Talaidh and Tomsleibhe, Glen Forsa

Iain Brown

Mull

Beinn Talaidh*; 761m; (OS Sheet 49; NM625347); *alluring* or *soothing hill*

BEINN TALAIDH*

The island of Mull has a complex volcanic history, with the centre of past activity situated in what is now hollow ground near Loch Ba. Beinn Talaidh forms part of the rim of hills surrounding this site. Although once considered a Corbett, revised OS data reduced the height

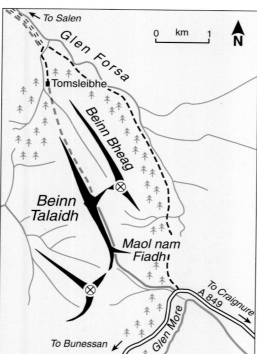

of the hill to 761m, demoting it from the Corbetts, but making it one of the highest Grahams. The hill is easily accessible from the A849 from Craignure to Bunessan and the Iona ferry at the head of Glen Forsa (643329). This point can be reached by bus from Craignure as services connect with the ferries.

Leave the A849 and head NW towards the prominent col, the Mam Bhradhadail, or the shoulder of Maol nam Fiadh on the south ridge of Beinn Talaidh. From there climb NNW to the summit without difficulty. (2.5km; 660m; 1h 40min).

An alternative approach to Beinn Talaidh is from the north, starting at Glenforsa airstrip 2km east of Salen. Go up the forestry track in Glen Forsa for 6km to Tomsleibhe and from there climb the long, easy-angled NNW ridge of the hill which leads directly to the summit. (9km; 760m; 3h 20min). A cycle might be used with advantage.

Gill Nisbet

Dun da Ghaoithe

Mull

Dun da Ghaoithe; 766m; (OS Sheet 49; NM672362); *fort of the two winds*

DUN DA
GHAOITHE

This very attractive hill rises above Craignure on the island of Mull, and overlooks both the Sound of Mull and the Firth of Lorn. Access from the mainland is by the ferry from Oban to Craignure.

Direct access from the pier at Craignure to the open hillside above is restricted by trees, and the nearest open ground is about 2km NW at Scallastle. Start at the farm on the A849 a few hundred metres beyond the bridge over the Scallastle River. Pass through a gate between the farm and the coach works and follow a path along the river to where it fords the river. Ascend SW to the corner of the forestry plantation then join the east ridge, Maol nan Damh, which is followed to the summit. (From Craignure pier: 5.5km; 770m; 2h 40min).

The descent can be made by going a short distance NW and descending the broad ridge of Beinn Chreagach eventually turning east between the Allt an Dubh-choire and the plantation back to the start. The views are possibly the best from any hill in Mull.

A better descent route can be made by going along the level ridge SE to Mainnir nam Fiadh (754m) and then east along the ridge above Creag Dubh to the upper telecommunications mast. From there follow the access track down to the A849, which is reached about 2km south of Craignure pier.

An even longer traverse is possible with the help of the bus service between Craignure and Tobermory. Leave the A849 at Fishnish Bay and climb SW to Maol Buidhe, the NW point of the long ridge which extends for about 8km to Dun da Ghaoithe. This ridge proceeds over a series of progressively higher hills, with quite small drops between them, and gives a fine walk.

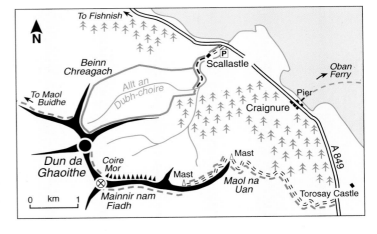

An Sgurr, Eigg

Eigg

An Sgurr*; 393m; (OS Sheet 39; NM463847); *the peak*

AN SGURR*

As seen from the Morar coastline, the Cuillin of Rum and Skye compete to hold the eye, but it is the striking profile of Eigg that captures attention. At a modest 393m, the Sgurr of Eigg does not feature in any list where height is the gauge of status. This massive thrust of primitive pitchstone, crowning one of the most beautiful islands in the Hebridean seas is quite without equal, the summit a 100m high tower of Dolomitic steepness.

From the pier at Galmisdale, An Sgurr totally dominates the landscape. Take a road then track leading up through wild garlic scented woodland and over an open field to a large white house. Crossing the track running west to Grulin follow a path over brown moorland towards the great pillar. Skirt to the north of the dark ramparts on a gentle path worn into the softer basalts eroded from around the base of the monolith. At the first obvious break a diagonal path leads through a stone gateway onto a grassy col. A switchback and short scramble give access onto the spine of An Sgurr where pitchstone column heads have weathered into a cobblestone pavement – a pathway in the sky. The summit trig pillar is perched close to the edge of a great void. (3.5km; 390m; 1h 15min). We know that we are standing at one of the truly magical places in the Western Isles. The return can be varied by heading west for 1km and dropping south to pick up the Grulin path/track back to Galimsdale.

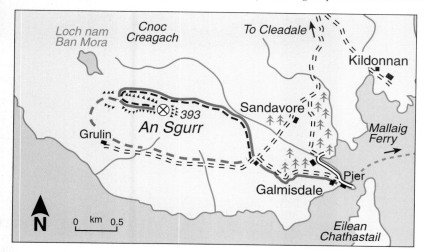

Askival

Rum

Askival; 812m; (OS Sheet 39; NM393952); *hill of the spear*
Ainshval; 781m; (OS Sheet 39; NM378943); *rocky ridge hill*

These two fine hills are the highest points of the Rum Cuillin, a ridge of five very distinctive peaks that bear comparison with their larger and more celebrated neighbours across the Cuillin Sound in Skye. The Black Cuillin of Skye may be higher, more numerous and more starkly rocky, but the Rum peaks have their own character and individuality. The traverse is comparable with the traverse of the Arran peaks described elsewhere. Both are mountaineering expeditions of exceptional character and beauty.

ASKIVAL

AINSHVAL

Sgurr nan Gillean, left, and Ainshval from the Dibidil path

Askival and Hallival from the sea

The island of Rum is a National Nature Reserve under the management of Scottish Natural Heritage, but climbing on the island is not subject to any restrictions, provided that no interference is caused to the research activities being carried out there, particularly on the red deer population. Climbers and hillwalkers should, however, be self reliant and not dependent on assistance from the SNH staff working on the island in the event of an accident.

Access to Rum is by boat. Scheduled services from Mallaig are operated by Caledonian MacBrayne (tel. 01687 462403). Charters from Mallaig are also available on request from Bruce Watt Cruises (tel. 01687 462283) and sailings from Arisaig are operated in summer by Arisaig Marine (tel. 01687 450224). Other operators who may be able to arrange sailings to Rum are Doune Marine (tel. 01687 462667) and Bella Jane Boat Trips, Elgol (tel. 0147 866244). Self catering hostel accommodation is available at Kinloch Castle and there is one bed-and-breakfast cottage in Kinloch village, Ferry Cottage, (tel. 01687 462767). In addition, camping by the shore in Loch Scresort is permitted and there is a bothy at Dibidil. There is a small shop and post office at Kinloch.

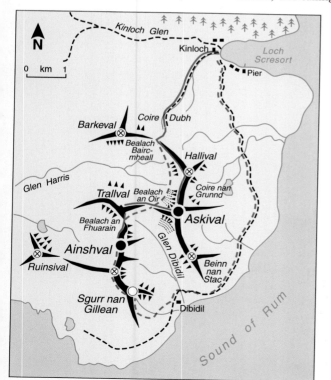

Although Askival and Ainshval are the only two Corbetts, they can be climbed as part of a complete traverse almost as easily as by separate ascents, and this traverse is described. The day can be shortened conveniently at one or two points.

From Loch Scresort go through the grounds of Kinloch Castle and take the well signposted path up Coire Dubh. At the head of the corrie the path goes up gravelly slopes to reach the broad Bealach Bairc-mheall. (The enthusiastic can make a detour to ascend Barkeval with its wind eroded summit rocks). From the bealach climb east then SE up the broad ridge to Hallival (723m), the upper part being quite steep and

Rum from Eigg

rocky. This is the first of five main peaks on the ridge, and there is a splendid view towards Askival, the highest summit on Rum.

Descend south, steeply at first down two or three rocky steps, then easily along a grassy ridge to the col. The north ridge of Askival is narrow and rocky, but quite easy until one reaches the Askival Pinnacle, a steep and narrow tower which can be climbed by a moderately difficult pitch on the west side. Above the Pinnacle the ridge leads up a few rock steps to the summit. The Pinnacle can be avoided by a traverse on the east side of the ridge to reach steep but easy rocks leading to the summit. (5.5km; 940m; 2h 50min).

Descend the steep west ridge of Askival to the Bealach an Oir (450m). At this point there is a choice of routes. The five peaks traverse goes up the east ridge of Trallval to its twin rocky summits (702m) and then makes a steep and rocky descent south to the Bealach an Fhuarain (510m). This is a worthwhile diversion, for Trallval is a fine peak, but a level traverse from the Bealach an Oir to the Bealach an Fhuarain across grassy slopes is the alternative.

From the Bealach an Fhuarain avoid the lower buttress of Ainshval's north ridge by going to the right (W) on scree and broken rocks to regain the crest at a level section. The upper half of the ridge is narrow and rocky, and may be quite awkward when wet, so go up a narrow path in the screes on the east side of the crest to reach the flat grassy summit close to the cairn of Ainshval. (Excluding Trallval: 7.5km; 1220m; 3h 50min. Including Trallval: 8km; 1410m; 4h 10min).

The quickest way back to Kinloch is to return to the Bealach an Fhuarain, traverse to the Bealach an Oir and from there make a long dipping traverse north below the west faces of Askival and Hallival to the Bealach Bairc-mheall, and the path back to Kinloch. The return from Ainshval takes about 2.5 to 3 hours.

The last of the Rum peaks, Sgurr nan Gillean (764m) can be reached from Ainshval by an easy walk along a broad grassy ridge over an intervening peak. Sgurr nan Gillean is a superb summit, the remotest in Rum but a long way from Kinloch. The return may be made by Ainshval and the route described above, or by descending to Dibidil bothy and walking back to Loch Scresort by the path above the eastern coastline. The latter route is no shorter, and involves a steep descent south from Sgurr nan Gillean to avoid the rocky slopes east of the summit. Whichever route one chooses, the long return from Kinloch will end a memorable day.

ASKIVAL

AINSHVAL

Beinn na Cailllich

Skye – The Eastern Red Hills

Beinn na Caillich*; 732m; (OS Sheet 32; NG601233); *hill of the old woman*
Beinn Dearg Mhor*; 709m; (OS Sheet 32; NG587228); *big red hill*
Beinn Dearg Bheag*; 582m; (OS Sheet 32; NG593219); *little red hill*

**BEINN NA
CAILLICH***

**BEINN DEARG
MHOR***

**BEINN DEARG
BHEAG***

The Eastern Red Hills are the trio of steep hills which rise abruptly from low-lying moorland just west of Broadford. Being among the most easterly hills in Skye, they are prominent in views from the mainland, particularly from Kyle of Lochalsh, and they dominate the view as one travels towards Broadford. Beinn na Caillich is the highest and boldest of the trio, more often admired than climbed, but the steep stony flanks are less arduous than one might expect and the summit view is as fine as any in Skye. From Beinn na Caillich a pleasant horseshoe walk can be made round Coire Gorm over the other two hills in the group.

The usual starting point is at Coire-chat-achan, which can be reached by a path across the moor from the B8083 between Broadford and Torrin. The name commemorates the wild cats which may once have been there, but are now exterminated on Skye. Pennant in 1772 made the earliest recorded ascent of Beinn na Caillich from Coire-chat-achan, the first recorded ascent of any Skye peak. Dr Johnson, staying there, made a familiar-sounding remark: "The hill behind us we did not climb. The weather was rough and the height and steepness discouraged us".

Present-day hillwalkers should not be so easily discouraged. From the ruins of Coire-chat-achan head WNW up the steadily steepening hillside. Higher up large boulders lend themselves to a fast and easy ascent and one reaches the east shoulder of the hill not far from the grassy summit. A Norwegian princess is reputably buried under the huge cairn. (3.5km; 700m; 2h).

Continue west for the traverse round Coire Gorm over the tops of Beinn Dearg Mhor and Beinn Dearg Bheag. The former also has a large cairn and a grandstand view of Blaven's east face. A chaos of scree leads down to the Bealach Coire Sgreamhach between the two hills, and a twisting ridge continues to the substantial cairn on Beinn Dearg Bheag. From there the east ridge gives an easy descent, and when the Allt Beinn Deirge is reached it is less tedious to follow the stream to Coire-chat-achan than to strike directly across the rough heather to reach the Strath Suardal road.

The circuit of the Eastern Red Hills is very much one to keep for a clear day, such as Pennant enjoyed: when he looked over the Black and Red Cuillin and pictured them coloured by "the rage of fire".

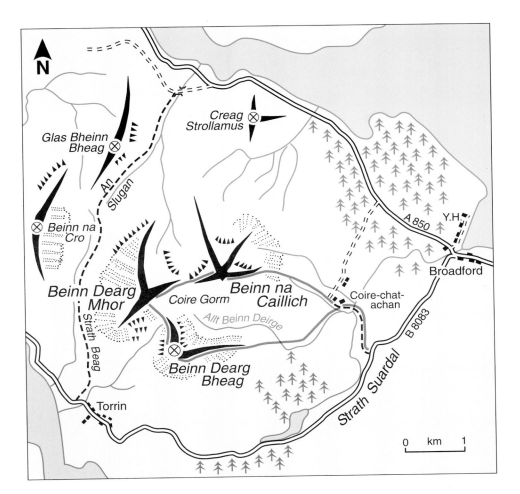

Beinn Dearg Mhor from the north-east

Alastair Matthewson

Garbh-bheinn summit

Jim Teesdale

Skye

Garbh-bheinn; 808m; (OS Sheet 32; NG531232); *rough hill*
Belig*; 702m; (OS Sheet 32; NG544240)

Although Skye is justifiably renowned for the Cuillin, there are many other fine hills on the island. This is evident to anyone travelling along the road beside Loch Ainort. The hills which encircle the head of the loch make an impressive sight with their bold outlines, contrasting dark gabbro cliffs and red screes. Garbh-bheinn, the highest of these hills, is the northern peak of the long ridge which extends from Loch Scavaig over Bla Bheinn to Loch Ainort, and Belig is a pointed outlier to its NE.

GARBH-BHEINN

BELIG*

The traverse of Belig and Garbh-bheinn can be made from the head of Loch Ainort, starting from the A850 at the bridge over the Abhainn Ceann Loch Ainort. Head south across the rising grassy slopes of Coire Choinnich, aiming for the foot of the north ridge of Belig. A steeper rocky section is best climbed on the left (east) side of the ridge and, above, the way continues up the narrow grassy crest to the sharply pointed summit. (2.5km, 700m; 1h 40min).

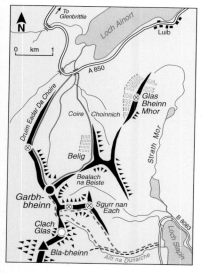

Descend the SW ridge, which is steep and quite rocky, with bouldery scree and the remains of a dry stone dyke leading down to the Bealach na Beiste. From there climb the NE ridge of Garbh-bheinn, easy at first, followed by steeper scree and finally a pleasant narrow ridge ending at the summit. (4km; 1050m; 2h 40min). On a clear day there is a very fine view of the whole Cuillin ridge to the west.

Return to Loch Ainort down the north ridge, leading to the Druim Eadar Da Choire. The lower slopes are rather rough peat and heather, but there is a path most of the way.

An alternative route to Garbh-bheinn from the head of Loch Slapin involves some good scrambling on the traverse of Sgurr nan Each (716m). Start from the B8083 road bridge over the Allt na Dunaiche and follow the path on the north side of the burn for 1km, then bear NW up grassy slopes to the steepening SE ridge of Sgurr nan Each. Scramble up to the first top (623m) and continue west along the rocky crest over the summit and down slightly to the foot of the SE ridge of Garbh-bheinn, which is narrow and rocky, but easy. (4km; 850m; 2h 30min). The return to Loch Slapin goes back down this ridge and a short distance further to the foot of the north ridge of Clach Glas. From there descend east down a steep slope of scree and boulders and continue down the burn to the Allt na Dunaiche path.

Glamaig

Skye

Glamaig; 775m; (OS Sheet 32; NG513300); *greedy woman*

Glamaig is one of the most outstanding summit viewpoints on Skye, one girded with steep slopes and some minor crags and scree. The classic view is from Sligachan, with Glamaig appearing as a huge cone rising beyond the old packhorse bridge. In 1899 a barefoot Gurkha ran from inn to summit and back in 55 minutes, the record at present being 46 minutes, 2 seconds.

The direct line up the hill can be seen and studied easily from below and presents no real problem other than unrelenting steepness with a ration of scree. This route has the diretissima advantage of landing you right on the summit, known as Sgurr Mhairi (*Mary's Peak*), 775m, named after a girl who was killed while searching for a lost cow. (3km; 775m; 2h).

A kindlier and more varied route is to ascend by the NE ridge over the minor summit of An Coileach. Most of the height is gained on very steep grass with some scrambly going over An Coileach. Park in a lay-by just south of the Moll coastal road junction and walk along the A850 to where a fence heads straight up the hill, which marks the line. Keep left of some crags until the main, highest, craggy area is reached where it is best just to pick a route through to land on An Coileach, 673m, *the cockerel*.

The ridge on to Sgurr Mhairi has fence poles dipping and rising onto the broader dome of the hill. The summit cairn lies off round the rim of the northern corrie. (3km; 835m; 2h 15min).

Descending, one can return down either of the ascent lines described but a circuit can be made via the Bealach na Sgairde, the gap to Beinn Dearg Mhor, which appropriately translates as the *loose* or *scree pass*. Head back along the summit crest to find where the fence line turns sharply: this forms an arrowhead pointing the way to go down. The bealach soon comes into view as do the slopes of unavoidable scree.

If returning to Sligachan, the way back to the inn leads by the attractive Allt Darach (*oak stream*) with its gorges and waterfalls; if returning to the Moll turn off car park, descend east and then flank along to circuit An Coileach's lower slopes on sheep tracks and reach the A850 where it bridges the river in the valley.

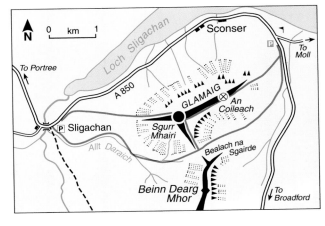

The Old Man of Storr

Skye – The Trotternish Hills

The Trotternish Traverse; (OS Sheet 23);
The Storr*; 719m; (NG495540); to **The Quiraing*;** 362m; (NG453692)

THE STORR*

THE QUIRAING*

Trotternish, the large north-eastern peninsula of Skye which reaches to the northernmost point of the island, has a backbone of hills which offers a long and classic traverse. The start and finish are at the two most interesting features of the area, The Storr in the south and The Quiraing in the north, and the walk from one to the other is in no way inferior to any day on the more famous Black Cuillin, and deserve better than just visiting in bad weather!

The twisting Trotternish escarpment in its entirety is nearly 30km long, constantly edged by sheer cliffs on the east, and rolling down in wind-swept grass slopes to the west. The complete walk from Portree to The Aird is a two-day venture. The following description is of a more feasible one-day journey which still entails 22km of walking, 1700m of climbing and may take 9 or 10 hours from end to end.

Some prearranged transport will also have to be organised, using the car parks below The Storr and at Flodigarry or the Bealach Ollasgairte. Start at the car park on the A855 by the north end of Loch Leathan (507527) and walk up, as indicated on current notices, by the forestry plantation to reach The Sanctuary of The Storr. A rising traverse from the corner of the plantation leads north to the famous Old Man of Storr and other strange pinnacles which are grouped below the vertical 200m cliffs of The Storr. The mountain flowers are a notable feature here and along the cliffs.

To reach the summit of The Storr (*the high hill*) keep on traversing north until easy ground is reached and one can turn back along the cliff-top on the edge of Coire Scamadal to curve up to the 719m trig point, the highest summit of the walk. The views are fantastic and remain so throughout the day.

Drop NW to the Bealach a' Chuirn and traverse the Norse-named Hartaval (668m) to the Bealach Hartaval. All the named passes on the ridge offer escape routes if need be. Many were regularly used by the population in centuries past. The walk, always edged by cliffs to the right (east) leads after 7km of dramatic bumps and dips to Beinn Edra (611m), the major peak of the middle section. A path and fence lead down to the Bealach Uige, once an important pass. There is a steep bluff to pull up to reach Bioda Buidhe where the landscape below suddenly takes on an element of the weird and wonderful, a landscape full of towers and lochans.

The continuation north leads to the Bealach Ollasgairte (439679), the only pass crossed by a road, which links Staffin and Uig. From the top of the pass one can climb Meall na Suiramach (543m), the most northerly hill on the Trotternish ridge, but this bypasses the extraordinary, unique world of The Quiraing. This should on no account be missed, so follow the path which leaves the road at its summit and traverses NE below the cliffs of Meall na Suiramach towards The Quiraing. This name means *fold* or *pen*, and imaginatively describes the towers, pinnacles, gullies and cliffs which enclose The Prison. The slender spire guarding the most obvious gully is The Needle, and scrambling upwards past it one comes to The Table, a perfectly horizontal platform of grass in the centre of The Prison. The Quiraing is certainly a place of atmosphere, a stark contrast to the view down to the comfortable crofting communities and turquoise waters of Staffin Bay. By continuing beyond The Quiraing it is also possible to break up and back to reach Meall na Suiramach, from which gentle slopes descend SW to the Bealach Ollasgairte.

The weird landscape of both The Storr and The Quiraing is due to land-slipping, and a descent from The Quiraing NE by Loch Fada and Loch Hasco towards Flodigarry takes one through country more reminiscent of Iceland than Scotland – an alternative finish.

Those who feel that the long traverse described above is over-strenuous can savour the best of Trotternish by making separate visits to The Storr and The Quiraing.

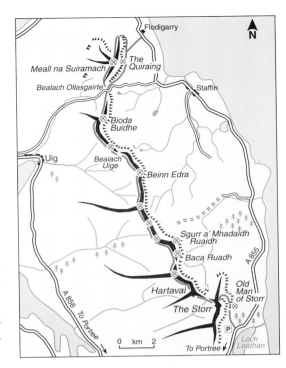

Quiraing - The Table

Alan Hall

Barra landscape from Ben Tangabhal

The Isle of Barra (Barraigh)

Sheabhal (Heaval)*; 383m; (OS Sheet 31; NL678994); *mound hill*
Thartabhal*; 356m; (OS Sheet 31; NL682001)

SHEABHAL
(HEAVAL)*

THARTABHAL*

The island of Barra (Barraigh) is surprisingly hilly, as one finds on looking north from the summit of Sheabhal. The ascent of this, the highest and most prominent hill on the island, is easily made from Castlebay (Bagh a' Chaisteil), where the ferry services from Oban and Lochboisdale arrive. Walk NE up the A888 road from the village, past scattered houses, and then either climb directly up steep grassy slopes to the rocky summit or take a slightly less steep line, passing close to the prominent white (Virgin of the Isles) statue, from a starting point 400 metres further east along the road. There is an easy scramble or two to be found among the short craggy terraces below the summit. (3km; 385m; 1h 30min).

From Sheabhal, the 'round' of the Barra Hills goes over Thartabhal and Grianan and then the lower hill Beinn Bheireasaigh, from where an easy descent can be found to the SW to reach Beinn Mhartainn. A better option is to return south from Beinn Bheireasaigh to the shallow bealach just north of Grianan (682017) and descend west to the interesting chambered cairn of Dun Bharpa and ascend Beinn Mhartainn from there. The grassy descent from Beinn Mhartainn SW to Borgh and a walk back along the road to Castlebay completes the round, involving almost 1000m of climbing. (15km; 960m; 5h 40min).

Beinn Tangabhal in the SW corner of Barra makes a pleasant climb from Castlebay, while the sea cliffs to the NW provides pleasant walking and contain some fine natural arches and caves well worth visiting. Likewise Beinn Chliaid north of the A888 makes a separate pleasant scramble from the road and both its summit and the lower Beinn Eireabhal give fine views of Traigh Mhor Airfield (on the tidal sands) and to the South Uist hills.

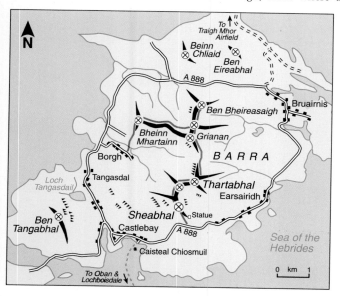

Peter Bailey

Ben Corradail from Hecla

South Uist (Uibhist a' Deas)

Beinn Mhor*; 620m; (OS Sheet 22; NF808310); *big hill*
Beinn Corradail (Ben Corodale)*; 527m; (OS Sheet 22; NF820329)
Hecla (Thacla)*; 606m; (OS Sheet 22; NF826345); *hooded* or *shrouded hill*

The three main hills of South Uist form a group running SW to NE along the east coast of the island. They are shapely, especially when viewed from the NW, as well as rugged, and are the most important hills in the Outer Hebrides outwith Harris and Lewis.

A full round of the three summits in either direction makes a fine excursion involving some 1200m of climbing. If transport can be arranged (by road or by sea) a traverse of the three from Loch Sgiopoirt in the north to Loch Aineort to the south makes a memorable day requiring 6 to 8 hours. Indeed, the most pleasing ascent of Hecla is by its long NE shoulder, reached from a starting point on the south shore of Loch Sgiopoirt; especially if a landing by boat can be arranged on the headland Ornais or in the exquisite rocky bay Caolas Beag, east of Caolas Mor. The driest route from the shore passes to the east of attractive Loch Bein to reach the bouldery slopes of Maol Martaig; then over Beinn na h-Aire to gain the east ridge of Hecla's lower NE summit (564m) and eventually the NE sharp grassy ridge leading to the higher table-like summit. (4.5km; 600m; 2h 10min).

Without the assistance of a boat an approach can be made from the tiny hamlet of Loch Sgioport, though taking some 40min longer to reach Hecla's summit from there. Follow the path (marked on the map but ill-defined) from the end of the road to the ruined shielings on the SW shore of Loch Sgiopoirt (833382); pass to the east of the small fresh water lochan there and head for Loch Bein, taking its drier SW shore to gain Maol Martaig and Beinn na h-Aire. There is no track or path from the shielings and the going is rough across ground which is a mixture of rocky bluffs and knolls, peat and heather, making a compass almost essential in mist.

For the shortest round of the three summits, start and finish at a point on the A865 near Loch Dobhrain (768345), where one or two peat-cutters tracks lead SE for a kilometre or so across the moor. The approach to Beinn Mhor is surprisingly dry. Aim for its long NW shoulder, Maola Breac to the north of prominent Coire Dubh, leading first to a small subsidiary peak (608m), 500 metres NW of the summit and identified by a stone circle cairn. From this cairn a narrow but easy grassy and rocky ridge leads to the summit trig point of Beinn Mhor. The final section of the ridge has several bouldery outcrops which in mist give the impression of false summits. (5.5km; 600m; 2h 20min). To continue the traverse of the three hills return to the 608m top and, a short distance beyond, descend east on a shoulder leading to the Bealach

BEINN MHOR*

BEINN CORRADAIL
(BEN CORODALE)*

HECLA (THACLA)*

Sheiliosdail. This shoulder is broken and rocky and the descent requires care in mist, especially on the section directly above the bealach where there are several short vertical steps. From Bealach Sheiliosdail the ascent of the south ridge of Beinn Corradail is straightforward, with only a small loss of height at the almost level Feith-bhealach before reaching the steep grassy slope to the bouldery summit. (8.2km; 800m; 3h 30min).

Beinn Corradail has a short summit ridge and a steep and rocky, although short, NNW ridge which then runs out NW towards a broad bealach to the east of Maoladh Creag nam Fitheach, at the heads of Gleann Uisinis and Gleann Dorchaidh. Just below the summit of Beinn Corradail this ridge has a deep almost vertical cleft dividing it into two moderately difficult buttresses. The descent northwards from the summit therefore requires care in mist to avoid these, by first seeking out a short scree gully which drops NE from the summit ridge some 50 metres east of the summit cairn. This scree gully leads to a sloping grassy shelf and thence to the broad shallow bealach above and NW of Loch Coradail. From there the ascent to Hecla's mostly grassy summit is steep but otherwise straightforward. (10km; 1220m; 4h 50min). The north side of Hecla is a mass of fractured rock, mostly Lewisian gneiss where the compass is unreliable. The return to the road should be made by retracing one's route SW to the same broad bealach and descending west down the spur of Maoladh Creag nam Fitheach across Gleann Dorchaidh, taking a fairly direct line back to the starting point near Loch Dobhrain. (15km; 1220m; 6h).

For an ascent of Beinn Mhor alone, the quickest way – although not a particularly rewarding climb – is from the hamlet Airidh nam Ban to its SW, on the north shore of Loch Aineort. A good path (not on the OS map) passes to the south of Loch nam Faoileann and then to the NE corner of this lochan. The going NE is boggy until the coarse heathery slopes of the Bealach Crosgard are reached, from where the ridge to the summit is mostly grassy. (4.2km; 600m; 2h 10m). This route provides an easy descent from Beinn Mhor following a traverse from Hecla or Beinn Corradail.

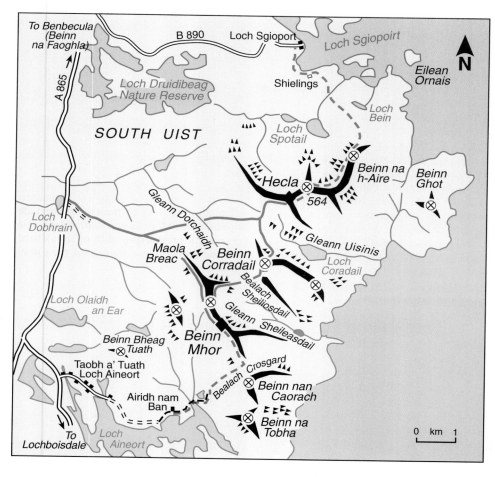

Douglas Scott

Oireabhal (left) and Sron Scourst from Gleann Mhiabhaig

North Harris (Ceann a' Tuath na Hearadh) – The Western Hills of Harris

Tiorga Mor*; 679m; (OS Sheet 13 or 14; NB055115)
Oireabhal (Oreval)*; 662m; (OS Sheet 13 or 14; NB083099); *Orri's* or *grouse hill*
Ulabhal (Ullaval)*; 659m; (OS Sheet 13 or 14; NB086114); *Ulli's (Olafs's) hill*

TIORGA MOR*

OIREABHAL
(OREVAL)*

ULABHAL
(ULLAVAL)*

The western hills of North Harris are grouped around Loch Chliostair; Tiorga Mor to its west and Oireabhal and Ulabhal to the east. All three can be climbed in a day, but it may be more interesting to climb them in two separate excursions.

Tiorga Mor is the highest and most rugged of the group, towering above Loch Chliostair, but is awkward to ascend from there except by the relatively steep and slabby SE ridge which is best approached from the dam at the south end of the loch. There is a private (hydro) track from the B887 to the south. Grassy gullies between the slabs make this SE ridge to the summit relatively straightforward, though steep. (4.8km; 670m; 2h 10min). Views from the summit are particularly fine. The SE ridge forms the western edge of Tiorga Mor's SE corrie, in which there is the hidden Loch Maolaig; while, looking NE, the dramatic overhanging cliffs of Sron Uladal – widely regarded as the most awe inspiring crag in the British Isles – are seen at their best. Descend from the summit NE to the bealach, Lag Glas, and then east by south to the north of Lag Glas Oireabhal, down fairly steep but easy grassy slopes to reach the Gleann Chliostair path back to the dam and the B887 near to Abhainn Suidhe (see OS Sheet 13), 3km NW from Cliasmol. (9km; 670m; 3h 10min).

For the quickest and easiest ascent of Tiorga Mor from the B887, take the private track (cycles can be useful here) leading to Loch Chliostair as far as the bridge over the Abhainn Leosaid, then branch NW onto the path up Gleann Leosaid for 1km before striking north up the steep but easy south flank of the hill. (4km; 680m; 2h 10min). A more pleasant route, is to continue along the Gleann Leosaid path for a further 1km as far as Gill Abaidh and climb the shallow glen from there to the bealach between Tiorga Mor and Ceartabhal, above the attractive Loch Braigh Bheagarais. From this bealach (see OS Sheet 13) both hills can easily be climbed.

The direct descent from Tiorga Mor to the Gleann Chliostair path is described above but, more interesting, continue north to Tiorga and descend east, keeping south of the steep slabs of Creagan Leathan, to reach the tiny fishermans bothy (072123) at the north end of Loch Aiseabhat. A short walk from there down Gleann Uladal provides superb views of Sron Uladal.

The bothy location is also the best connecting point at which the hills to the west and east of Loch Chliostair can be combined in a day's excursion.

The summits of Oireabhal and Ulabhal, to the east of Loch Chliostair, form the two highest points of the 7km ridge which extends northwards from Caolas Shodhaigh, in Loch a' Siar, to the great overhanging promontory of Sron Uladal. The traverse of these hills including a visit to look at the impressive overhang of Sron Uladal above Loch Uladal probably ranks second, in the Harris Hills, to the An Cliseam (Clisham) horseshoe.

From the hamlet of Cliasmol on the B887, climb Cleiseabhal (511m) by its SW shoulder, just west of the short low-lying crags of Mulla Chlieseabhal. This gives a pleasant ascent to the stony summit which is a fine view point. Crags drop steeply to the north, as well as eastwards from the NE shoulder which one descends with care to reach a bouldery bealach. From there a stony and grassy ridge veers north to the grassy subsidiary summit of Bidigidh (500m). Apart from this short stony descent from Cleiseabhal, the rounded ridges and shallow bealachs of the group, extending north over Oireabhal, and then Ulabhal and Muladal (454m) to the summit of Sron Uladal (442m), give easy walking on grass. This route to Sron Uladal is probably more interesting than along Gleann Chliostair, though slightly longer. (7km; 800m; 3h 10min).

From the summit of Sron Uladal descend by the east flank, then NW to view in profile, if weather permits, the spectacular overhanging cliff above Loch Uladal. From this NE side the overhang is best seen – albeit requiring a short detour – from the SW slopes of Mullach na Reidheachd. An alternative route of return from Loch Uladal is to take the glen rising SE over the bealach north of Gormal Mor and descend from the attractive unnamed lochan towards Loch Bhoisimid, passing to the south of Lochan an Fheoir to reach the private well made track down Gleann Mhiabhaig and back to the B887, 3km east of the Cliasmol starting point. (16km; 1100m; 5h 40min). Otherwise, circle under Sron Uladal for the Gleann Chliostair path back to the B887 2km west of Cliasmol.

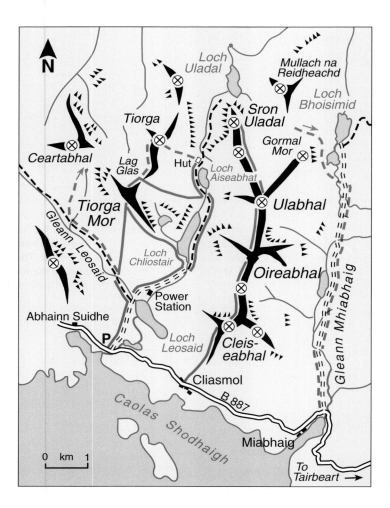

The north-west ridge of Uisgneabhal Mor

North Harris (Ceann a' Tuath na Hearadh) – The Central Hills of Harris

Uisgneabhal Mor (Uisgnaval Mor)*; 729m; (OS Sheet 13 or 14; NB120085)
Teileasbhal (Teilesval)*; 697m; (OS Sheet 13 or 14; NB125091)
Stuabhal (Stulaval)*; 579m; (OS Sheet 13 or 14; NB133122); *sheiling hill*

To the east of deep Gleann Mhiabhaig and between this glen and the An Cliseam horseshoe, separated by the continuous narrow glen formed by the Abhainn Loch a' Sgail, Loch a' Sgail and the Allt a' Sgail, is a small but significant and shapely group of Central Harris hills of which Uisgneabhal Mor is the highest. This peak forms a twin summit with Teileasbhal, its close neighbour to the NE. Viewed from the south the pair appear as one, lying directly west of the narrow and deep glen formed by the Allt a' Sgail which flows north into the Abhainn Langadail and eventually to Loch Langabhat (Harris's largest freshwater loch). Stuabhal, 3.5km north of this pair, is joined with them into one massif by a fairly rugged though pleasantly grassy and bouldery line of ridges and bealachs.

From the head of Loch Mhiabhaig, where the B887 crosses the Abhainn Mhiabhaig, the 2km long SSW ridge of Uisgneabhal Mor provides an easy and pleasant way of ascending both this hill and Teileasbhal - as well as being the start for a round of the entire group. Head first for the shoulder east of Creag na Speireig, above Loch Brunabhal, and then keep well above and west of the line of bouldery crags forming Craig Uilisgeir, which drops steeply to Loch a' Sgail. The ridge leads directly to the summit of Uisgneabhal Mor (3.8km; 730m; 2h 10min); and thence to Teileasbhal, only some 600 metres to its NE with a drop of 150m to the grassy bealach between the two. (4.5km; 880m; 2h 50min). Both summits are stony, with pleasant grassy ridges; one running NW from Uisgneabhal Mor to the steep promontory of Sron Scourst, another north from Teileasbhal around the head of Coire Sgurra-breac to Stuabhal. A descent from Sron Scourst can readily be made SW, from the bealach some 500 metres to the SE of its summit, leading directly down to Loch Scourst in Gleann Mhiabhaig. (6.4km; 930m; 3h 30min).

From Teileasbhal the ridge above Coire Sgurra-breac leads NNW to Creag Stulabhal and Sron Ard; from there an easy descent SW can also be made to Gleann Mhiabhaig, but to complete the interesting round of the three summits, take the grassy east ridge from Creag Stulabhal, above the north-facing crags, to reach the bealach at the head of Gleann Stuladail. The ascent from this bealach to the summit of Stulabhal is straightforward but, to descend, return to this same bealach from where the easiest line of descent is north of Loch Stuladail to reach the Gleann Stuladail path down to Loch Bhoisimid, and thence by the well made track along Gleann Mhiabhaig back to the starting point on the B887.

UISGNEABHAL MOR (UISGNAVAL MOR)*

TEILEASBHAL (TEILESVAL)*

STUABHAL (STULAVAL)*

An Cliseam

Gill Nisbet

North Harris (Ceann a' Tuath na Hearadh) – An Cliseam (Clisham) Hills:

AN CLISEAM
(CLISHAM)

MULLA-FO-DHEAS*

MULLA-FO-
THUATH*

MULLACH AN
LANGA*

An Cliseam (Clisham); 799m; (OS Sheet 13 or 14; NB155073); *rocky hill*
Mulla-Fo-Dheas*; 708m; (OS Sheet 13 or 14; NB143076); *south summit*
Mulla-Fo-Thuath*; 708m; (OS Sheet 13 or 14; NB140084); *north summit*
Mullach an Langa*; 614m; (OS Sheet 13 or 14; NB143094); *long summit*

To the east of the central hills of North Harris, between Gleann Mhiabhaig and the A859 from Tarbert (Tairbeart) to Stornoway (Steornabhagh), is a compact group that includes the highest peak in the Outer Isles, An Cliseam. This mountain with its two immediate neighbours, Mulla-Fo-Dheas and Mulla-Fo-Thuath, plus the lower hills Mullach an Langa and Tomnabhal, form a fine prominent horseshoe ridge enclosing the small Loch Mhisteam at the head of the Abhainn Scaladail. When seen from the south or SW, An Cliseam is a gracefully shaped hill, with the edge of the steep crag of Aonaig Mhor, on its north flank, just visible but well defined; while the fine ridge joining the summit to Mulla-Fo-Dheas is also distinct, forming the skyline above the broken tiers of rock at the head of Coire Dubh.

The climb of An Cliseam can be readily made from almost any point on the A859, which flanks the south and east sides of the hill and gains a height of almost 200m. The nearest approach is from either the bridge crossing the Abhainn Maraig (173058), or from 1km NW where the road crosses the Allt Tomnabhal. Both locations have good parking available. There is no clear path, but by following either stream NW for 400 metres, and skirting westwards to gain the SE flank of An Cliseam, north of the craggy Sron Carsacleit, the SE shoulder to the summit is easily reached. The bouldery summit ridge of An Cliseam, running SE to NW, is rocky and quite narrow; its width being almost completely taken up by the large walled cairn surrounding the trig point. (3km; 630m; 1h 50min).

For a traverse of the summits enclosing Loch Mhisteam, including Tomnabhal (552m), the best start is near the bridge where the A859 crosses the Abhainn Scaladail. The clearly marked track on the map, running SW from the road (186096) and skirting to the NW of Caisteal Ard, provides easy access to Tomnabhal and thence to the grassy bealach to the NE of An Cliseam;

from there the slope to the summit is easy, though steep, at first grassy, then stony. (4km; 720m; 2h 20min). The SE-NW short summit ridge has a 500 metre rocky north spur running out to Aonaig Mhor, which calls for care in mist; though it provides a splendid viewpoint in fine weather.

From the NW end of An Cliseam's summit ridge, a rounded stony slope drops steeply west to a long grassy bealach, from where a short easy ascent leads to the subsidiary (east) summit of Mulla-Fo-Dheas, (named An t-Isean on the OS 1:25,000 map). Beyond this distinct but subsidiary summit, the ridge narrows again, dropping first to a small green and bouldery bealach and then rising to the rocky main summit of Mulla-Fo-Dheas. (5.2km; 870m; 2h 40min). From Mulla-Fo-Dheas, the descent by the NW ridge, to reach the bealach to its north, is easy though narrow and bouldery; with care needed to avoid the rocky crags that drop steeply to the east. The ascents of Mulla-Fo-Thuath and Mullach an Langa are mostly grassy and relatively straightforward. Return to the start skirting south of Creag Mo then descending to the Abhainn Scaladaill and the A859. (12km; 1800m; 8h).

An interesting alternative from the summit of Mulla-Fo-Dheas, if suitable transport can be arranged, is to descend south down the Mo Buidhe shoulder and then across the Abhainn Thorabraidh to join the well marked path to the west side of Creag Ghreinebridh, leading to the derelict whaling station at Bun Abhainn Eadarra. This makes for a shorter day than the full round of summits above. (9km; 870m; 3h 40min).

Note: Names throughout the Hebrides are given as on the latest OS maps which may not always be consistent, eg. Stuabhal should perhaps be Stulabhal, Mulla-Fo-Dheas; Mulla-fo-Dheas, etc.

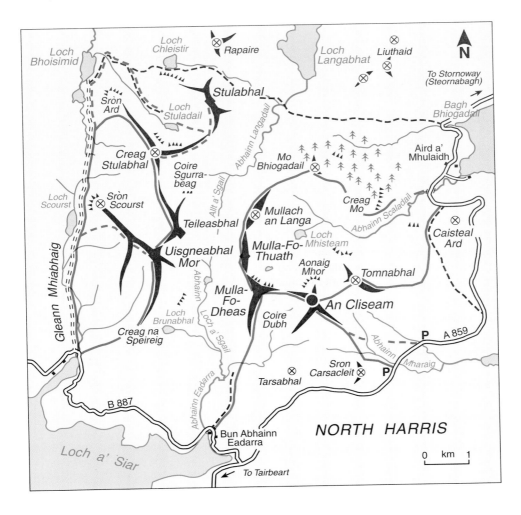

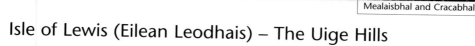

Mealaisbhal and Cracabhal

Derek Sime

Isle of Lewis (Eilean Leodhais) – The Uige Hills

Mealaisbhal (Mealisval)*; 574m; (OS Sheet 13; NB022270); *honey hill*
Cracabhal (Cracaval)*; 514m; (OS Sheet 13; NB029253); *crow hill* or *creviced hill*
Tahabhal*; 515m; (OS Sheet 13; NB044265)

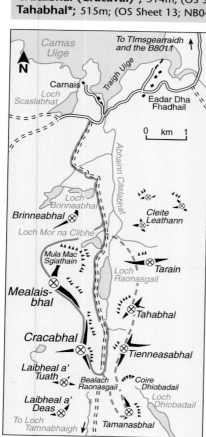

The Uige hills, near the west coast of Lewis (Leodhais), form a compact group of low, rough and rocky hills. This rugged nature and not any height gives their great character. Two ridges run south - north, separated by deep Gleann Raonasgail. The bealachs between the hills are quite deep so there is plenty of climbing on any traverse.

The highest of the group (prominent viewed across the renowned Uige sands) is Mealaisbhal, west of Loch Raonasgail. A round of Mealaisbhal, Cracabhal and Loch Raonasgail makes a good introductory outing. Start up the track from the minor coast road (032313) and follow this to Loch Mor na Clibhe. Circle north of the loch and west of Mula Mac Sgiathain to climb Mealaisbhal from the NW. (Any direct line over Mula Mac Sgiathain is best left to those with climbing skills). (7km; 570m; 2h 30min). Descend SE to the 293m bealach and climb the rocky north ridge of Cracabhal. (9km; 790m; 3h 20min). Take the SE slopes of Cracabhal down to pick up the estate track at its highest point. Follow this north by Loch Raonasgail to the start. (14km; 720m; 4h 20min). An impressive addition after reaching the track is to climb SE and add Tamanasbhal (467m) then, passing impressive Coire Dhiobadail, traverse northwards over the succession of eastern hills, Teinneasabhal (497m) and Tahabhal (515m) to skirt Tarain from where a slabby descent NW leads back to the track and the start. (26km; 1250m; 8h 10min).

Index of Corbetts

Index of Other Hills

Beinn Damh from Beinn Liath Mor

Walkingwild in Scotland

Before you go why not check out VisitScotland's dedicated walking site **www.walkingwild.com** – Scotland's premier website for walkers. Put together by walkers for walkers it will help you plan your trip whether you fancy a short stroll with the kids or a multi day trek through some of Scotland's wildest areas – some of these Corbetts are pretty remote! You can even get a better idea of what each area is like with the excellent photography and our virtual walks.

In addition, the Walkingwild website will help you with:
- **Walker friendly accommodation** – accommodation that offers all those essential features such as drying facilities, packed lunches and weather forecasts.
- **Walking holidays and guides** – Details of companies specialising in organising it all for you, or helping you to gain new skills.
- **Special Offers** – the place to get a good deal on your accommodation or walking holiday.
- **Travel information** – How to get here and how to get around.
- **Events** – Everything from mountain festivals and walking festivals to wildlife walks.
- **Suggested walks** – Fancy a day off from Corbett bagging or a bad weather alternative – we give a range of suitable walks.
- **Stalking information** – Advice and contact details to help you get the most out of the hills during the stalking season.
- **Online shop** – You can buy your OS maps here along with a range of other walking guides.

www.walkingwild.com

For general information on holidays in Scotland check out

www.visitscotland.com

Hillphones

The Hillphones service offers hillwalkers recorded telephone messages detailing stag stalking in various parts of the Highlands from August 1st to October 31st. The messages indicate where stalking is taking place and which walking routes will be unlikely to affect stalking, as well as giving a forecast of stalking activity over the next few days. Recorded messages are generally updated by 8.00 a.m. each day, and calls are charged at normal rates. It usually helps to have a map to hand when calling. There is no stag stalking on Sundays.

The Hillphones service is supported by the Access Forum, and has been organised by the Mountaineering Council of Scotland, Scottish Natural Heritage and the participating and aims to improve communications between stalkers and hillwalkers.

Leaflets detaling the precise areas covered by the various Hillphones are updated annually and are available from The Mountaineering Council of Scotland, The Old Granary, West Mill Street, Perth, PH1 5QP, (t) 01738 638 227. Further details can also be found on the MCofS's website: www.mountaineering-scotland.org.uk

1. Grey Corries/Mamore
including Sgurr Eilde Mor and Stob Coire Easain on OS Map 41.
Tel: Kinlochleven (01855) 831 511

2. Glen Dochart/Glen Lochay
including Meall Glas and Sgiath Chuil on OS Map 51.
Tel: Killin (01567) 820 886

3. North Arran
covering the northern half of the island (north of the B880) on OS Map 69.
Tel: Brodick (01770) 302 363

4. South Glen Shiel
including the Saddle and the South Cluanie Ridge on OS Map 33.
Tel: Glenshiel (01599) 511 425

5. Drumochter
including Geal-charn and A' Bhuidheanach Bheag on OS Map 42.
Tel: Dalwhinnie (01528) 522 200

6. Glen Shee
including Carn a' Gheoidh and Creag Leacach on OS Map 43.
Tel: Blairgowrie (01250) 885 288

7. Callater and Clunie
including Carn an t-Sagairt Mor and Carn an Tuirc on OS Maps 43 and 44.
Tel: Braemar (013397) 41997

8. Invercauld
including Ben Avon and Beinn a' Bhuird on OS Maps 36 & 43.
Tel: Braemar (013397) 41911

9. Balmoral/Lochnagar
including Lochnagar and White Mounth on OS Map 44.
Tel: Ballater (013397) 55532

10. Glen Clova
including Broad Cairn and Tom Buidhe on OS Map 44.
Tel: Clova (01575) 550 335

11. Paps of Jura
including Beinn Chaolais, Beinn an Oir and Beinn Shiantaidh on OS Map 61.
Tel: Jura (01496) 820 151

12. Atholl and Lude
including Beinn a' Ghlo and Beinn Dearg on OS Map 43.
Tel: Blair Atholl (01796) 481 740

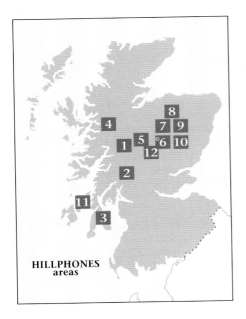

HILLPHONES
areas

SCOTTISH MOUNTAINEERING CLUB
SCOTTISH MOUNTAINEERING TRUST

CLIMBERS' GUIDES
Scottish Winter Climbs	£17.95
Arran, Arrochar and Southern Highlands	£14.95
Ben Nevis	In preparation
The Cairngorms Vol. 1	£11.95
The Cairngorms Vol. 2	£11.95
Highland Outcrops	£14.95
Lowland Outcrops	£14.95
North-East Outcrops	In preparation
Northern Highlands Vol. 1	£13.95
Northern Highlands Vol. 2	£13.95
Skye and the Hebrides (2 Vols)	£19.95

HILLWALKERS' GUIDES
The Munros	£18
The Munros CD-ROM	£40
Munros GPS data disk – from SMC website	£10.48
The Corbetts and Other Scottish Hills CD-ROM	In preparation
The Cairngorms	£17.95
Central Highlands	£17.95
Islands of Scotland Including Skye	£19.95
North-West Highlands	In preparation
Southern Highlands	£16.95
Southern Uplands	£16.95

SCRAMBLERS' GUIDES
Skye Scrambles	£12

OTHER PUBLICATIONS
Munro's Tables	£15.95
A Chance in a Million? Avalanches in Scotland	£14.95
The Munroist's Companion	£16.00
Heading for the Scottish Hills	£6.95
Scottish Hill and Mountain Names	£9.95
Ben Nevis – Britain's Highest Mountain	£14.95
Ski Mountaineering in Scotland	£12.95

Visit our website for more details and to purchase on line:
www.smc.org.uk

Distributed by:
Cordee Ltd, 3a De Montfort Street, Leicester LE1 7HD
(t) 0116 254 3579 (f) 0116 247 1176
www.cordee.co.uk

These publications are available from bookshops and mountain equipment suppliers.